The Most Sublime Hysteric

The Most Sublime Hysteric

Hegel with Lacan

Slavoj Žižek

Translated by Thomas Scott-Railton

polity

First published in French as *Le plus sublime des hystériques. Hegel avec Lacan* © Presses Universitaires de France, 2011

This English edition © Polity Press, 2014

INSTITUT
FRANÇAIS
ROYAUME-UNI

This book is supported by the Institut français (Royaume-Uni) as part of the Burgess programme.

Polity Press
65 Bridge Street
Cambridge CB2 1UR, UK

Polity Press
350 Main Street
Malden, MA 02148, USA

ISBN-13: 978-0-7456-6374-6
ISBN-13: 978-0-7456-6375-3(pb)

A catalogue record for this book is available from the British Library.

Typeset in 10.5 on 12 pt Sabon
by Toppan Best-set Premedia Limited
Printed and bound in Great Britain by Clays Ltd, St Ives PLC

The publisher has used its best endeavours to ensure that the URLs for external websites referred to in this book are correct and active at the time of going to press. However, the publisher has no responsibility for the websites and can make no guarantee that a site will remain live or that the content is or will remain appropriate.

Every effort has been made to trace all copyright holders, but if any have been inadvertently overlooked the publisher will be pleased to include any necessary credits in any subsequent reprint or edition.

For further information on Polity, visit our website: www.politybooks.com

Contents

Introduction: Impossible Absolute Knowledge

Foucault once suggested that we define philosophy as such with anti-Platonism. Precisely because Plato was the thinker whose work cleared the ground for the field of philosophy, every philosopher, beginning with Aristotle, would define his project by distancing himself from Plato. In a similar way, we can think of philosophy in the last two centuries as defined by taking distance from Hegel. Hegel is the incarnation of the "panlogical" monster, the total dialectical mediation of reality, the total dissolution of reality in the self-movement of the Idea. Faced with this monster, various ideas have been advanced that would supposedly be capable of escaping the mediation of the concept. This procedure is already visible in the three great post-Hegelian reversals that opposed the absolutism of the Idea in the name of the irrational abyss of the Will (Schelling), in the name of the paradox of individual existence (Kierkegaard), and in the name of the productive process of life (Marx). When siding with Hegel, even the most favorable commentators refuse to step over the line into accepting Absolute Knowledge. Thus, Jean Hyppolite emphasized that the post-Hegelian experience permitted the irreducible opening of the historico-temporal process through an empty repetition that destroyed the framework of the progress of Reason. Even among partisans of Hegel, their relationship to the Hegelian system is always one of "Of course, but still . . ." – of course Hegel affirmed the fundamentally antagonistic character of effectivity, the de-centering of the subject, etc., but still . . . ; this fissure is finally canceled through the self-mediation of the Absolute Idea that heals

all wounds. The position of Absolute Knowledge, of the final reconciliation, plays the role of the Hegelian Thing. It is the monster that
is both frightening and ridiculous, from which one would do best to
keep one's distance. It is both impossible (Absolute Knowledge is, of
course, unattainable, an unrealizable Ideal!) and forbidden (Absolute
Knowledge is terrifying, because it threatens mortification of all the
richness of the living through the self-movement of the concept!). In
other words, any identification with Hegelian thought implies a
moment where this identification will break down – the Thing must
always be sacrificed.

For us, this image of Hegel as "panlogicist," devouring and mor-
tifying the living substance of the particular, is *the Real of his critics.*
"Real" in the Lacanian sense: the construction of a point that does
not actually exist (a monster unrelated to Hegel himself) but that,
nonetheless, must be presupposed in order to legitimate our position
through negative reference to the other, by distancing ourselves.
Where does this terror that grips the post-Hegelians in the face of
the monster of Absolute Knowledge come from? What is concealed
in the fascinating presence of this phantasmic construction? A hole,
an empty space. It is possible to define this hole by undertaking
the reading of Hegel *with Lacan*, which is to say against the background of the Lacanian problematic of the lack in the Other, the
traumatic emptiness around which the signifying process articulates
itself. From this perspective, Absolute Knowledge reveals itself to be
the Hegelian name for what Lacan attempted to pin down with the
term "the pass" [*la passe*], the final moment of the analytical process,
the experience of the Lack in the Other. If, according to Lacan's
famous formulation, Sade gives us the truth of Kant, then Lacan
himself could give us access to the fundamental matrix that gives
the movement of the Hegelian dialectic its structure; Kant with Sade,
Hegel with Lacan. What then is the relationship between Hegel and
Lacan?

Today, things seem clear-cut. While no one denies that Lacan owes
a certain debt to Hegel, at the same time it is widely accepted that
Hegel's influence was limited to certain theoretical borrowings, which
occurred during a very fixed time frame. Between the late 1940s and
the early 1950s, Lacan attempted to articulate the psychoanalytic
process in the terms of the intersubjective logic of the recognition of
desire and/or the desire for recognition. Already at this time, Lacan
had taken care to distance himself from the closure of the Hegelian
system, from the Absolute Knowledge that he associated with the
inaccessible ideal of a perfectly homogenous discourse, complete and
sealed in upon itself. Later on, the introduction of the logic of the

*pas-tout** and the concept of the barred Other would render this initial reference to Hegel obsolete. Is it possible to imagine a more incompatible contradiction than between Hegelian Absolute Knowledge – the sealed "circle of circles" – and the Lacanian barred Other – knowledge as irrevocably lacking? Is Lacan not the anti-Hegel *par excellence*?

It is the critiques of Lacan in particular that bring out his debt to Hegel. Lacan has been criticized for remaining a prisoner of logophallocentrism, allegedly because of an underlying Hegelianism that confined textual dissemination within the teleological circle. In response to this critique, Lacanians reply, as they will, by drawing attention to Lacan's break with Hegelianism, struggling to save Lacan by emphasizing that he is not and was never a Hegelian. Now is the moment to take on this debate in a novel way, by articulating the relationship between Hegel and Lacan in an unprecedented manner. To my eyes, Lacan was fundamentally Hegelian, but did not know it. His Hegelianism is not to be found where we might expect it to be, in his overt references to Hegel, but rather in the final stage of his teachings, in the logic of the *pas-tout*, in the importance he placed on the Real, on the Lack in the Other. And, reciprocally, a reading of Hegel through the lens of Lacan gives us a picture of Hegel that is radically different from the commonly accepted view of him as a "panlogicist." It will bring out a Hegel of the logic of the "signifier," of a self-referential process articulated as the repeated positivation of a central Void.

This reading changes the very definitions of the two terms involved. It washes away the alluvium of panlogicism and/or historicism and uncovers a Hegel of the logic of the signifier. On the other side, it makes it possible to isolate the most subversive of the core elements of Lacanian doctrine, that of the constitutive Lack in the Other. This is why this book is, at its roots, dialogical: it is impossible to develop a positive line of thinking without including the theses that are opposed to it. In this case, these are the commonplaces regarding Hegel that I've already mentioned, which see Hegelianism as the quintessential example of the "imperialism of reason," a closed economy in which the self-movement of the Concept sublates all the differences and dispersions of the material process. Similar commonplaces can be found in Lacan. But these are accompanied by a different conception of Hegel, one that is not found in Lacan's direct

---

* *Pas-tout* is often translated as "not-all" or "not-whole," and although the latter comes closer, it doesn't quite capture the meaning of the French original, which contains elements of both.

references to Hegel – which is why I will, for the most part, ignore these references. In my reading, Lacan "did not know where he was a Hegelian," because his reading of Hegel followed in the tradition of Kojève and Hyppolite. Therefore, in order to articulate the link between the logic of the dialectic and of the "signifier," we must, for the time being, put aside all of Lacan's explicit references to Hegel.

It seems that today the terms themselves of the philosophical debate have changed. The debate no longer draws on the "poststructuralist" themes of de-centering the subject, but rather on a kind of renewal of the Political (human rights, critiques of totalitarianism) through a theoretical return to a position that could generally be described, in its various different forms (up to and including Habermas's communicative ethics), as Kantian. This return to Kant has allowed for philosophy to be rehabilitated, rescuing it from "symptomal readings" that had reduced it to an ideological-imaginary effect and conferring a new credibility on philosophical reflection, while still avoiding the "totalitarianism of Reason" (which it identifies with post-Kantian idealism), which is to say, while still keeping the horizon of historical progress open. And so, the second part of this work will develop an implicit dialogue with this point of view, at several levels, through references to three fields of philosophy.

First of all, the Kantian field itself. Starting with Lacan, I will describe the dimension of Kant that has not figured in the renewal of his thinking, the Kant whose truth is Sade, the Kant whose impossible superego imperative hides the injunction to *jouissance*,* the Kant who was radicalized by Schelling in his theory of original Evil.

Second, owing to the influence of the return to Kantian philosophy, Marx has been largely forgotten. What can we salvage from Marx after the experience of "totalitarianism"? There remains the man who invented the symptom (as Lacan argued in the "RSI" seminar), who can help us understand the fundamentally unconscious nature of ideology, the relationship of the symptom to the fantasy, and so on.

Third, according to received *doxa*, analytic philosophy is the radical opposite of Hegel. However, I will argue that this novel understanding of the core of the Hegelian dialectic is more present in certain strains of analytic philosophy (Kripke's anti-descriptivism, for example) than it is in the different versions of straight Hegelianism.

---

* Although it could be roughly translated as enjoyment, *jouissance* is a more specific term with a sexual connotation. For a more in-depth discussion of how to translate the term, see Dylan Evans, *An Introductory Dictionary of Lacanian Psychoanalysis* (Routledge 2002), p. 150. Evans defines *jouissance* as "an excessive quantity of excitation which the pleasure principle attempts to prevent."

Using this three-part dialogue as its base, the second part of this book will sketch the outlines of a Lacanian theory of the politico-ideological field that will allow us to diagnose the phenomenon that has been labeled "totalitarian," while at the same time pinning down the fundamentally paradoxical nature of democracy.

The final thesis of this book is that Lacanian doctrine contains the framework for a theory of the politico-ideological field. This framework has not been fully fleshed out, and this is one of the great enigmas of contemporary thought. Perhaps the solution to this great enigma coincides with the solution of another: why has the true character of Lacan's Hegelianism been consistently misrecognized?*

This book presents the re-edited text of the doctoral thesis "Philosophy Between the Symptom and the Fantasy," completed under the direction of Jacques-Alain Miller and defended in November 1982 in the Psychoanalysis Department of the Université de Paris-VIII. I extend my thanks to Professor Miller and other colleagues in the Freudian field who provided their support for this work.

---

* I have generally translated *méconnaissance* (literally mis-knowledge) as "misrecognition," and also once or twice as "misunderstanding," depending on the context. Although it is often left untranslated, it seems not to lose anything essential in its translation. For a more in-depth discussion, see Evans, *An Introductory Dictionary*, p. 112.

Book I

Hegel with Lacan

1

"The Formal Aspect": Reason versus Understanding

The story of an appearance

The first "materialist inversion of Hegel"? It can be pinpointed precisely: Nuremberg's central square, May 2, 1828. On that date, a peculiarly dressed young man appears in downtown Nuremberg. His countenance and his gestures are markedly stiff. The only words he knows are a few fragments of the Lord's Prayer that he has memorized and an enigmatic – and slightly ungrammatical – sentence: "I would be a horseman, like my father was," the first hint of an identification with an Ego-Ideal. In his left hand, he holds a paper bearing his name – Kaspar Hauser – and the address of a cavalry captain in Nuremberg. Once he learns to speak, Kaspar tells his story. He had spent his life alone in a "dark cellar" where a "man in black" brought him food and water, until the day when this man brought him to Nuremberg, teaching him along the way the few sentences Kaspar knew.

Placed in the care of the Daumer family, Kaspar was quickly "humanized," learned to speak "properly," and became a celebrity. He was the subject of philosophical, psychological, pedagogical, and medical interest, as well as the focus of political speculation as to his origins. After a few years of quiet life, he was found on the afternoon of December 14, 1833, with a fatal stab wound. On his deathbed, he claimed that his assailant was the "man in black" who had brought him to Nuremberg (see Hörisch 1979). Although Kaspar's sudden appearance provoked a brutal encounter with an "impossible-reality" that ruptured the symbolic circuit of cause and effect, the most surprising thing was that, in a certain sense, *the moment was awaiting him*. As a surprise, he "arrived right on time." Kaspar was an incarnation of the age-old myth of the child of royal descent abandoned in the wilderness and then found as an adolescent, and the rumor soon spread that he was the Prince of Baden. The fact that the only objects he remembered from the cellar were a few toy animals carved from wood was itself a poignant re-enactment of the myth of a hero who is rescued and cared for by animals. But above all, toward the end of the eighteenth century the theme of the child living outside of human society had become the subject of an ever-increasing number of literary and scientific works, as the pure embodiment of the distinction between the "nature" and "culture" of man.

Kaspar's emergence was, from a "material" point of view, the result of a series of unexpected accidents. But from the *formal* point of view, it was fundamentally necessary; the structure of contemporary knowledge had prepared a space for him. Because this empty space had already been constructed, his appearance caused a sensation, whereas a century before or after it would have passed unnoticed. To grasp this *form*, this empty space that precedes the content that will come to fill it, is the work of *Reason* in the Hegelian sense. That is to say, Reason as opposed to Understanding, in which the form expresses a positive and predetermined content. In other words, far from being overtaken by his "materialist inversions," Hegel is the one who, ahead of time, gave them their meaning.

Wanting to say and saying

According to orthodox dialectics, Understanding supposedly treats categories, conceptual determinates, as abstract moments, frozen and removed from the living totality, reduced to the specificity of their fixed identity. Reason, on the other hand, goes beyond the level of Understanding by deploying the living process of subjective (self-) mediation whose "dead" and rigid abstract moments, whose "objectifications," are the categories of Understanding. Where Understanding sees only rigid categories, Reason sees the living movement that generates them. The Understanding/Reason distinction is therefore seen through the Bergsonian opposition between the flexible, moveable, vital force and the inert matter it produces that is accessible to Understanding.

A view such as this completely misses the true significance of the distinction between Understanding and Reason. Reason is not something "in addition" to Understanding, a movement, a living process that escapes from the dead skeleton of the categories of Understanding. Reason is Understanding itself in the sense that nothing is missing from Understanding, in the sense that there is nothing beyond it. It is the absolute form outside of which there exists no content. We remain at the level of Understanding so long as we think there is something "beyond" it, a force that eludes Understanding, an unknown inaccessible to the "rigid schematics" of the categories of Understanding – *and so long as we give the name "Reason" to this beyond!* By making this step toward Reason, we are not adding anything to Understanding; rather, we are *subtracting* something from it (the phantom of the object that persists beyond the form). We are reducing it to its formal process. We "go beyond" Understanding when we recognize that Understanding is already in itself the living movement of self-mediation that we were searching for outside of it.

Already, this can help us to correct a misunderstanding of the Hegelian critique of "abstract thought" (cf. Hegel 1966).

All that is usually retained from this critique is the idea that common sense, Understanding, proceeds by abstraction, by subsuming all of an object's richness under a specific determination. A feature of a concrete network is picked out from the fullness of the living – a man, for example, is identified by the determination "thief" or "traitor" – and the dialectical approach is supposed to compensate for this loss, by allowing us to return to the richness of the concrete living world. But, as Gérard Lebrun (1972) has pointed out, this is not the case: once we're in the domain of *logos*, the loss is irremediable – what is lost is lost. To use Lacan's words, once we've spoken, the gap between the Real and its symbolization is irreducible. But instead of bemoaning this loss, Hegel's fundamental move is to praise this incredible power of Understanding, this capacity to "abstract," to divide up the immediate unity of the living world:

> The action of separating the elements is the exercise of the force of Understanding, the most astonishing and greatest of all powers, or rather the absolute power. The circle, which is self-enclosed and at rest, and, *qua* substance, holds its own moments, is an immediate relation, the immediate, continuous relation of elements with their unity, and hence arouses no sense of wonderment. But that an accident as such, when cut loose from its containing circumference, – that what is bound and held by something else and actual only by being connected with it, – should obtain an existence all its own, gain freedom and independence on its own account – this is the portentous power of the negative; it is the energy of thought, of pure ego. (Hegel 1977: 23)

To put this another way, the concreteness of thought is completely different from the immediate concreteness of the fullness of the living. The "progress" of dialectical thought in regard to Understanding is in no way the reappropriation of this pre-linguistic richness; rather, it can be reduced to the experience of its fundamental nullity – the richness that is lost through symbolization is already in itself something ephemeral. The error of Understanding is not that it wants to reduce the richness of the living to the abstract determinations of thought. Its great error is the very opposition between the richness of the concrete and the abstractness of the network of symbolic determinations, the belief in an original fullness of the concrete living world that supposedly escapes the network of symbolic determinations. Those worn-out formulations, according to which Reason puts the rigid categories of Understanding "in movement" and introduces dialectical dynamism, lead to a misunderstanding: far from "passing beyond the limits of Understanding," Reason marks the point of reduction where all the content of thought is immanent within Understanding. The categories of Understanding "become fluid," and "dialectical movement" is introduced when we no longer think of them as frozen moments, as "objectifications" of a living process that is always overflowing from them – that is to say, when we locate their motive force *in the immanence of their own contradiction.*

"Contradiction as the agent of dialectical movement" has once again become a platitude that is often used to sidestep efforts to give an exact definition of this contradiction. Therefore we must ask: what is, in a strict sense, the "contradiction" that "pushes" the dialectical process forward?

An initial approach would be to say that it is the contradiction of universality *with itself*, with its own specific content. Among the specific elements of each universal totality, posited as a thesis, there will necessarily be "at least one" that *negates* the universal trait defining the totality in question. This is the "symptomal point," the element that, from within the field of this universality, serves as its outside, a point of exclusion from which the field establishes itself. Therefore, we do not compare the universality of a thesis to a Truth-in-Itself to which it supposedly corresponds; we compare it with itself, with its own concrete content. Exploring the concrete content of a universal thesis subverts it retroactively, out of the structural necessity of an element that "extrudes" and that functions as its constitutive exception. Take Marx's *Capital*: a society of private property in which individual producers are themselves owners of the means of production, when developed fully, to its radical conclusion, gives us its immanent negation, capitalism, which implies the expropriation of the majority of producers who are forced to sell their own labor in the marketplace, rather than the fruit of their labor; and then, capitalism, developed all the way to its radical conclusion, gives us socialism (the expropriation of the expropriators themselves).

Second, we must specify the character of this comparison of universality to itself, to its concrete content. Ultimately, it is a matter of the comparison of what the subject who uttered a universal thesis *wanted to say* and what he really *said*. One subverts a universal thesis in such a way as to show the subject who formulated it how, *by his own formulation*, he was saying something completely different from what he "wanted to say." As Hegel makes clear, the most difficult thing in the world is to utter, to articulate, what one "really said" by formulating a proposition. The most basic form of this dialectical subversion of a proposition by self-reference – by putting the proposition in the context of its own formulation – can be seen in Hegel's treatment of the proposition of identity. The subject "wants to say" that identity has nothing to do with difference, that it is something radically other than difference. But by doing this, he *says* the precise opposite of what he wanted to say; he determines identity as radically *different* from difference. As a result, difference is inscribed into the core itself, *into the identity itself* of identity:

> It is thus to an empty identity that they cling, those who take it to be something true, insisting that identity is not difference but that the two are different. They do not see that in saying, "*Identity is different* from difference," they have thereby already said *that identity is something different*. (Hegel 2010: 358)

This is why, for Hegel, truth is always on the side of what one says and not what one "intended to say." Already in the beginning of the *Phenomenology of Spirit*, in the case of "sense certainty," the literalness of the spoken subverts the intention of signification (the consciousness "wanted to say" an absolutely specific here-and-now, but, in fact, it spoke the greatest abstraction, any here-and-now whatsoever). Hegel knows that we always say too much or else too little, always *something else*, as opposed to what we *wanted* to say. This discord is the energy that powers the dialectical movement; it is this discord that subverts every proposition.

This crucial distinction between what the subject "wants to say," what he "thinks [*meint*]," and what he "actually says" – a distinction that corresponds perfectly to Lacan's distinction between *signification* and *signifiance** – can be explained in relation to the dialectic of essence and appearance. "For us," for the dialectical consciousness that observes the process afterwards, the essence is *the appearance as appearance* [*die Erscheinung als Erscheinung*], which is to say the movement of appearance's self-transcendence, the movement through which appearance is posited as such, as something that, in fact, "is only appearance." However, "for the consciousness," for the subject caught in the process, essence is something beyond appearance, a substantial entity hidden by deceptive appearances. The "significa-tion" of the essence, what the subject "wants to say" when he speaks of essence, is therefore an entity that transcends appearance. But what he "actually says," the "*signifiance*," can be reduced to the movement of the self-abolition of appearance. Appearance does not have its own substance; it is a chimerical entity continually in the process of dis-solving itself. The "*signifiance*" of essence can therefore be reduced to the path traveled by the subject, to the process through which appearance becomes for him appearance of the Essence.

An exemplary instance of this dialectic can be seen in the Hegelian interpretation of the aporias that Zeno of Elea tried to use to dem-onstrate the non-existence of movement and of the Many. Zeno "wanted to say," of course, that movement does not exist, that all that exists is the One, being that is unchanging, indivisible, etc. But what he in fact demonstrated was the contradictory nature of move-ment; movement *exists only through self-dissolution*, which is not the same thing as saying that *there is no* movement. The crucial point here is to capture the *self-referential* character of movement. Move-ment coincides with (the movement of) its own dissolution. The infinite One, the unchanging Absolute, is not an entity that transcends the multitude of the finite; it is instead the absolute, self-referential movement, the movement itself of the self-dissolution of the finite, the Many.

Zeno's paradoxes

The paradoxes employed by Zeno in his attempt to disprove the hypothesis of movement and the existence of the Many – which is to say, that he uses to prove the existence of the One, of unchanging

---

* Here I have left the French word "significance" in its original form, although it has also been translated as "signifierness," "signifyingness," or "meaningfulness." For a more in-depth discussion of the various translations of the term, see Lacan 2006: 318.

being, via the absurd consequences that result from the affirmation of movement – are especially interesting from the point of view of our argument. Jean-Claude Milner's brilliant "fictional detective work" (Milner 1985) showed us that Zeno's four arguments (Achilles and the tortoise, the arrow in flight, the Dichotomy, the stadium) were arrived at not through a purely formal logical approach, but rather through a kind of literary technique. Let us examine the exact nature of the literary examples that served as reference points for Zeno. Take the most famous paradox, that of Achilles trying in vain to capture the tortoise (or Hector). According to Milner, the paradox is drawn from the following passage of *The Iliad*:

> As a man in a dream who fails to lay hands upon another whom he is pursuing – the one cannot escape nor the other overtake – even so neither could Achilles come up with Hector, nor Hector break away from Achilles. (Homer 1999: 264)

How can we not recognize in the paradoxical relationship of the subject to the object the well-known dream in which one is continually approaching an object that remains eternally out of reach? As Lacan already pointed out, the object is inaccessible not because Achilles cannot pass the tortoise (he can overtake the tortoise and leave it behind him), but because he cannot reach it. The object is a limit that is never reached, located between a "too early" and a "too late" – reminiscent of the well-known paradox of happiness in Brecht's *Threepenny Opera*; by pursuing happiness in too ardent a manner, we overtake it and leave it behind. The topology of this paradox is the paradoxical topology of the object of desire that escapes us, that draws away at our very approach. Similar literary contexts can easily be found in Zeno's other paradoxes. For the paradox of the arrow in flight, which cannot be in motion because at each moment it occupies a specific point in space, Milner finds the model in this description of Heracles in *The Odyssey*:

> He looked black as night with his bare bow in his hands and his arrow on the string, glaring around as though ever on the point of taking aim . . . naked bow in his grip, an arrow grooved on the bowstring, glaring round him fiercely, forever poised to shoot. (Homer 2012: 178)

Heracles fires and the arrow flies, but in a perpetually repeated manner, in such a way that it is continually beginning its movement over again, and, in this sense, remains immobile through its very movement. Once again, we cannot miss the connection with a very common dream experience – that of "immobile movement" in which, despite your frenzied activity, you remain in some way blocked, immobile, stuck in a fixed point, where, through your very movement itself, you seem "not to move." You are constantly repeating the same gesture, and even though the act is accomplished again and again, its effect is canceled out. As Milner notes, the location in which this episode occurs is not insignificant: it takes place in the Underworld, where Ulysses encounters a whole series of famous tortured figures who are doomed to continually repeat the same action again and again: Tantalus, Sisyphus, etc. For the time being, we can leave aside the figure of Tantalus, whose torture is the physical embodiment of the Lacanian distinction between need and demand (in satisfying one's need to drink, one does not satisfy the demand that is contained within thirst, and this is why thirst persists into infinity). The "rock of Sisyphus" is directly relevant to our theme:

> With hands and feet he tried to roll it up to the top of the hill, but always, just before he could roll it over on to the other side, its weight would be too much for him, and the pitiless stone would come thundering down again on to the plain. (Homer 2012: 177–8)

This is the literary reference point for the third paradox, called the "Dichotomy": one can never cross distance X, because, before doing so, one must travel half of this distance, etc., on to infinity. The goal (in Sisyphus' case, the top of the hill) becomes further away once reached and moves again; the whole path, once traveled, is revealed to be only the half of it. The actual goal of Sisyphus' activity is the path itself, the circular movement that consists in pushing the rock uphill and letting it roll back down. It is clear that here we have the basic framework of *a drive*, with its pulsation and its circular movement. The true aim of a drive is not its stated goal: it is nothing more than "the return into the circuit of the drive" (Lacan 1998a: 178). And the final paradox:

> two rows of bodies, each row being composed of an equal number of bodies of equal size, passing each other on a race-course as they proceed with equal velocity in opposite directions, the one row originally occupying the space between the goal and the middle point of the course and the other that between the middle point and the starting-post . . . half a given time is equal to double that time. (Aristotle 2006: 87)

Or, to quote Plato's general formulation: "the half is worth more than the whole" (Plato 1992: 141). Where can we find such an experience, in which the influence of an object is reinforced and increased as it is diminished – the more it diminishes, the more important the remaining part becomes? Consider the way in which the figure of the Jew – the quintessential libidinal object – functioned in Nazi discourse: "the more we eliminate and destroy them, the more dangerous the rest become. . . ." The more we attempt to repel the horrifying object of desire, the more it looms, frightening, in front of the subject.

The general conclusion we can draw from this is that there is a domain in which the paradoxes of Zeno take on their full value, a domain that operates in a perfectly homologous way to Zeno's paradoxes of movement themselves. This is the domain of the object of desire, of the "impossible" relationship of the subject to the object-cause of his desire and the compulsion that circles around this object. The topology of Zeno's paradoxes is that of the relationship of the subject to the object-cause of his desire. The domain ruled out by Zeno – I am even tempted to say foreclosed – as "impossible" in order to establish the reign of the One, is the Real of compulsion and the object that it circles around. Omitting the *object a* is constitutive of the field philosophy as such: "the object is the one lacking in philosophical consideration in order to situate itself, that is: in order to know that it is nothing" (Lacan 1987: 110). This is why the paradoxes Zeno used in order to prove the impossibility of movement and from there its non-existence are the other side of the existence of the One, of what Parmenides – the "first philosopher" – called unchanging Being.

The *object a* is simultaneously the purest semblance, a chimera "without substance," the fragile positivation of nothingness, and also the Real, the hard kernel, the rock upon which symbolization is dashed. This explains the paradox of philosophy: philosophy lacks the *Real* because of its very attempt to find true being through exclusion, through ruling out false appearance [*semblance*], which is to say, by setting about drawing the line of separation between true being and the semblant. The lack of consideration given to the Real core takes the paradoxical form of the fear of being taken in by false appearances, of succumbing to the power of the semblant. The pure semblant appears horrifying, because it announces a Real that threatens to explode the ontological consistency of the universe.

To bring this back to Hegel, we can reformulate his reading of Zeno's paradoxes in the following way: Zeno's "intention" is to exclude the paradoxical circuit of compulsion, the paradoxical nature of the *object a* that grows through its very own diminution, that keeps its distance through our very approach. However, what he "actually does" is define in a very neat and concise way the paradoxical topology of the impossible-Real object, the phantasmic relationship of the subject to the object-cause of desire ($ ◊ a).

Truth as loss of the object

This Hegelian reading of Zeno demonstrates the fundamental error of the standard view of the *in-itself* [*An-sich*] category. The in-itself is normally thought of as the transcendental substantial content that eludes consciousness and therefore, according to the Kantian model of the thing-in-itself, has not yet been "mediated" by it. To return to Zeno, what is the in-itself of his argument? Zeno takes his argument to be a *reductio* proof of the existence of unchanging being, which persists in itself beyond the misleading appearance of movement. And so already, "for the consciousness" (for Zeno himself), there is a difference between what is only "for it," for the ordinary consciousness, and what exists "in itself." Movement is a false appearance that only exists for the naive, pre-philosophical consciousness, while "in itself," there only exists unique and unchanging being. This is the first correction we must make to the aforementioned standard view: the difference between what is "for it (the consciousness)" and what exists "in itself" *is a distinction that takes place within the "naive" consciousness itself*. The Hegelian subversion consists only in relocating this distinction and showing that it *is not where the "naive"* (or, "critical," which is nothing more than the supreme form of naivety) *consciousness posits it*.

"For the consciousness," for Zeno, there is a distinction between the contradictory, self-dissolving appearance of movement and unchanging being, unique, identical to itself, existing in itself. Zeno's "truth," his "in-itself-for-us," is that the entire content of unchanging being, all that Zeno "actually says," can be reduced to the movement of movement's self-sublation. Unchanging being, beyond appearance, is the process of movement's self-dissolution through contradiction. This is the crucial point: "for the consciousness," for Zeno, this argumentative approach is fundamentally *exterior to the "thing-itself,"* it is only *our* path to the One, to unchanging being that is supposed to persist in-itself, unaffected by our methods – to use the well-known metaphor, it is like the ladder that we kick away after using it. "For us," on the other hand, the entire content of being resides in the argumentative path that brought us to it; "for us," unchanging being is only an objectification, a fixed figuration of the method through which we came to see movement as misleading appearance. The passage from that which is only "for the consciousness" to the "in itself or for us" is therefore in no way a passage from misleading, superficial appearance into the Beyond that exists in itself. On the contrary, it is a question of recognizing that what the consciousness took to be a path toward the truth, exterior to the truth (Zeno's argumentative approach, for example), *is already the truth itself.*

In a certain sense, "everything is in the consciousness." The true In-itself is not hidden in some transcendent Beyond. The error of the consciousness consists entirely in failing to notice that what it took for a procedure exterior to the object is already the object-itself. Here we can see the whole weight of the category of the "formal aspect [*das Formelle*]" introduced by Hegel in the *Introduction to the Phenomenology of the Spirit*. The truth of a moment in the dialectical process consists in its form itself, in the formal procedure, in the path by which the consciousness reached it:

> The *content*, however, of what presents itself to us does exist *for it* [for the consciousness]; we comprehend only the formal aspect of that content, or its pure origination. *For it*, what has thus arisen exists only as an object; *for us*, it appears at the same time as movement and a process of becoming. (Hegel 1977: 56)

Contrary to the classical representation of an external form that supposedly obscures the true content, the dialectical approach conceives of the content itself as a "fetish," an objective given whose inert presence *hides its true form*. The truth of Eleatic Being is the formal approach that demonstrated the inconsistency of movement. That is why the Hegelian dialectic implies the experience of the fundamental nullity of the "content" – meaning this *X*, this core of the in-itself that we supposedly approach through the formal procedure. We must come to recognize in *X* an upside-down effect of the formal process itself. If Hegel criticized Kant for his formalism, it's because he was not "formalist" enough, which is to say, because he retained the postulate of an In-itself that supposedly escapes the transcendental form, not realizing that this was in fact a pure "thing-of-the-mind."

The dialectical path toward the "Truth" of an object therefore implies the experience of its *loss*. The object, its rigid form, dissolve into the network of "mediations," of formal procedures. That the dialectical "truth" of an object consists in the network of its mediations is nothing new – but, as a rule, people forget the other side of the immediacy of the object's passage toward the network of its mediations: the *loss* of the object. By grasping the "Truth" of Eleatic Being as the movement itself of the demonstration of the non-existence, the self-dissolution of movement, we lose "being" as an entity existing in itself. In place of Being – a fixed reference point, identical to itself – all that remains is the vertiginous movement of the bottomless maelstrom, the self-dissolution of movement, a procedure that at first seemed to be an exterior path to being. This is Heraclitus as the "truth" of Parmenides (see Dolar 1986).

And it was the concept of truth itself that Hegel famously reversed: truth does not consist in the correspondence of our thought (the proposition, the concept) to the thing (the object), but rather the correspondence of the object itself to the concept. Heidegger (2002) replied that this reversal remained trapped in the same metaphysical framework of truth as correspondence. But what escaped from Heidegger's critique was the radically *non-symmetrical* character of the Hegelian reversal. For Hegel, we are dealing with three elements, not just two. "Knowledge," the dual relationship between "thought" and its "object," is replaced by the triangle of (subjective) thought, the object and the concept *that is in no way the same thing as thought*. We might say that the concept is in fact the *form of the thought*, form in the strictly dialectical sense of the "formal aspect" as the truth of the "content." That which remains "un-thought" [*impensé*] in a thought is not a transcendental surplus, an unseizable X of its objectual "content," but its form itself. The encounter between an object and its concept (concept in a strictly dialectical sense, not some abstract-universal Platonic Idea) is therefore necessarily a *missed* encounter. The object can never correspond to its concept, because *its existence, its very consistency*, depends on this non-correspondence. "The object" itself, as a fixed, inert point, that is to say, as a non-dialecticized presence, is in a certain sense non-truth incarnate and, as a point, plugs the hole in the truth. This is why the path to the truth of an object entails its loss, the dissolution of its ontological consistency.

2

The Retroactive Performative, or How the Necessary Emerges from the Contingent

One-grain-more, one-hair-less

Doesn't the dialectical procedure entail the total dissolution of the positive object into the absolute form of the concept? And isn't this dissolution simply Hegelian "panlogicism" in action? Such hasty reasoning overlooks the fact that the Hegelian concept of totality is fundamentally *pas-tout*; there must always be a "grain of sand" that functions as a foreign body. What is this grain? It is, of course, the same one as in the paradoxes of one-grain-more and one-hair-less. Which grain is it that makes a collection of grains of sand a pile? Which hair is the one whose removal makes someone bald? The only possible answer involves inverting the Lacanian concept of "anticipated certainty." That what we have in front of us is already a pile is something that can only be recognized *too late*, after the fact – the moment can never be quite right. At a particular moment, we simply recognize that what we have in front of us was, *at least one grain earlier*, a pile. In other words, the validity of our observation is retroactive; it remains true if we remove a grain, if we add a hair . . . Why is this? What we are dealing with here are *symbolic* determinations, which refuse to be reduced to descriptions of positive traits, positive properties, which always involve a certain distance from positive reality. A symbolic determination ("pile," for example) will never seamlessly coincide with reality. We can only notice, *after the fact*, that the state of things in question already existed, *beforehand*. The paradox is, of course, that this "beforehand," this effect of "already there," results retroactively from the symbolic determination itself. The excess, superfluous grain that makes a pile (superfluous, because the pile would remain a pile even if we removed the last grain we added) embodies the function of the signifier in reality. I am tempted to say that it represents the subject for all the other grains. This paradox of inevitable superfluousness, of necessary excessiveness, is a good illustration of the fundamental nature of the symbolic order. Language is always excessive, it is always added as a surplus – but if we take away this surplus, we lose the very thing that we had hoped to capture in its "naked form," without the superfluous element: "reality in itself."

This is a good point from which to approach the fundamental paradox of the Hegelian dialectical process, which is characterized by two traits that seem, at first, to contradict – perhaps even mutually exclude – each other. The principal thrust of Hegel's critique of the theory of "naive" knowledge – "common sense" – is that it sees the process of acquiring knowledge as a discovery, a penetration into a universe of pre-existing facts. We supposedly gain knowledge of reality as it existed prior to this process. This "naive" theory misses the constructive nature of the relationship of the process of knowledge in regard to its object, the way in which knowledge itself modifies the object, giving it, through the act of knowing, the form that it takes as an object of knowledge.

The key thrust of Hegel's critique bears on something completely different from the Kantian critique, which emphasized the constitutive role of transcendental subjectivity. For Kant, the subject gives universal form to a substantial content of transcendental origin (the "Thing-in-Itself"). Kant remained within the framework of the opposition between subject (the transcendental network of the possible forms of experience) and substance (the transcendental "Thing-in-Itself"), whereas for Hegel we must treat the substance itself as subject. Knowledge is not breaking through to the substantial content – content that would supposedly be unaffected by the knowing process – the act of subjective knowledge is already included in its substantial "object"; the path to the truth is part of the truth itself. In order to illustrate the point Hegel is making here, let me give an example that might initially seem surprising, but that testifies to the Hegelian legacy in historical materialism and that confirms Lacan's thesis that Marxism is not a "world view" (Lacan 1998b: 30). The fundamental claim of historical materialism is that the proletariat has a revolutionary role and a historical mission. But the proletariat only becomes an effective revolutionary subject through the recognition and acceptance of its true historical role. Historical materialism is not "objective knowledge of the historical role of the proletariat" – its knowledge requires the subjective position of the proletariat; it is in this sense self-referential, included in its own object of knowledge. Therefore, the first point we must address is the question of the "performative" character of the process of knowledge. When the subject goes behind the curtain of appearance to search for the hidden essence, he thinks he will discover something that was always there; he does not realize that in passing behind the curtain, he is bringing with him the very thing that he will find.

And yet, elsewhere in Hegel we can find an argument that seems initially to directly contradict this conception of the "performative" nature of the dialectical process. While the idea of "performativity" is today a commonplace in Hegelian interpretations, this other thesis receives significantly less attention from Hegelians. When Hegel describes the decisive reversal of the dialectical process, he constantly makes use of the same stylistic device: things are "already there," or were "always already." This implies the *recognition* of a pre-existing state of affairs. The reversal is reduced to the realization that "it's already like this" – *we already have* the thing we were looking for; what we aspire to *is already the case*. The passage from the scission to the dialectical synthesis is therefore in no way an ordinary "synthetization" of opposites – a productive act that reconciles the opposites, that erases the scission. Rather, it can be reduced to the realization that, in fact, the scission *never existed*, that it was an effect of our perspective. This in no way implies a position of abstract Identity that would nullify all differences, a night in which "all cows are black." Rather, what Hegel emphasizes is that it is the scission itself that unites the opposing poles: the "synthesis" that we were looking for beyond the scission *was already realized by the scission itself*.

Take the example of the "unhappy consciousness" in the *Phenomenology of the Spirit* (Hegel 1977: 119). It is "unhappy" because it feels the pain of the scission between the Absolute and itself, (a) finite consciousness, excluded from the Absolute. What would it take to bridge this scission? How does the "unhappy consciousness" succeed in overcoming this scission? Not by succeeding, at long last, in arriving at the transcendent Absolute, finally satisfying its fervent aspirations by fusing itself with the Absolute. Instead, "overcoming" this scission requires only the simple recognition that the "unhappy consciousness" is already the medium, the field of mediation, the unity of the two opposing moments, because the two moments *occur in it* and not in the Absolute. In other words, the very fact that the "unhappy consciousness" suffers the pain of this scission proves that it is in itself the unity of the two opposing moments, of itself and the Absolute, which is not an Absolute that exists in serene indifference.

How then should we think of these two sides of the dialectical process? On the one hand, we have its "performative" character, which we must be careful not to treat as if it were the movement toward some pre-existing In-Itself. On the other, there is its "constative" character, according to which the scission is overcome because it never existed, the obstacle vanquished because it was never an obstacle. Herein lies the proof that the Hegelian dialectic is none other than the logic of the signifier. The concept of the signifier can be found in the paradoxical unity of these two traits, in the paradox of *retroactive performativity*. Let us return to our example of the pile of sand. The recognition that there is a pile is a performative one. The determination "pile" is not reducible to description using only positive properties. And, as we saw earlier, out of structural necessity, this recognition can only occur after the fact. It is always "at least one grain too late," implying that what we have before us *was already* a pile "one grain earlier." This is the signifier's performative "temporal reach," which *retroactively* makes the thing in question (the pile, for example) *what it already was*.

The *Witz* of the synthesis

Is this kind of structure of retroactive performativity the key to the fundamental paradox of the dialectical process? Do we achieve the infinite goal by realizing that it was already achieved, erase the scission by recognizing that it was already erased, that, in a certain sense, it never even existed? Does the antithesis proceed to the synthesis through the realization that it was already, in itself, the synthesis it was searching for in vain outside of itself? Let us take as an example the following, quite Hegelian, *Witz*: Rabinovitch (a legendary figure in Jewish *Witz* from the Soviet Union) enters the Emigration Office in Moscow and declares that he wishes to emigrate. The bureaucrat on duty demands that he justify his request. Rabinovitch replies: "There are two reasons. The first is that I'm frightened that communist rule in the Soviet Union will collapse, and once the reactionaries are back in power, they will blame all the ills of socialism on the traditional scapegoats: the Jews. There will once again be pogroms . . . ." The bureaucrat interrupts him: "But that's absurd – communist rule in the Soviet Union is invincible, it will last forever, nothing will change the Soviet Union. . . ." "And that is the second reason," Rabinovitch calmly replies.

What is essential to notice here is that the *Witz* only works because of its dialogic economy. If Rabinovitch simply listed the two reasons – (1) because, if Soviet power collapses, there will be pogroms; (2) because Soviet power will never collapse – we would only have a non-sequitur similar to the famous Freudian "kettle logic," it would lack the twist necessary for it to be a *Witz*. The genius of this *Witz* lies in including the listener's reaction to Rabinovitch's first reason. There are two reasons: the first is offered, the other person protests, produces arguments against the first reason, and there you go, he himself has given the second reason. This is the logic of the thesis-antithesis-synthesis in its pure form. The thesis is the first argument ("I want to emigrate because I am afraid of the pogroms that would follow the collapse of Soviet power"), the bureaucrat's objection is the antithesis ("Soviet power is indestructible"), the synthesis is *exactly the same* as the antithesis – the bureaucrat's reply becomes its own opposite, it becomes the reason itself. The synthesis is the antithesis, the only step between the two is a reversal in perspective, a retroactive realization that the solution can be found in what we originally saw as the problem. The pass is what had initially seemed to be the impasse. The Hegelian performative makes it so that the thing in question is, in the end, what it had always-already been. A good example of this retroactive performativity can be found in Jean-Claude Milner's commentary on the Leninist-Maoist theory of the "weakest link" and the "principle contradiction":

> What was impossible for them is that an act could create the conditions that would, retroactively, make it just and timely. However, it has been shown that this is in fact what happens and it is not that we must try to see more clearly, but rather that we must blind ourselves sufficiently so as to be able to strike in just the right way, which is to say, in a way that would break things open. (Milner 1983: 16)

This idea – first we examine the state of affairs and determine the principle contradiction and the weakest link through "objective" analysis, and then, armed with our correct understanding, we strike at this very point – is an error of perspective. All acts, all interventions, are fundamentally shots in the dark. In a final analysis they are only grounded on themselves. It is through these acts, these interventions, that the point that was struck becomes "the weakest link." Hegel, in his interpretation of tragedy, already emphasized this link between acting and blindness. This is why acting is fundamentally tragic and why it can only accomplish its true goal through its own failure, through missing its immediate aim.

The above error in perspective is not unrelated to the transfer; in fact it coincides with the retroactive illusion of supposition ("the subject who supposedly knows") that is characteristic of the phenomenon of the transfer. For proof of this, we don't need to look any further than the retroactive character of love. When you fall in love, you necessarily fall prey to the illusion that, in a certain sense, *you had always-already* been in love. All of your life leading up until that point comes to seem like a chaos that was waiting for the creative gesture of love, a chaos that is only legible through the arrival of this love that would retroactively give it its signification, which is to say, that would help us detect the signs that foretold its arrival. Love is like the hero in one of the stories from *The Arabian Nights* who is wandering aimlessly through the desert, and, by pure happenstance, enters a cave. There, three wise men awaken from their deep slumber and greet him: "There you are! We've been waiting for you for more than three hundred years!" If you situate it within a linear sequence of events, the encounter with the loved one appears completely accidental, the result of pure happenstance. But afterwards, one gets the sense that it was, from the very beginning, destined to happen, and one cannot help feeling a little surprised, like in the old joke: "My mother was born in Brest, my father in Marseille and I was born in Paris – what a stroke of luck that we ever met!"

Hegel and the contingent

We can already begin to see how the paradox of retroactive performativity allows us to dispel the mirage of Hegelian "panlogicism," of conceptual Necessity that governs the contingency of events. The habitual counterargument proffered against Hegel's alleged "panlogicism" is the irreducible fact of existence. As Schelling emphasized, logical necessity only deals with reality's *conditions of possibility*, reality in the guise of the possible – it cannot capture the positive given form of reality, its *quod est* – the thing that is left over once we have removed its rational form. The most infamous version of this is "Krug's quill." Krug, a minor philosopher and a contemporary of Hegel, offered the following challenge to speculative idealism: deduce from the logical movement of the Absolute the quill with which I am writing at this very moment. To which Hegel replied: far from claiming the ability to deduce all individual content, speculative philosophy is in fact the only philosophical theory that can acknowledge the idea of *absolute happenstance*, that includes the contingent in the very concept itself of essence.

Nature is quintessentially the domain of happenstance. That there are 122 and not 123 breeds of dog, and so forth, is the product of happenstance. Non-conceptual contingency overflows from logical necessity and this is the necessary consequence of the development of the Idea, which externalizes itself and gives free range to its particular moments. Let us recall Hegel's famous reply when one of his students criticized him because an empirical detail did not fit with his theory: "too bad for nature." This incessant overflowing, the transgression of natural forms in regard to the rational order, the never-ending production of bastards, the intermixing of different species: these are not reflections of the creative power of nature, but rather its fundamental *powerlessness*, its inability to attain the level of the concept. The concept, in its self-development, divides itself and necessarily posits its externality as the domain of happenstance: "The necessity is *contingency* . . . not *the contingent*. This is why determinate/particular content is not the object of substantial theoretical interest" (Henrich 1971: 168). This is the difference between Hegel's position and that of Kant or Fichte, for whom the subject is dedicated to the infinite task of mastering contingency, reducing it, suffusing it with rational necessity:

> The correct attitude of the subject towards happenstance is not in the endless drive to dissolve the contingent into the concept, but rather the renunciation of such an understanding. Happenstance is, as natural content, allowed to roam free, already surpassed by the Idea and therefore posited as uninteresting. (Henrich 1971: 169)

This shift that Hegel represents in relation to the Kantian-Fichtian position can best be understood against the background of the Lacanian logic of *pas-tout*. The Kantian position is that of a Whole, a Universality of the formal-transcendental conditions of all possible experience and from there of all objects of experience. This Universality entails an Exception – there is something that escapes from the universal framework of the transcendental form: the noumenon, the transcendental Thing-in-Itself. According to the traditional interpretation of the passage from Kant to Hegel, the latter supposedly "radicalized" the above position of Kant and Fichte. In this view, Hegel's famous formulation, "the real is the rational," is taken to mean that, from this moment on, "everything without exception" is encompassed by the circle of rational self-mediation, every contingency is suppressed-recovered as a moment in the necessary movement of the concept. But, as we have seen, to think that the formulation "the real is rational" contains the program for the total dissolution of contingent reality in the necessity of *logos* is to completely miss the point.

"The real is rational" (and vice versa) should not be read as "*all that is real is rational*," but rather "*there is no thing of the real that is not rational*" – the price of this "no-exceptions" being that, in fact, *all is not rational*, the domain of the contingent escapes conceptual deduction.

By *excluding* the contingent from necessity, by *giving up on* conceptually deducing the contingent, Hegel takes a first step in what seems like the other direction, presenting us with an exemplary case of the logic of the Whole and the Exception. If All is rational, we must exclude something from the necessary movement of the rational Totality – the contingent. But such a reading gives the contingent an importance that is incompatible with Hegel's conceptualization. This would make the contingent the opposite pole, the corollary equivalent of the necessary. However, Hegel emphasizes that it does not follow from "all is not rational" that a positive-substantial thing exists that would be an exception, a thing that "would not be rational." What escapes from the self-determination of the concept, the thing that makes it the case that "all is not rational," is indeed the contingent. But the contingent in itself is simply a nullity, an expired moment with no substantial weight, disappearing on its own, self-dissolving.

This difference from Kant and Fichte is especially conspicuous in the domain of ethics. Kant saw ethics as a continual battle against everything inert, non-rational, contingent in man, against his "pathological" inclinations, a never-ending and constant effort to *reduce* the role of the contingent. Hegel, meanwhile, held that we must *exclude happenstance but without opposing ourselves to it*. If we oppose ourselves to "pathological" happenstance, if we make this opposition the principal terrain upon which the ethical battle is fought, we are according far too much weight to happenstance, we are taking it for precisely what it is not, for the essential rather than the peripheral. The only proper attitude toward happenstance given its peripheralness is to *see it as such*, indifferently, "dispensing with the contingent without opposing it." To stoop to the level of the contingent by believing that the basis for an ethical life is the infinite battle against the contingent will always implicate positing the contingent as essential.

What is the difference between this Hegelian position and Stoicism, which also regards the contingent course of the world with indifference? According to Hegel, the Stoic *logos* is an empty formal identity, without content, that is unable to specify itself, to alienate itself as particular content. In other words, it is not yet a "concrete universality." This is why Stoicism culminates in the homeostasis of an isolated and abstracted individual, whereas, for Hegel, the form ethical duty takes is always dictated by the historical situation of the social community, the *polis*. There is therefore a development inside the field of ethics – the "battlefield of the spirit against itself" – that arrives in the form of the necessary conflict of duties (the confrontation of two ethical positions, that of Antigone and Creon in *Antigone*, for example). In these situations, "pathological" particularity re-emerges at the very heart of the ethical edifice: Good itself, posited as exclusive, coincides with absolute Evil.

Necessity as a retroactive effect

The concept that, through its self-development, divides itself and necessarily posits its externality as the domain of happenstance, evokes the idea of an essential Necessity that realizes, self-mediates, and "expresses" itself through a multitude of contingent conditions. This brings to mind two standard examples from Marxist theory. The development of capitalism occurs according to the necessity of its internal logic, but it will be realized through a multitude of contingent circumstances that arise out of "primitive accumulation," which will differ from country to country. Over the course of the French Revolution, the passage to empire was a historical necessity, and therefore a figure *like* Napoleon was necessary, but it was only by happenstance that this necessity was realized precisely in the person of Napoleon. Normally, the Hegelian theory of happenstance is reduced to just this: necessity is realized through a series of contingent conditions, contingency is therefore the form through which hidden necessity reveals itself. This necessity is the unity of itself and its contradiction, it encompasses and sublates [*aufhebt*] happenstance. It's impossible to miss the big themes of the "poststructuralist" critics of Hegel (Derrida, for example), who saw the Hegelian dialectic as the extreme form of "metaphysics of presence," in which identity mediates and suppresses all difference, necessity mediates and suppresses all contingency. The Hegelian idea of a necessity that retroactively puts in place its own necessary preconditions allows for a different, and more interesting, reading of Hegel from a Lacanian perspective:

> Contingency is the way in which possibility is posited as realized. Something that exists only in the mode of the possible is – when it is able to exist effectively – in relation to this possibility alone effectuated in a contingent manner. (Henrich 1971: 162)

How then do we pass from the contingent to the necessary? If we are dealing with a possibility that has been realized, the conditions of its realization are certainly contingent. If we look at the process of effectuation/realization *from the point of view of its result*, we see necessity. That is to say, the effective result that comes from the realization of a possibility appears necessary in that it locates its own necessary preconditions, in that it designates them as the conditions of its realization: "The possible that has become effective is not contingent but necessary because it posits its own conditions itself" (Henrich 1971: 163).

When a thing occurs as a result of a series of contingent conditions, it produces the *retroactive* impression that it was teleologically necessary, as if its development had been preordained from the very beginning. From the vantage point of the end result, it appears to have posited its own preconditions. The key for Hegelian "teleology" would therefore be to search inside the retroactive movement of the signifier for the point at which the appearance of a new master-signifier retroactively bestowed signification upon the chain that preceded it. Hegelian "necessity" is precisely the necessity of an S1 that "miraculously" turns chaos into a "new harmony," that transforms a series from a *lawless* to a *lawlike* series. The "dialectic" is, in its essence, the science of "how necessity emerges from contingency." The "dialectical unity of happenstance and necessity" simply consists in the fact that the emergence of the S1, the gesture that creates necessity, is in itself *radically contingent* – not because necessity is the all-encompassing unity of itself and its opposite (happenstance), but because necessity itself depends on a radical contingency. All the effort of the dialectical approach is directed to guarding against falling prey to the retroactive illusion that the final result was preordained from the outset, and thus to not losing sight of the contingency upon which the arrival of Necessity depends. This is why Brecht's concept of "alienation" [*"Verfremdung"*] is a constitutive part of dialectical analysis; that which is most "familiar," most "natural," must always appear to be a totally contingent and fictional order.

How should we understand this contingency? We should not take the retroactive character of necessity to mean that the way in which a story unfolds will appear necessary as soon as we know how it will end, nor that contingency will reappear if we present events in their linear order, from beginning to end. In his play *Time and the Conways*, J. B. Priestley presents the destiny of the Conway family in three acts. The first act finds them spending an evening together as a family, full of enthusiasm and projects for the future. The second act takes place 20 years later and they are all reunited once again. It is a meeting of

desperate, failed lives. The third act takes us back 20 years, to immediately following the action of the first act. The extremely depressing
effect this play has is not the result of the passage from the first to
the second act (passionate projects, then disillusionment), but rather
the transition from the second to the third act, when, after having
glimpsed the end result (complete failure), we see the same people
full of hope, unaware of what awaits them.

Rather than giving rise to a feeling of fatalism – that "all is already
decided in advance, that the characters are only puppets marching
unknowingly toward their sad fates" – the process of inverting the
linear succession of events and telling the story from ending to beginning brings out the fundamental contingency of the ending. The fact
that only this kind of anticipatory knowledge of the ending can dena-
ture the appearance of an organic succession of events can be shown
a contrario regarding the film *Casablanca*. It's a well-known fact that
even during shooting, the writers kept delaying making a choice
between several variants of the final denouement. Should Ingrid
Bergman leave with her husband or stay with Bogart? Will Bogart
have to die? And so on. When one watches the film, the end the
authors settled on (Bergman leaves with her husband) seems "natural,"
as if it was the logical result of the events that led up to it. But a different end (the death of Bergman's husband, for example) would be
no less "convincing"; it would produce the same impression of an
"organic succession" that comes when a story is presented to us in
linear order. The final "Quilting" [*"Capitonnage"*] automatically
confers on the preceding events a "natural" character. If, however, we
knew the end in advance, at each turning point in the story the
anguishing question would come up: will what must happen actually
happen? What if things turn out differently? We find ourselves split:
"I know what is going to happen, but still. . . ." Just as the teleology
makes use of evolutionism to support itself (this was Lacan's argument in the *Ethics of Psychoanalysis*), in the same manner fundamental contingency is most effectively concealed in a linear narrative.

From king to bureaucracy

Structural-necessity's dependence on contingency is to be taken literally. It is only through a contingent element, through its inert, given,
positive material form, that the formal structure can realize itself.
The scattered, as of yet unstructured, network of elements becomes
a "rational" structure through the emergence of a fundamentally
"irrational" element that functions as the S1, the master-signifier

with no signified, which is in its given material form the pure stupidity of reality, a scrap of contingent waste. Take the Hegelian monarch, for example, a totally arbitrary scrap of reality, determined by the completely arbitrary logic of heredity who, nevertheless, "is" the embodiment-itself of the effective form, the actualization, of the State as a rational totality, which is to say, the figure *in* whom the State attains its determinate existence [*Dasein*]. This type of paradoxical conjunction of a rational totality and an absolutely particular, inert, non-dialectical moment is the object of Hegelian "speculative judgment." The spirit is a bone; Napoleon, that arbitrary individual, *is* "the spirit of the world"; Christ, that unfortunate individual, crucified between two criminals, *is* God. Or, to give a more general formulation: the signifier, that tiny, senseless scrap of the real, *is* the signified, the exuberant abundance of meaning. The greatest "speculative mystery" of the dialectic is not the mediation of all particular contents through the process of rational totalization, but the way in which *this rational totality, in order to actualize itself, must once again incarnate itself in an absolutely particular moment, in pure waste*. In short, the "speculative mystery" is conceptual Necessity's dependence on a radically Contingent "scrap of reality." Hegel was quite right to underline the fact that the concept of the Monarch, of a particular individual who is the State, is "therefore extremely difficult for ratiocination – i.e. for the reflective approach of understanding – to grasp" (Hegel 1991a: 318).

In his *Elements of the Philosophy of Right*, Hegel was probably the last classical thinker to develop the idea of the necessary function of a symbolic, purely formal point of unfounded "irrational" authority. A constitutional monarchy is a rational Whole headed by the strictly "irrational" instance of the royal person. What is essential, here, is the irreducible chasm between the naturally articulated rational Whole of the State's constitution, and the "arbitrariness" of the person who embodies supreme Power, through which Power achieves subjectivity. In response to the criticism that the fate of the State should not be left up to the psychological disposition of the monarch, his wisdom, honesty, courage, etc., Hegel argues:

> [T]his objection is based on the invalid assumption that the monarch's particular character is of vital importance. In a fully organized state, it is only a question of the highest instance of formal decision, and all that is required in a monarch is someone to say 'yes' and to dot the 'i'; for the supreme office should be such that the particular character of its occupant is of no significance. . . . In a well-ordered monarchy, the objective aspect is solely the concern of the law, to which the monarch merely has to add his subjective "I will." (Hegel 1991a: 323)

The essential nature of the monarch's act is therefore completely formal. The framework for his decisions is determined by the constitution, the concrete contents of his decisions come from his expert-councilors, so that "he often has nothing more to do than to sign his name. But this name is important: it is the ultimate instance and *non plus ultra*" (Hegel 1991a: 321). It is all already there: the monarch is the "pure" signifier, the master-signifier "without signified." All of his "reality" (and authority) rests upon a *name*, and this is why his "given reality" is arbitrary, why it can be left up to hereditary biological contingency. The monarch is the One who, as the exception, as the "irrational" summit, makes the amorphous (*"pas-tout"*) masses into the "people," into a concrete moral totality. Existing as the "pure" signifier, he constitutes the Whole in its "organic articulation" [*"organische Gliederung"*]. He is the "irrational" surplus necessary for the rational Totality, the "pure" signifier without signified necessary for the organic Whole of the signified-signifier:

> *Without* its monarch and that *articulation* of the whole which is necessarily and immediately associated with monarchy, *the* people is a formless mass. The latter is no longer a state, and *none* of those determinations which are encountered only in an *internally organized* whole (such as sovereignty, government, courts of law, public authorities [*Obrigkeit*], estates, etc.) is applicable to it. (Hegel 1991a: 319)

In this sense, the monarch's authority is purely "performative." It is not based on any "existing" features of his person. The councilors, the ministers, the whole bureaucracy of the State, on the one hand, are chosen specifically for their competences (wisdom, know-how, etc.). This preserves the decisive *gulf* between State employees who operate according to their capacities and the head itself, the monarch as the pure point of signifying authority. This gulf prevents a short-circuit between (symbolic) authority and "actual" competence, the illusory fusion of a "rationally founded authority":

> the multitude of individuals is a folkgroup [*Volksmenge*] juxtaposed to one of its individuals who is the monarch. They are many – movement, fluidity – while he is the immediate, the natural. He alone is the natural element, i.e., the point to which nature has fled, its last residue as positive. The royal family is the one positive element, the others are to be abandoned. The other individual [i.e., the citizen] counts only as externalized, cultivated, as that which he has made of himself. (Hegel 1983: 161)

The paradox of the Hegelian monarch is that in a certain sense, he *is* the point of madness within the social system. The king is

defined by his royal origins, by biological fact, he is therefore the only
individual who is already "by his very nature itself" what he is –
everyone else must make themselves, which is to say, must give
content to their determinate existence through their actions. Saint-
Just was right – as usual – when, in his famous indictment, he
demanded the execution of the king not because of what he'd done,
but *because he was the king*. From the radical republican point of
view, the ultimate crime is *being* king.

The key Hegelian point here is more ambiguous, perhaps even
more cynical, than it might appear. His conclusion is basically the
following: if the Master is indispensable to politics, we should not
stoop to the level of common sense that tells us "let him at least be
the most able, wise, courageous. . . ." On the contrary, we must
preserve to the greatest extent possible the distance between symbolic
legitimation and "effective" authority, relegating the position of the
Master to a point rejected from the Whole, where it matters little if
he is incompetent, stupid, cowardly, etc. In the very place where he
seems to be singing the praises of monarchy, Hegel accomplishes a
kind of *separation* between S1 and *a* (the Lacanian notation for the
Freudian definition of hypnosis). The power that the King has to
fascinate comes from covering over the difference between S1 and *a*.
Hegel separates them and shows us, on the one hand, S1 in its
tautological folly as an empty name, without content, and, on the
other hand, the monarch's physical form as pure waste, the name's
appendix.

In other words, Hegel is saying the same thing here as Lacan is in
The Other Side of Psychoanalysis (the 1969–70 seminar). The gulf
between the State bureaucracy and the monarch corresponds to the
gulf between the field of "knowledge" (S2, bureaucratic "know-
how") and the quilting point (S1, the "unary" master-signifier).
Bureaucratic "knowledge" needs a unary point to "quilt" its discourse, to totalize it from the outside, to shoulder the moment of
decision and give discourse its performative dimension. Our only
hope is to isolate S1 as much as possible, to make it an empty point
of formal decision, without any concrete weight, which is to say, to
preserve as great a distance as possible between S1 and the register
of authority due to ability. If this exceptional point fails, bureaucratic
knowledge "becomes crazed," the neutrality of knowledge comes to
seem "malevolent." Without a "quilting point," its very "indifference" provokes in the subject the impression of a superego imperative
– we arrive at rule by totalitarian bureaucracy.

It is the logic of the signifier that can account for the necessity of
this One, of the exceptional point of an empty name.

3

The Dialectic as Logic of the Signifier
(1): The One of Self-Reference

The "quilting point" ["*point de capiton*"]

In the opening act of Racine's *Athaliah*, Abner laments the cruel fate that awaits followers of God under Athaliah's rule, to which Joad replies with the famous lines:

> He who can rein in the fury of the waves
> Knows also how to check the base one's plots:
> Submit with reverence to His holy will.
> Dear Abner, I fear God, and no one else
> I have to fear.

These lines have a transformative effect upon Abner. From an impatient *zealot*, and as such worried and uncertain, he turns into a calm *believer*, confident in himself and in the almighty power of God. How does evoking the "fear of God" manage to operate this miraculous "conversion"? Before this transformation, Abner saw in the earthly world only a multitude of dangers that filled him with fear, and he was waiting for his side, God and His representatives, to lend him their aid and help him to vanquish the world's many difficulties. Faced with this opposition between the earthly realm of dangers, uncertainty, worry, etc. and the divine kingdom of calm, love, and confidence, Joad doesn't just try to convince Abner that the forces of God are powerful enough to triumph over earthly chaos. He assuages Abner's fears in quite a different manner, by presenting their opposite, God, as more frightening than any worldly danger. And – this is the "miracle" of the quilting point – this one-fear-more, the fear of God, retroactively changes the character of all the other fears:

> [It] completes the sleight of hand that transforms, from one minute to the next, all fears into perfect courage. All fears – *I have no other fear* – are exchanged for what is called the fear of God, which, however constraining it may be, is the opposite of a fear. (Lacan 1993: 267)

The traditional Marxist view that religious consolation is an "imaginary compensation" for worldly misery is therefore to be taken literally. We are dealing with a dual, *imaginary*, relationship between terrestrial earth and celestial heaven, without any other *symbolic* "mediation." According to this conception, religion works by compensating for worldly horrors and uncertainties with the bliss that awaits us in the other world – all of Feuerbach's famous formulations of heaven as an inverted mirror image of earthly suffering. In order for this operation to "succeed," a third moment must intervene that would, in a certain sense, "mediate" between the two opposing poles. Behind the multitude of worldly horrors we can make out the infinitely more terrifying wrath of God, so that all the misfortunes of the world take on a new dimension and become so many manifestations of divine anger. The same operation takes place in fascism. In *Mein Kampf*, how does Hitler go about explaining to Germans the calamities of the era (the economic crisis, moral "decadence," etc.)? He constructs a new subject that is infinitely more terrifying, a single cause behind the multitude of misfortunes, the "Jewish conspiracy" that "explains everything." Just like that, all the problems of the world, from the economic crisis to the crisis of the family, become manifestations of the "Jewish conspiracy"; the Jew is Hitler's "quilting point."

The "Dreyfus Affair" is a paradigmatic example of the "miraculous twist" in discourse that is produced by the intervention of a quilting point. Its role in French and European political history already resembles that of a quilting point – it restructured the entire world of politics and sparked, directly or indirectly, a whole series of shifts that, still today, define the political landscape: the final separation of Church and State in bourgeois democracies, the socialist collaboration with bourgeois governments and the resulting schism between social democrats and communists, the birth of Zionism, the rise of anti-Semitism as the defining feature of "right-wing populism," etc. But here, I will focus only on locating the decisive turning point in the course of the affair itself, the intervention that turned a judicial dispute over the legality and fairness of a verdict into the focal point of a political battle that would shake the entire nation. This turning point is not, as it is often thought, the famous *"J'accuse"* that appeared in the *Aurore* on January 13, 1898, in which Zola simply recapitulated all the arguments in defense of Dreyfus and denounced corruption in official circles. Zola's intervention remained inside the framework and language of bourgeois liberalism, calling on the defense of liberties and the rights of citizens, etc. The true turning point only occurred in the second half of 1898. On August 30, Lieutenant-Colonel Henry, the new head of the *Deuxième Bureau*, is arrested, accused of having forged one of the secret documents that led to Dreyfus's conviction for high treason. The next day Henry commits suicide in his cell.

Public opinion is shocked by this news. If Henry confesses his guilt like this – what other signification could his suicide be given? – it must be that the charges leveled against Dreyfus were fundamentally flawed. Everyone expected that the trial would resume and that Dreyfus would be acquitted. At that moment – and here I will defer to Ernst Nolte's "poetic" description:

> Then in the midst of the confusion and consternation, a newspaper article appeared which altered the situation. Its author was Charles Maurras, a thirty-year-old writer hitherto known only in limited circles. The article was entitled "The first blood." It looked at things in a way which no one had thought or dared to look. (Nolte 1966: 56)

What is it that Maurras did? He neither introduced new evidence nor refuted the evidence that already existed. What he provided was a reinterpretation that put the whole "affair" in a completely different light. Henry became a heroic victim who preferred patriotic duty to abstract "justice." After seeing how the Jewish "Treason Syndicate" was exploiting a legal technicality in order to undermine the foundations of French life and break the strength of the Army, Henry quickly told a patriotic "white lie" in order to stop the nation from going over the edge. What was really at stake in the affair was not the fairness of a sentence, but the weakening and sapping of the French national *élan vital* by Jewish financiers who hid behind corrupt liberalism, the freedom of the press, the independence of the judiciary, etc. As a result, the real victim was not Dreyfus, but Henry himself, the lone patriot who risked everything for the well-being of France and whose superiors, at the decisive moment, turned their backs on him. This was the "first blood" drawn by the Jewish conspiracy. Just like that, this intervention changed the entire perspective on the event. The right rallied its forces and "patriotic" unity quickly won out over disarray. Maurras provoked this reversal by manufacturing a triumph – this myth of the "first victim" – *out of the very same elements that, prior to his article, had provoked the deepest disorientation and astonishment* (the false documents and, as a result, the unfair sentence, etc.), elements that he did not even try to dispute – far from it. It is no surprise, therefore, that he maintained up until his death that this article was the greatest achievement of his life.

The fundamental operation of the "quilting point" lies in this "miraculous" twist, in this shift in identities when what had been, at a given moment, the source itself of distress is transformed into proof and evidence of a triumph – just as in the first act of *Athaliah*, where the intervention of "one-fear-more," the fear of God, transforms all fears into their opposite in one fell swoop. This is a creative gesture in the strictest sense; it is a gesture that shapes chaos into a "new harmony," that suddenly makes things "legible" that up until then had been senseless – even terrifying – confusion. There is a very clear parallel here to Christianity. Not so much God's act of turning chaos into an ordered world, as the decisive turning point that resulted in the definitive form of Christianity, in the form inscribed and revered in our tradition: the break effected by St Paul. St Paul centered the entire Christian project on exactly the point that up until then had seemed, to the disciples of Christ, to be a horrifying, "impossible," traumatic event that couldn't be symbolized or integrated into their field of signification: his shameful death on the cross flanked by two criminals. Out of the complete and utter defeat of his earthly mission, which destroyed any hope of deliverance (of the Jews from Roman oppression), St Paul fashioned the act itself of His salvation. Through His death, Christ redeemed, saved, humanity.

We can shed some more light on the logic of this operation through a brief detour into detective fiction. What is the main "charm" of detective fiction in terms of the relationship between the law and the transgression of the law, crime? On the one hand we have the rule of law, tranquility, and security, but also boredom, the ennui of everyday life. On the other hand we have crime, which, as Brecht already said, is the only adventure possible in the bourgeois world. Detective stories operate through a sleight of hand, which did not go unnoticed at the time by Gilbert Keith Chesterton:

While it is the constant tendency of the Old Adam to rebel against so universal and automatic a thing as civilization, to preach departure and rebellion, the romance of police activity keeps in some sense before the mind the fact that civilization itself is the most sensational of departures and the most romantic of rebellions. . . . When the detective in a police romance stands alone, and somewhat fatuously fearless amid the knives and fists of a thieves' kitchen, it does certainly serve to make us remember that it is the agent of social justice who is the original and poetic figure, while the burglars and footpads are merely placid old cosmic conservatives, happy in the immemorial respectability of apes and wolves. The romance of the police force is thus the whole romance of man. It is based on the fact that morality is the most dark and daring of conspiracies. (Chesterton 2012: 77)

The fundamental mechanism of detective stories is presenting the detective himself – the one who works in defense of the law, in the name of the law, to re-establish the rule of law – as the greatest adventurer. In comparison to him, the criminals themselves look like indolent petty bourgeois, prudent conservatives. Once again we have this miraculous sleight of hand. There are, of course, a multitude of transgressions of the law, crimes, adventures that break the monotony of loyal and calm everyday life. But the only true transgression, the only true adventure, the one that changes all other adventures into petty bourgeois prudence, is the adventure of civilization, of the defense of the law itself.

Lacan saw things in a quite similar manner. For him as well, the greatest transgression, the most traumatic, senseless thing, is the law itself, the mad law of the superego, that inflicts, that demands *jouissance*. It is not that we have, on one side, the multitude of transgressions, perversions, aggressions, etc. and, on the other, the universal law that regularizes, normalizes the dead end of transgression, that makes the peaceful coexistence of subjects possible. The greatest madness is the other side, the other face, of pacifying law, the face of the law that so often goes unseen, a stupid injunction to *jouissance*. We might say that the Law necessarily splits itself in two, into a pacifying law and a mad law. The opposition between the Law and its transgressions is repeated inside the Law itself. We have here the same operation as we do in *Athaliah*. For Chesterton, the law, faced with the transgressions of ordinary criminals, appears as the only true transgression. In *Athaliah*, looking upon worldly fears, God appears to be the only thing truly worthy of fear; He divides Himself into a pacifying God, a God of love, calm, and grace, and a ferocious, enraged God, a God who evokes the most terrible fears.

This twist, this moment of inversion where the law itself appears to be the only true transgression, corresponds exactly to what is called, in Hegelian terminology, the "negation of the negation." First, we have a simple opposition between a position and its negation – in our case, between the positive, pacifying Law, and the multitude of specific transgressions of the Law, of crimes. The "negation of the negation" is the moment when we understand that the only true transgression, the only true negativity, is the Law itself, which changes all ordinary, criminal transgressions into indolent positivity. This is why Lacanian theory is irreducible to any variant of transgressivism, anti-Oedipalism, etc.; the only true anti-Oedipus is Oedipus himself, his super-egotistical side. This "Hegelian" economy is present even in Lacan's organizational decisions. Dissolving the *École freudienne de Paris* and creating *La Cause freudienne* might appear to be a liberating gesture – out with bureaucratization, rules, and regulations, now there would only be the Cause itself, freed from all mundane constraints. But it soon became clear that this action led to the re-establishment of an *École* of the Cause, far stricter than any other school – just as the transcendence of earthly fears through divine love necessarily requires the fear of God, more terrible than any worldly fear.

The dialectical return-to-the-self

The triad, the ternary structure in which universality, confronted with its particular contents, divides itself into positive and negative, inclusive and exclusive, "pacifying" and "destructive," offers us the basic matrix of the dialectical process. When confronted, mediated by the multitude of particular differences, the initial position reveals itself to be pure difference. When confronted, mediated by the multitude of particular negativities, the initial position reveals itself to be pure, absolute negativity. To give two more "concrete" examples: confronted with the multitude of specific crimes, the universal Law reveals itself to be the absolute, universalized Crime; confronted with the multitude of horrors on earth, God Himself, paragon of calm and love, is revealed to be absolute fury, total horror.

At first glance, this matrix seems to confirm Derrida's analysis (cf. Derrida 1986). Is it not the case that such a coincidence of absolute negativity with absolute positivity, of identity with absolute difference, etc. reduces difference to the self-movement of identity, reduces negativity to the self-mediation of positivity? The circle appears to be closed. Starting with identity, we pass to difference, and once we've pushed difference to its point of self-reference, difference is recuperated by identity. However, this reading misses the decisive point of the dialectical movement. It is not difference that ends up being reduced to the self-movement of identity, but identity that is reduced to absolute, which is to say self-referential, difference. *"Identity" is the name for difference taken to its point of self-reference.* To return to the example of the universal Law and the specific crime: it is not that universalized crime coincides with the Law, but *that it is the "truth" of the Law itself that it is nothing more than crime universalized.* "Truth" is therefore on the side of crime and not the side of the Law. Crime is not recuperated in the self-movement of the Law, reduced to a subordinated moment of its self-mediation. It is rather the Law itself that self-divides as it is caught up in the movement of the specific crime, insofar as it emerges out of its own self-reference. The "Law" is crime universalized. In the middle of a concrete analysis of the revolutionary process in *Class Struggles in France*, Marx develops the perfect example of the Universal splitting when confronted with its specific contents. Discussing the role of the "Party of Order" during the revolutionary events of the mid-nineteenth century, he writes:

> The secret of its existence, the coalition of Orleanists and Legitimists into one party . . . the nameless realm of the republic was the only one in which both factions could maintain with equal power the common class interest without giving up their mutual rivalry . . . if each of their factions, regarded separately, by itself, was royalist, the product of their chemical combination had necessarily to be republican. (Marx 2008: 79)

Following this logic, the republican is a species inside the royalist genus and, as such, it serves as the genus itself for the species that are subsumed within the genus. The royalist family is therefore divided into three species: Legitimists, Orleanists, and republicans. We can understand this conjuncture as a question of choice: a royalist is faced with the choice between Legitimism and Orleanism. Can he choose royalism in general, the medium itself of the choice? Marx replies: yes – if he chooses to be a republican, to place himself at the intersection itself between the Orleanist and Legitimist groups (see figure 1). This paradoxical element, this third option that cannot itself be selected, is the unsettling point where the universal genus *encounters itself* among its specific species. In other words, the proposition "the royalist is a republican" is a tautology whose

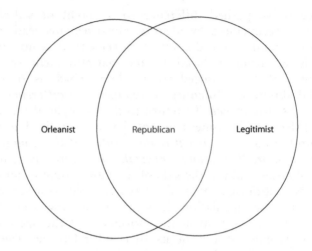

Figure 1

structure corresponds perfectly to that of the proposition "God is God," which Hegel exposed as pure contradiction:

> If anyone opens his mouth and promises to announce what God is, and says that "God is . . . God," expectation is cheated, for a different determination was anticipated. . . . Let us take a closer look at what makes such a truth tedious. So, the beginning, "The plant is . . . ," makes moves in the direction of saying something, of adducing a further determination. But since only the same is repeated, the opposite has happened instead, nothing has occurred. Such talk of identity, therefore, contradicts itself. (Hegel 2010: 359–60)

The key to this paradox – which Hegel discusses in the following section – rests with *the form of the proposition*. Such a form produces an "expectation" that the second half of the equation will include a determination-specification of the initial neutral universality. This expectation demands that the second half of the equation provide a *species* of genus, a *determination* of the abstract universality, a *marker* inscribed in the location, an *element* of the ensemble. But instead of that, what do we get? Identity, that fastidious point where the ensemble encounters itself among its own elements, where the genus encounters itself among its own species. More precisely, instead of finding itself exactly, what the initial moment stumbles upon is its own absence, the ensemble encounters itself as an empty ensemble. If the first God ("God is . . .") is the positive God, the genus that encompasses all its species, all its particular contents, the God of calm, of reconciliation and love, then the second God (". . . God") is the negative God, the one who *excludes* all these predicates, all these specifications, all the particular content, the God of hate and destructive fury, the mad God. In the same way, in the proposition "the royalist is a republican," "republican" embodies royalism in general while excluding all its particular content (the different species of royalism). The only way to *actually* be a royalist *in general* is to proclaim oneself to be a republican. This is what Hegel means by the "identity of opposites": far from being reducible to a simple aberrant identification of mutually exclusive predicates (such as "this rose is at the same time both white and blue"), its target is the *self-reference of the universal*. The universal is the opposite of itself insofar as it refers to itself as a particular, insofar as it attains its being-for-itself in the form of its opposite.

This contradictory effect can only be produced within the framework of a dialogic economy. The first part ("God is . . .") provokes in the interlocutor an *expectation* that is determined by the form itself of the proposition (we expect a predicate that is different from the subject, a specific determination of divine universality: God is all-powerful, infinitely good and wise, etc.). This expectation is disappointed by the second half (". . . God"), in which the same term returns. This dialogic economy requires logical *temporality*, a temporal cut, a lag between the two parts of the tautological proposition, between the moment of expectation and the moment of its disappointment. Without this temporality and this dialogic economy, the proposition A = A would remain a simple affirmation of identity and would not be experienced as pure contradiction.

The universal as exception

The fact that self-reference functions in this manner, with the universal genus encountering itself among its species, the ensemble encountering itself among its elements, implies that we should be able to reduce the structure of the ensemble to a "limit case" [*cas limite*]:

> that of the ensemble to an element: the element can only split off from the ensemble as an emptiness, which is only as its own lack (or as its location as such, or as the mark of its place – which is simply to say that it is cloven). The element must exist in order for the ensemble to exist, it must exclude itself, make itself an exception, it must be a deficit or a surplus. (J.-A. Miller 1975: 6)

Specific difference no longer functions as the difference between elements against the backdrop of the neutral-universal, it becomes the difference itself between the universal ensemble and its particular element. In this way, the ensemble ends up *placed at the same level as its elements*, it functions as one of its own elements, as the paradoxical element that is absence itself, the element that is lacking. Once we are dealing with a differential network of signifiers, we have to insert into the network of differences the difference between the signifier and its absence as a signifying opposition, which is to say, *we must consider its own absence as part of the signifier*. We must posit the existence of a signifier that is the very lack of a signifier itself, which coincides with the signifier's place of inscription. This difference is, in a certain sense, self-reflexive. It is the paradoxical, but necessary, point where the signifier not only differs from another signifier but from itself as a signifier.

We have already arrived at the very heart of the Hegelian dialectic. The fundamental feature of the Hegelian relationship between the Universal (the ensemble) and the Particular (its elements) can be found in the fact that the Universal has only one Particular, in the fact that the genus has only one species, which is to say in the fact that specific difference coincides with the difference between the genus and the species. At first, we have abstract Universality, and we arrive at the Particular not because abstract Universality requires the Particular as a counterpoint, but because *it is already in itself particular*: it is *pas-tout*, and the thing that eludes it (in that it is *abstract*, which is to say, it is a universality that we arrive at through the abstraction of the particular) is precisely the Particular.

Therefore, at the heart of the Hegelian dialectic there is a constitutive discord between the Universal and the Particular, an encounter that will always be missed, and it is this very "contradiction" between the Universal and its Particular that is the true motive force of the dialectic. In relation to the Universal, the Particular is always deficient and/or excessive. Excessive, because it escapes from the Universal, because the Universal – as an abstraction – cannot encompass it. Deficient, because – and this is simply the same thing from a different perspective – it is never enough to "fill" the Universal. The "contradiction" between the Universal and the Particular would be "resolved," it would achieve the tranquil stillness of a satisfied encounter, if the disjunction, the division of the genus universal into its specific species, were *exhaustive*, if it were a division that left no *remainder*. But, the disjunction/division of the signifying ensemble is never complete, never exhaustive. There will always remain an empty space occupied by the "excess" element that is the ensemble itself as an empty ensemble. "Classifying" signification therefore differs from ordinary classification. In it, we find, outside the "habitual," "normal" species of the genus, a supplementary species that acts as the genus itself.

We have now arrived quite close to the logic of *pas-tout*. To make a collection of particular elements into a totality, we must add (or subtract, it amounts to the same thing; determining an element as an exception) a paradoxical element that, through its very particularity, embodies the universality of the genus, while at the same time serving as its negation. The universal genus of "royalism" is only totalized when we add republicanism to it as the embodiment of royalism in general. That royalism functions as a universal implies the existence of "at least one" thing that functions as its exception. This means that *scission and division are on the side of the universal rather than on the side of the particular*. The standard view is that it is the particular content that introduces scission, division, and specific difference into the neutral framework of universality. But for Hegel, it is the universal that constitutes itself through the subtraction, the "abstraction," of a particular that embodies it as such. The Universal emerges out of a radical scission, the scission between the richness of the particular and the element that, from inside the Particular, embodies the Universal. This is also the logic of sexual difference. The ensemble of women is a particular, non-totalized, non-universal ensemble. This multitude acquires its universality (the universality, in fact, of the human genus), once we have *excluded* an element that begins to function as the immediate embodiment of the human genus: man. If Woman does not exist, then man is Woman pretending to exist. The universalization of the "human genus" therefore introduces sexual difference, the difference between its two species. Man represents the moment of *scission* within the non-differentiated feminine collectivity, while simultaneously embodying, in regard to its opposite feminine-particular, the moment of its *universality*.[1]

The common point shared by pre-Hegelian idealism and materialist nominalism is that both misrecognize this kind of difference, which, far from being reducible to a specific difference against the backdrop of the neutral universality of the genus, constitutes this universality itself. It is a paradox of this kind that is the focus of the

---

1   In "Woman does not exist," "existence" should be understood in the sense it is used in Hegel's *Logic*, in which it is not just a simple synonym of being. The discussion of the category of existence is found near the end of the second half of the *Logic* that deals with essence. The term that is paired with existence is not essence (which is coupled with appearance), but foundation, Ground [*das Grund*]. Existence is defined as the effect, the appearance of a foundation, of a reason, of an essential and unique principle, it is being appearing insofar as it is posited and understood as the effect of a foundation. It is precisely in this sense that "Woman does not exist": she has no unique foundation, she cannot be totalized in the framework of a unique principle of which she would be the expression.

category of overdetermination, although normally this is seen as a conjuncture that supposedly escapes from the Hegelian dialectic: each totality contains a particular paradoxical element that, through its very particularity itself, "gives the tone" to the entire totality and dyes it with a "specific coloration." Here is an example of this from Marx:

> In all forms of society there is one specific kind of production which predominates over the rest, whose relations thus assign rank and influence to the others. It is a general illumination which bathes all the other colours and modifies their particularity. It is a particular ether which determines the specific gravity of every being which has materialized within it. (Marx 1993: 106–7)

This is what overdetermination is: the determination of the All by one of its elements that, according to the order of classification, is only supposed to play a subordinate role – a paradoxical particular that is part of the structure, but that at the same time structures the entire structure. When, in the totality of production, distribution, exchange, and consumption, Marx assigns this role to production, he is in fact making use of the Hegelian category of "opposite determination" [*gegensätzliche Bestimmung*]: "production imposes itself on its opposite determination as much as it does on the other phases" (Marx 1968). "Opposite determination" is therefore the point where the Universal encounters itself in the domain of the Particular, where production chances upon itself among its four species. This is why the Hegelian formula, "*the Truth is the Whole*," can be misleading if we interpret it as referring to classical "holism," according to which any particular content is only a subordinated, passing moment of an integral Totality. Hegelian "holism" is far more paradoxical, it is a "holism" that can best be described as self-referential. For Hegel, *the Whole is always a part of itself*; it always numbers among its own elements. The "progress" of the dialectic has nothing to do with the simple differentiation of an initial non-differentiated totality, which would make it nothing more than diversification into a network of increasingly rich concrete determinations. Rather, its mechanism consists in a Whole that always adds itself to its own elements, as in the joke cited by Lacan: "I have three brothers, Paul, Ernest, and myself."

The subjectified structure

It is through this "surplus element" that embodies universality in its negative form, this element in which universality encounters itself under its "opposite determination," that the structure subjectivizes itself. The subject only exists in this discord between the Universal and the Particular, in the missed encounter between the two. The Particular is always lacking; there is not enough of it to fill the extension of the Universal. Yet at the same time it is excessive, overabundant, superfluous, because it always adds itself as the surplus element that plays the role of the Universal itself. As soon as we do away with this short-circuit between the Universal and the Particular, this Möbius strip in which the Universal and the Particular end up "on the same side," as soon as we have a pure structure of classification in which the Universal could divide itself into its Particulars without paradoxical remainder, we would be dealing with a flat "objective" structure, without any representation of the subject.

It might seem as if this is the same thing as Lacan's formulation of the subject of the signifier. Isn't this the paradoxical Particular that, among the other Particulars, serves as the Universal, the signifier that represents the subject for the other signifiers? To extend this to the example of royalism and republicanism, republicanism would represent royalism-in-general for the (other) species of royalism. But this is not at all the case. In such a simplistic reading, the dialectic of lack and excess remains concealed. The surplus-Particular is the *negative embodiment* of the Universal; it fills the lack, the Void, the deficiency of the Particular in regard to the Universal. The surplus, the excess, is therefore the form which lack takes, and it is only at this point that it becomes legitimate to introduce the formula of the subject. This excess, this surplus element that fills the Void, is the signifier that represents the subject. Take the following passage from *The Science of Logic*: "I have concepts, that is, determinate concepts; but the 'I' is the pure concept itself, the concept that has come into determinate existence" (Hegel 2010: 12.17, 514). The "I" (which Hegel uses here as synonymous with the subject) is therefore placed at the intersection between being and having. If the universal concept simply *had* predicates, it would still be a substantial universality, it would not yet be the universality specific to the subject. And this universality is quite paradoxical indeed. The subject is, on the one hand, pure negative universality. As an identity-with-itself, it abstracts all of its own determinate contents (I am none of my determinations, I am the universality that both encompasses and denies them). Yet at the same time, it is the abstraction *that came into determinate existence in the very domain of its determinations*. As such, it is the very opposite of universal identity-with-itself; it is an ephemeral point, its own other, it eludes any determination, it is a point of pure singularity. It is precisely this "pulsation" between abstract-negative universality (the abstraction of all determinate contents) and the ephemeral punctuality of pure singularity, "this absolute *Universality*, which is just as immediately absolute *singularization* . . . this universality constitutes the nature of the 'I' and of the concept . . ." (Hegel 2010: 514–15). Hegelian *individuality*, far from being located as the opposite of the Universal, is in fact the precise designation of the paradoxical point of "pulsation," this point where pure ephemeral exactness coincides with the universality that abstracts all determined contents.

We can also draw out the subject by returning to the thing that makes the dialectical process "work." At first, we have the inscription of the unary trait, outside of which there is "nothing" – that is to say, there is only the place of inscription. The opposition between the trait and the place is already an opposition at the level of the trait; which is to say, it is an opposition between the unary trait and the lack of the trait (the unary trait is not only "one," but more specifically unary – this is why its counterpoint is not another "one" signifier, but the empty $. If the trait and the place (the lack) were not posited at the same level like this, if the place was not inside the field of the S (signifier) as $, there would be no reason for the chain to progress to another signifier. The chain of inscriptions is "pushed forward" precisely because the initial and unary inscription is already in itself – to put it in Hegelian terms – mediated by $, because its identity already represents pure difference. The initial inscription therefore contains in itself the – so to speak – "absolute" discord between the identity of the unary trait and pure difference, between the unary signifier and the subject. This "absolute" discord pushes the process toward ulterior inscriptions. All the other signifiers are just so many attempts to resolve this discord, to inscribe the place itself in the trait, to inscribe pure difference into the identity of the signifier (cf. J.-A. Miller 1975).

These three moments – the positive Universal (royalism as a genus), the Particular (its different species: Orleanism, Legitimism, . . .) and the Exception that embodies the Universal in its negative form (republicanism as the only means of being a royalist in general) – require a fourth, a nothingness, an emptiness that is filled by the paradoxical, "reflexive," element that embodies the Universal within the Particular. We have already seen this emptiness at work in Hegel's subversion of the proposition of identity. The tautology of identity-with-itself is in itself pure contradiction, the lack of a particular determination; where we had hoped to find a specific determination, a predicate, we find a nothing, the absence of determination. Far from indicating a self-sufficient fullness, the tautology opens an emptiness that is then filled by the element-exception. This emptiness is the subject, and the element-exception represents it to the other elements. If I say "God is God," then I am adding something to the divine predicates (all-powerful, wise, good . . .), a "nothing," a lack of determination that subjectivizes it – that is why it is only the Judeo-Christian God, the God of the tautology "I am that I am," that is subject.

The starting point of the dialectical process is therefore not the abundance of self-sufficient substance, identical with itself, but rather absolute contradiction. Pure difference is always already the impossible "predicate" of the tautology, of identity-with-itself. This absolute contradiction "resolves" itself through the exclusion of a "reflexive" element that embodies the emptiness, the lack of determination specific to tautology. *The subject is the emptiness, the lack of a predicate of the universal "substance."* The subject is the "nothing" that is introduced by the tautological reference-to-the-self of the "substance," this intermittent fourth moment that has vanished from the final result, the completed triad. In the final chapter of his great *Logic*, Hegel describes the fundamental matrix of the dialectical process. He emphasizes that the process could be seen as having either three or four moments. The subject is the additional moment that "does not count":

> In this turning point of the method, the course of cognition returns at the same time back into itself. This negativity is as self-sublating contradiction the restoration of the first immediacy, of simple universality; for the other of the other, the negative of the negative, is immediately the positive, the identical, the universal. In the whole course, if one at all cares to count, this second immediate is third to the first immediate and the mediated. But it is also third to the first or formal negative and to the absolute negativity or second negative; now in so far as that first negative is already the second term, the term counted as third can also be counted as fourth, and instead of a triplicity, the abstract form may also be taken to be a quadruplicity; in this way the negative or the difference is counted as a duality. (Hegel 2010: 746)

The first moment is the immediate positivity of the starting point. The second moment, the mediation, is not simply the opposite pole, the contradiction of the immediate. Rather, we produce it as soon as we try to seize the immediate "in itself and for itself," "as such." In this way, we already see it as the other of the mediation, and therefore as mediated by the mediation. More precisely, the second moment is not the negative or the other of the first; it is the first moment as *its own other*, as its own negative. As soon as we try to take hold of the first moment "as is," it becomes its other (as soon as we try to take hold of being "as such," it evaporates into nothing, etc.).[2] This is why we have to count negativity twice. If we want the second moment in its "for-itself" and not simply as the alterity of the first, we must reflect on it in-itself, and negativity's reference-to-the-self gives us absolute negativity, pure difference – the paradoxical moment that is the *third* moment because it was already the *first* moment that, as soon as we tried to take hold of it "as such," became its own *other*. The first "as such" is already the "other of the other" (this is the only way of grasping it intellectually); this is why the second is, in its for-itself, the third, and the final mediated identity is the fourth. If we are only counting the "positive" moments, there are only three: the immediate, the mediation, and the final synthesis, the mediated imme-diacy – what we lose is the excess, the elusive surplus of the pure difference of the $, which "does not count," but nonetheless adds itself by making the process work, this "emptiness" of substance that is at once both the "receptacle [*Rezeptakulum*] for all and for each one" (Hegel).

The Hegelian "one One"

Here we should examine one of the decisive moments of Hegelian logic, the passage from the finite determinate-existence [*Dasein*] to the being-for-itself [*Fürsichsein*] with the being-for-one [*Sein-für-Eines*] as its specification. Hegel starts with the formula used in German to inquire as to the quality of a thing: *Was für einer?* For example: *Was für ein Ding ist das?* (literally, "for what one thing is this?"). By viewing the one [*einer*] not as an indefinite article but as the one of unity, the one as opposed to the other, he asks what is this "one" that the thing in question is for. His first answer emphasizes that this One is in no way the same thing as the Something [*Etwas*]. The correlate of Something is Something-else [*ein Anderes*]; this all takes place at the level of finite reality and its network of reciprocal determinations, where a thing is always linked to other things, inter-laced with them, limited by them, mediated by something else.

2　It follows from this that the Hegelo-Lacanian view is fundamentally incompatible with recent "poststructuralism" and "postmodernism," which consist of attempts to counter "totalitarian," "monologic," "universalizing," "repressive," etc., reason with another reason, one that is plural, polycentric, dialogic, baroque, feminine. Such a move toward a different reason is simply *superfluous*: it is already the first ("mono-logic") reason that reveals itself to be *its own other*, as soon as we try to take it as such, in its form (in the strictly dialectical sense), in what it "does," and at the level of the process of its enunciation.

Something is therefore always a being-for-another [*Seinfüranderes*]. We only reach One when this other – the other-thing for which the something is – is reflected in that thing-itself as its own ideal unity, when something is no longer for another thing, but *for itself*. In this way, we pass from the being-for-another to the being-for-itself [*Fürischsein*]. The One is the ideal unity of the thing beyond the multitude of its real properties. The thing as an element of reality is sublated [*aufgehoben*] in the One. The passage from Something to the One coincides with the passage of reality to ideality; the One *for which* the thing as a thing-of-the-real *is* ("for what *one* is this?") is the thing itself in its ideality.

I need hardly mention that this passage implies entry into the symbolic order. This passage is only possible if the One, the ideal unity of the thing beyond its real properties, is again embodied, materialized in its signifier. The thing as an element of reality is "killed," canceled, suppressed, and at the same time elevated to its symbol, which places it as One above the multitude of its properties by reducing it to a single trait – the unary trait, its signifying mark. In other words, the passage from being-for-another to being-for-itself entails the radical de-centering of the thing in relation to itself. The "self" of the for-itself, the most intimate kernel of the thing, is simultaneously externalized into an arbitrary signifying mark. Being-for-itself means the existence of the thing for its own symbol; the thing is "more itself" in its exterior symbol than in its reality, in its immediate reality.

If the correlate of Something is Something-else, what is the correlate of One? Let us not forget that in regard to the sequential order of Hegelian logic, we are still only at the level of *quality*. The One in question is not yet that of quantity, the One to which we can add the second, the third, etc. For this reason, the correlate of the One is not the Other but the *Void* [*das Leere*]. The correlate of the One cannot be the Other, cannot be something-else, because the One is already the unity, reflected in itself, with its other – it is the thing itself as *its own other*; the other for which the thing is, is itself – as a One – its ideal unity. For that reason, the correlate of the One can be none other than the Void. The One is ideal unity, the reflection-in-itself of some thing. The Void is the reflection-in-itself of alterity, a pure alterity that is not "*something-else.*"

However, at this level there is still the possibility for confusion. We normally think of the relationship of the One and the Void inside the framework of external coexistence – for example, the atoms and the Void around them, between them. And the fact that for Hegel the atomist philosophy of Democritus is the historical exemplification of the category of the being-for-itself may seem to confirm this. But no, the Void is not outside the One. It is at its very core. The One is in itself empty; the Void is its only "content." Here we can appeal to the logic of the signifier. The One is conceptualized as the pure signifier, without signified, the signifier that does not designate any positive, real property, the signifier whose quintessential example is the proper noun, the tautological signifier that only references the pure Unity of the object, its being-one [*être-un*], the Unity that is, for its part, performatively constituted by the signifier itself. And what is this Void, if not precisely *the signified of the pure signifier*? I am even tempted to determine this Void, the signified of the One, of the pure signifier, as the *subject* in the sense of the subject of the signifier. The One represents the Void (the subject) for the other signifiers – what others? It is only against the background of this qualitative One as being-for-itself that we can arrive at the One of quantity, the one as the first element in the chain of counting. No surprise, then, that we find in both Hegel and Lacan the same paradoxical expression: the "one One [*das eine Eins*]" (cf. Lacan 1998a: 141; Hegel 2010: 141). First, we must have the One of quality, the unary trait, in order to then be able to count, to say "we have one one, we have another one, we have three ones . . ."

The passage from being-for-another to being-for-itself makes use of a figure of speech that is unique to the German language (*Was für eines?*), which is liable to elicit the comment that "for Hegel, the Absolute speaks German. . . ." It is true that a whole series of Hegelian concepts and developments are founded on specific features of the German language. The *Aufhebung* depends on the three components of the signification of this German word (cancel, preserve, elevate), the passage to the category of Ground [*Grund*] is accomplished through reading the verb *zugrunde-gehen* (falling into ruin, decomposing) as *zu Grunde gehen* (arriving at the foundations), etc., etc. However, the key here is not that Hegel is privileging the German language. Rather, he is explicitly emphasizing that we are dealing with fortuitous encounters where, purely by chance, the signification of a word (more precisely, its split signification) expresses its speculative meaning. The ordinary signification of words operates at the level of "understanding," and the supposed precise, scientific definitions do nothing more than consolidate and harden the fundamentally non-dialectical nature of signification. Speculative meaning, at least in principle, belongs neither to words (concepts) nor to propositions, but can only be uncovered through the entire movement of the syllogism. This meaning can, sometimes, erupt, break through, at the level of the words through the means of these fortuitous encounters, and this is the only support possible for speculative truth.

Here we have a Hegel who is very far from the conventional depiction of him as a "panlogicist." For him, "speculative truth" can only articulate itself at the level of words through chance encounters. Hegel radically subverts the Platonic opposition (from *Cratylus*) between the natural character and the arbitrary character of language – an opposition that would in modern thought take the form of two distinct fundamental conceptions of the nature of language. There is the "rationalist" conception, which reduces language to a system of signs that are fundamentally arbitrary, external, disposable, whose signification is based on free association and is therefore without any intrinsic value. On the other hand, there is the "romantic" conception, according to which language does not allow itself to be reduced to a simple tool or a means, but carries in itself the value of an intrinsic truth, a foundational and profound signification, although this may have been lost in subsequent developments. Hegel's position toward these two alternatives is paradoxical: language certainly contains an intrinsic truth, but we should not search for it in obscure origins, in foundational roots that have been lost through progressive instrumentalization. Instead, this truth is the result of a chance encounter that came afterwards. *In principle*, language "lies," it hides the true dialectic of the concepts, their speculative movement. But sometimes, *by accident*, chance encounters, fortuitous coincidences (double meanings, plays on words, etc.), speculative content breaks through. It is not at the level of the universality of principles that we should look for the truth, but rather at the level of the contingency of the particular. The truth articulates itself through puns and double meanings.

4

The Dialectic as Logic of the Signifier (2): The Real of the "Triad"

Lalangue and its boundary

It follows from the differential character of the signifier that for each "Whole" there is "at least One thing" that – as an exception – constitutes this Whole. Theoretically, we could constitute as many "Wholes" as there are signifiers, as each signifier can, in turn, play the role of the exception that holds the Whole together. This is reminiscent of the quip, "let us discuss every possible subject, and a few others as well." It is precisely this "as well" that should draw our attention, the thing that must be excluded in order for the bounded field of "every possible subject" to constitute itself. What we can never obtain is the ensemble of all signifiers *without exception, without exterior* – this total ensemble would be an inconsistent ensemble, unbounded, gaping open, a togetherness that "does not hold together," and therefore an ensemble that is *"pas-tout."*

This kind of unbounded totality is inconsistent in the manner of a Möbius strip. It is a "One in Two" in which the Whole is the exception, in which the interior and the exterior encounter each other on the same surface. An inconsistent "totality" such as this has no exterior and is therefore *pas-tout*. And this is where Hegelian "concrete totality" lies. It is precisely such a "One in Two," an "absolute totality," and thus, in other words, "contradictory and split" (J.-A. Miller 1975: 7). This is why formulations of concrete universality coincide so neatly with formulations of *la-langue.** One might say that abstract universality, which excludes the Particular, functions as a Whole that bases itself on an exception, while concrete universality is a totality with no exterior, "absolute," and therefore contradictory.

Moreover, if, as it is claimed, nothing exists that could place a limit on lalangue, we should see this limitlessness as an indication of *circularity*. Lacking a reference point outside of itself, *as a last resort the signifier refers to itself*. This is precisely the difference between the differential and the arbitrary. We are dealing with the arbitrary so long as we can place an external *limit* on *signs* (and this is what makes them signs) in relation to which they are arbitrary (reality, pure thought, immediate sensory experience, etc.). When this limit disappears, when we are no longer able to construct it, we find ourselves in the abyss of circular movement, without the foothold of differentiation. The signifier is only different in relationship to other signifiers, and because what is true for one is true for all, the signifiers never form a consistent Whole; the signifying ensemble goes in circles, trying in vain to reach – what? Its "pure" self, which is to say, itself as pure difference. The inaccessible is not – as it is in the order of the sign – an "external reality" that is "trans-linguistic." Rather it is the "pure" signifier itself, the difference between signifiers, their *inter-diction*. It is because of this internal boundary that the movement of the signifier is circular, folded in on itself, which has nothing to do with the *exception*. We should look for the *exception* in the expulsion (or, if you will, the ex-pulsion) of this interior limit, the expulsion that allows the *"ics"* (unconscious/inconsistent [*incon-scient/inconsistant*], according to the work of Jacques-Alain Miller) and self-referential ensemble to "purify" itself into a whole and consistent ensemble.

In the circular movement of lalangue, in its very limitlessness – which is to say, in its lack of a reference point – we run into a limit. This limit has a name: *"pure" difference/the "pure" signifier* that holds the abyss of the signifying order open as a differential order, and therefore as one without reference point. We should therefore make sure not to conflate the relationship of lalangue to the "pure" signifier (Difference itself) with the relationship of the Whole to

---

* A neologism coined by Lacan, "to refer to these non-communicative aspects of language which, by playing on ambiguity and homophony, give rise to a kind of jouissance. . . . Lalangue is like the primary chaotic substrate of polysemy out of which language is constructed, almost as if language is some ordered superstructure sitting on top of this substrate" (Evans, *An Introductory Dictionary*, p. 100).

the Exception (the "at least One") that constitutes it. Difference is precisely what underpins the "*ics*" character of the *pas-tout* ensemble, which is fundamentally distinct from the Exception that guarantees the closure of the Whole as well as its universality.

"Not everything can be said" is the best example of the difference in question. Philosophy, from Plato all the way to Schelling, has always based the possibility of *logos*, of the Universal speaking, on some kind of ineffable trans-categorical surplus (for Plato, the Idea of the good; for Kant, the Thing-in-Itself, etc.) which, as an exception, would guarantee the universality of this speech. Here, "not everything can be said" means: the necessary condition for rational speech is an ineffable surplus. In the order of lalangue, on the contrary, "not everything can be said" means that the field of lalangue could never be traversed. Insofar as nothing exists that could limit it, speech is a circular movement of self-reference without solid foothold. It is, in other words, chasing its own tail. The thing that continually escapes the signifying movement of differentiation is not the unreachable trans-symbolic Identity, but difference itself. The impassable boundary already at work in the order of lalangue is an internal boundary, folded back in on itself. What is lacking from speech is not the thing but speech itself. The (external) limit of language is reality; the (internal) limit of lalangue is Difference itself. The limit of the sign is the "thing," the limit of the signifier is the "pure" signifier itself. It is not a coincidence that Marx developed the same formulation of an internal limit when discussing capital; for Marx, the limit of capital is capital itself, which is to say, the very mode of capitalist production. We can only attain the Whole through the expulsion, the externalization, of this interior limit – the internal boundary of the ensemble that makes it a holed ensemble – in the Exception. To avoid relying on the usual examples (for example, that the sign can "signify everything" on the condition that it does not signify itself), let us return to Marx and his critique of political economy. The necessary condition for the universalization of the function of commodity is the advent of a commodity-exception, labor, whose exercise – and here we have another self-reference, as it is the conjunction of exchange value and use value – is what produces (exchange) value.

This expulsion can also operate at the level of the distinction between interdiction as inter-diction and interdiction as a prohibition. With the expulsion of the limit, the inter-diction (the immanent blockage that prevents the thing from "becoming itself," of fully realizing itself) transforms itself into an interdiction that prohibits "something." For example, the inter-diction of incest (the blockage, the immanent impossibility of the sexual rapport)* becomes the positive prohibition against sleeping with one's mother, the Exception that constitutes the universal ensemble of "women I can sleep with." This prohibition resolves the dead end, the impasse of inter-diction. The truth can be "*tout*," we can resolve the dead end of its "*pas-tout*" quality, but only if we do not think of it as *adaequatio* to an external object-limit ("the thing," "the concept," etc.). Saying that "the truth is *pas tout*" specifically means that truth is not to be sought out in the relationship between the signifier and a reference, but within the signifier itself.

Where can we find the Real in the circular movement of lalangue? This is where the distinction between reality and the Real becomes of paramount importance. Reality is, as we have seen, the external limit that allows us to totalize language as a system that is always-already bounded and given, while the Real is *the internal limit of lalangue*, the unseizable boundary that prevents it from becoming itself, of attaining its identity-with-itself, the twist that causes it to return in on itself, to turn in circles.

This is the fundamental paradox of the relationship between the symbolic and the Real. The bar that separates them is *inside the symbolic field*, it is the bar that prevents the symbolic from becoming *itself*, from achieving its full realization. The problem for the signifier is not that it can never reach the Real, but rather that it can never reach itself – what is missing from the signifier is not just the object that is outside-signification, but the Signifier itself, the signifier that would be "unique to the subject," the non-barred absolute Performative. In more speculative terms: the signifier does not just miss the object, it already *misses itself*, it never realizes itself as a signifier, *and it is in this missed encounter that the object is inscribed*. The positivity of the object is nothing more than the positivization, the incarnation, the materialization of the impassable bar that prevents the signifier from "becoming itself."

Coincidentia oppositorum

It quickly becomes clear that the Lacanian Real is the conjunction of a series of opposite determinations.

* The standard translation of Lacan's famous statement is "the sexual relationship does not exist," or "there is no sexual relation," but it seems that "rapport" captures what Lacan is saying slightly more precisely than "relationship." There are many kinds of alienated relationships, relationships in which no true intimacy occurs (relationships of power, formal relationships, etc.), whereas a rapport implies a somewhat more personal connection.

The Real is the *starting point*, the foundation of the process of symbolization (in this sense, we can talk about the "symbolization of the Real"). In a way, it precedes the symbolic, it is the "raw substance" structured by the symbolic, which has caught it in its net. Symbolization mortifies, "empties," separates the Real from the living body. But the Real is also the *waste product* of the process-itself of symbolization. It is the surplus, the remainder that eludes symbolization and as such is produced by it. In Hegelian terms, we could determine the Real as both *presupposed* and *posited* by symbolization. Insofar as the core of the Real is made out of the *jouissant* substance, this duality takes on the form of jouissance and surplus jouissance. Jouissance, the body that is jouissant, is the fundamental "Void," structured, dissected, quartered by symbolization – and this operation produces the remainder: surplus jouissance.

The next opposition is linked to the first. The Real is the *plenitude* of inert, positive presence. "Nothing is lacking" in the real, lack being introduced by symbolization. At the same time, the Real is the *Void*, the hole at the heart of the symbolic, the central lack around which the symbolic structures itself. The Real as a presupposed starting point is positive plenitude, lacking nothing. As a product, it is the Void encircled by the symbolic. We can see the same opposition at work in negation. At first glance, the Real designates the "hard" core, *indifferent to negation*, an inert positivity that does not allow itself to be caught in the net of dialectical negativity. But right away we must add that this is because, in its positivity, the Real is nothing more than *the positivation of the Void*. The Real object is just as precarious as the sublime object, the object that embodies the hole in the Other. If it does not allow itself to be denied, if negation cannot reach it, it is because this positivity is itself nothing more than the positivation of an absolute "negativity." It cannot be denied because, as a "positive," *it is already* negation incarnated.

The third opposition in this series comes from the fact that, unlike reality, we first grasp the Real as a *hard kernel*, that which "always returns to the same place," the rock against which symbolization is dashed, or, to use Kripke's terminology, the kernel that would remain the same in every world, in all possible symbolic universes. On the other hand, we have the fundamentally precarious status of (symbolic) reality that can, at any moment, dissipate, losing its consistency. And as soon as we try to grasp the Real object in its positivity, it evaporates through our fingers. It is a *pure semblance* that can only exist in the shadows, as a failed, non-realized, purely chimerical being, as the promise of itself, an emptiness encircled by the structure. This conjunction between contrary determinations can be most clearly seen in the case of trauma. The traumatic event, the hard kernel that resists assimilation into the symbolic, is never given in its positivity. Its entire consistency depends on a fantasmic construction that obfuscates the Void, the entirety of its effectivity consists in its effects. It matters little whether the trauma "occurred in reality," its decisive role lies in its structural effects.

And it is in fact the concept of traumatism that will make it possible for us to outline the fourth pair of opposite determinations – which is actually the first in a second series, which Jacques-Alain Miller described as the Real object's passage from *contingency* to *logical consistency*. At first, the Real identifies itself with the fortuitous encounter, with the intrusion of the contingent that derails symbolic automatism, the grain of sand that blocks the machine's circuit. However, precisely because it is the intrusion of a contingency that subverts the equilibrated automatism of the symbolic machinery, it never allows itself to be pinned down in its positivity; it can only be *constructed*, granted the purely logical consistency of an X that eludes the structure, but is at the same time only discernible through its role in the structure (the repetitions, displacements, etc. produced by a traumatic X).

This leads to the next opposition. The Real is, according to the definition that has already become the standard, that which never stops not writing itself, and is therefore the impossible, *that which eludes writing* (the sexual rapport, for example), but at the same time, from a certain point of view, *writes this impossibility itself* in its difference from the signifier. The written is therefore on the side of the object, its status is therefore Real and not symbolic: it is identifiable with that which, in a language, "always returns to the same place," beyond, or more precisely below, possible subjectifications. As such, it does not represent the subject.

And finally, the last opposition in the second series can be presented as follows: if we attempt to place the Real against the background of Kripke's critique of the theory of descriptions (the distinction between the *quid* and the *quod*, between the properties of a universal-symbolic nature that we can predicate to the object and its given form as a "that" that eludes the network of symbolic determinations), the Real appears to be the surplus of the *quod* over the *quid, the pure "that" of an object without properties*. The example of traumatism, however, requires us to invert this relationship. Isn't the traumatizing Real precisely the paradoxical object *that does not exist, but that nonetheless has a whole series of properties?*

Namely, traumatism – as fundamentally chimerical, as a phantasy projection on the Void in the symbolic Other – is an entity whose existence we must refuse, it does not withstand the "test of reality," but this does not prevent it from having a multitude of properties that we can discern through its effects in the symbolic universe of the subject.

For Freud it was the primordial crime (patricide) that played the role of the Real. Even though we do not find any trace of patricide in prehistoric reality, we must construct it in order to explain the emergence of culture. For Hegel it was the "fight to the death" between the (future) Master and the (future) Slave. It would be a waste of time to search for the moment this fight occurred in pre-historic reality; it is not a fact to be discovered through anthropological research. It is a phantasy scenario, and as such it is *always already implicated, it is presupposed by the very fact of labor.* Labor presupposes a certain intersubjective conjuncture – the "fight to the death" between two subjects for recognition – and its result, the defeat of one of them who then becomes the slave laborer. Labor is, a priori, formally – or, in Hegelian terms, in its very concept – work *for a Master* (whether he is "real," as in the person of the Master, or a symbol, God, Death as the absolute Master, etc.), and for a Master in front of whom one does not dare show one's jouis-sance. Labor is therefore, a priori, formally structured as an *obsessive* activity.

Here Hegel was well ahead of his critics – Habermas, for example – who tried to resolve the problem of the relationship between labor and intersubjectivity by differentiating between two sides of human activity. On the one hand, Habermas (1971) argued, there is labor – the relationship of the subject to the object, to nature – and on the other, symbolic interaction – the relationship of subjects to each other. Hegel, ahead of time, answered the question that is repressed by such distinctions: what is the intersubjective (symbolic) economy of work itself, of the instrumental relationship to objectivity? The Hegelian dialectic of the Master and the Slave goes against Marxism in an analogous manner. In Marxism, social relationships of domination operate at a level determined by the development of productive forces, and therefore of labor, and these relationships operate as a function of the development and the organization of the productive force of labor. For Hegel it is exactly the opposite: labor itself depends on a particular intersubjective conjunction. What makes this opposition even more interesting is that Marxists often refer to the chapter on the Master and the Slave as the section of the *Phenomenology of the Spirit* where Hegel comes closest to historical materialism (the truth is on the side of the slave laborer, etc.).

The missed encounter is the object

Let me pick up where I left off. We have a series of opposite determinations that coincide with the concept of the Real and that could be grouped into two triads, that of *the presupposed/posited* (the starting point and the remainder; the inert plenitude that lacks nothing and the lack itself; the hard kernel and pure semblance) and that of *the structure's remainder/the structure itself* (contingency and logical consistency; that which does not allow itself to be written and the written itself; a thing without properties and at the same time an object with properties that does not exist). While a few of these oppositions can be located on the diachronic axes of the different stages of Lacan's doctrine (in the way that, as Jacques-Alain Miller showed, the emphasis shifts from the contingent to logical consistency), the key issue is the following: how do we think about their *simultaneous* conjunction, because *it is precisely this immediate conjunction of opposite determinations that defines the concept of the Real?* Perhaps the only philosophical precedent for this would be the Hegelian critique of Kant, of the Kantian "Thing-in-Itself" [*Ding an sich*], in which Hegel showed how the Thing-in-Itself, the surplus of objectivity over thought, that inaccessible, transcendent X, passes immediately into the pure immanence of thought and immediately coincides with the "thing-of-thought" [*Gedankending*], with the void of our thinking that is all that is left over once all the phenomenal determinations of the object have been taken away.

We should distinguish between the imaginary, the symbolic and the Real modes of the coupled opposites. The imaginary mode is the *complementary* relationship in which the two poles complete each other in a harmonious Whole, each one providing the other with what it lacks, which is to say, each one filling the lack in the other (for example, the fantasy of the harmonious sexual relationship in which the Woman and the Man would constitute an accomplished Whole). The symbolic mode is a *differential* relationship, in which each pole's identity is reduced to its difference from the others. Far from filling the lack in the other, from completing it, a given element serves as the lack, as the absence in its other. Through its very presence it presentifies the other's lack, and, in this sense, we could say that each of these elements returns the other's own lack to it. The Real is, in the end, the *immediate conjunction* of these opposites, the zero-point of the dialectical process when an opposite passes immediately into its other. For example, the unity of being and nothing (at the beginning of Hegel's *Logic*) is neither a complementary relationship nor a differential relation (being consisting only in the difference with nothingness and vice versa) but only in the way in which being, when you try to grasp it as such, in itself, is nothing.

This reference to Hegel is particularly important because it may be that the Hegelian dialectical process offers us the key to the logic at work in the conjunction of these opposite determinations. That is to say, in order to pierce the secret of this conjunction, we must start with the Lacanian thesis according to which "the Real can only be inscribed on the basis of an impasse of formalization" (Lacan 1998b: 93). The Real is, of course, that which "never stops not writing itself," the rock against which formalizing inscription is dashed. However, it is through this impasse – the very impossibility that we could touch it through the written – that we can locate its empty space. In other words, even though the inscription of the Real is impossible, we can inscribe this impossibility. The implication of this reversal of the impossibility of inscription into the inscription of impossibility is that the Real does not persist in some beyond, as a transcendental X, inaccessible to its inscription. *Rather, it coincides, radically, with its own impossibility*. The Real is nothing more than the impasse, the failure of its own inscription. We don't just miss the Real object but, as Lacan said, "the essence of the object is failure" (Lacan 1998b: 58).

Let us return to traumatism. Its whole effectivity consists in the series of its structural effects, in the series of impasses and missed encounters that it produces in the symbolic structure – its missed encounter with symbolization retroactively encircles its empty space. We can see the same mechanism at work with regard to jouissance. The entirety of its effectivity consists in the surplus jouissance, in the remainder, in the waste product produced by the symbolic process, in the signifying mortification of the jouissant body. Instead of thinking that we *missed* the object, we should understand the object as this *missed encounter*. This also allows us to make sense of Jacques-Alain Miller's thesis that the subject itself should be seen as one of the "responses of the Real." The subject, of course, does not have its own signifier; its *Real* status is defined by the *impossibility* of its signifying representation. But in no way does this mean that the subject is a positive, transcendent entity that persists ineffably beyond the signifying chain. The subject *is nothing more* than the impossibility of its signifying inscription; it is the retroactive effect of the missed encounter with its signifying representation. Herein lies the temporal paradox of the subject of the signifier: it is represented by a signifier, missed by this signifier, *and it is this missed encounter that is the subject.* Here we have the Hegelian distinction between the substance and the subject, what is truly at stake in the thesis that the substance must be seen as subject. We remain at the level of substance so long as we grasp the X that causes the failure of symbolization as a positive, transcendental entity. We pass to the level of subject once we realize that, despite the failure of symbolization, there is nothing beyond it that is not the empty space surrounded by the missed encounter itself.

It may seem that by thinking of substance as the big Other, as the signifying order on which the subject depends – from whose hole the subject emerges – we end up in contradiction with Lacan. In *Encore*, didn't he define substance as jouissance, as the jouissant body, and therefore precisely as the non-symbolic, extimate,* core of the Other (cf. Lacan 1998b: 21–2)? There is no need for us to try to resolve this problem by introducing an additional conceptual distinction – say, between "substance in the sense of the big Other" and "substance in the sense of the jouissant body" – because, here again, the problem is already its own solution, which is to say, this ambiguity *is already part of the concept of substance.* "Substance" is, first of all, the big Other, the order that gives birth to the subject. But the very heart of this order is outside of it; its core is a foreign body. This ambiguity means that the proposition "we should see the substance as subject" has a dual meaning.

First, it means that substance (the big Other), because it is holed, always-already includes the subject. The subject is internal to substance as its constitutive Void, as its blockage, as its immanent impossibility.

Second, it articulates the dimension that is enunciated and represented by the matheme $\$ \lozenge a$: the subject is correlative to the object that embodies the hole in the Other, to the surplus jouissance that makes its kernel extimate. In other words, it is correlative to substance in the sense of the jouissant body, and as such, it is its opposite side.

---

* Extimate is a translation of the Lacanian neologism *extime*, which refers to the external quality of even the greatest intimacy. For more in-depth discussions, see J.-A. Miller, "Extimité", in M. W. Alcorn, Jr., M. Bracher, R. J. Corthell, and F. Massardier-Kenney (eds.), *Lacanian Theory of Discourse. Subject/Structure/and Society* (New York University Press, pp. 74–87) and P. Kinsbury, "The Extimacy of Space," *Social & Cultural Geography* 2/8 (2007): 235–58.

Forbidding the impossible

It is true that this problematic was only articulated rigorously by the Lacan of the 1970s, the one who introduced the difference between reality and the Real and who focused on the impossibility of the Real. But we can find the impossible Real at work in the Lacan of the 1950s, well before he ever put it directly into words – although he articulated it using different terms. Take the following passage, for example, from *Seminar II*:

> Throughout his life, Oedipus is always this myth. He is himself nothing other than the passage from myth to existence. Whether he existed or not is of little importance to us, since he exists in each of us, in a palely reflected form, he is ubiquitous, and he exists far more than if he really had existed.
>
> One can say that a thing does or doesn't *really* exist. On the other hand, I was surprised to see, regarding the archetypal cure, one of our colleagues opposed the term *psychic reality* to that of *true reality*. I think that I have put you all in enough of a state of suggestion for this term to seem to you a contradiction *in adjecto*.
>
> Whether a thing *really* exists or not doesn't much matter. It can perfectly easily exist in the full sense of the term, even if it doesn't really exist. By definition, there is something so improbable about all existence that one is in effect perpetually questioning oneself about its reality. (Lacan 1991b: 229)

In a certain sense, "it is all already there." There is the difference between reality (that which "truly exists") and the Real (the phantasy "myth," whose true existence is irrelevant), the disjunction between the order of the true and that of the Real (which is what makes the expression "true reality" a contradiction *in adjecto*), and the determination of the Real as impossible (the "improbable" character of every existence). Traumatism presents us with an exemplary case of a Real for which it "matters little whether it truly exists or not." What matters is solely the fact that it exercises its effectivity, that it functions as a point that must be constructed in order to make sense of the current state of affairs. The Real is a little bit like the joke Freud told about Wellington: "Is this the spot where the Duke uttered that famous line? – Yes, this is indeed the spot, although he actually never said those words." A list of such examples of a non-existent entity to which we nonetheless attribute properties could go on forever: "God has all the perfections except one, he does not exist"; "Z did not believe in spirits, and he went so far as to not even be afraid of them."

If, therefore, we can construct the Real as a reference point that, despite "not truly existing," possesses a whole series of properties, it becomes clear that the quintessential Real is jouissance. The final sentence in the above citation from Lacan retroactively takes on its full importance if we replace "existence" with "jouissance." "By definition, there is something so improbable about all *jouissance* that one is in effect perpetually questioning oneself about its reality." An experience that, as we all know, is at the root of the obsessive position. And it is perhaps this difference between existence and properties – which is to say the determination of the Real as an entity that does not exist but that nonetheless possesses a whole series of properties – that gives us the key to the paradoxical interdiction whose presence unambiguously signals that we are dealing with the Real: the interdiction of an impossible thing. In Lacan's *Encore*, he produces the formula for other jouissance (other in relationship to phallic jouissance): "Were there another one, it shouldn't be/could never fail to be that one" (Lacan 1998b: 60).

This other jouissance therefore does not exist (because, as Lacan underlines, only phallic jouissance exists), but it nonetheless possesses a property, that of being excessive and therefore forbidden: "It is false that there is another one, but that doesn't stop what follows from being true, namely, that it couldn't be/could never fail to be that one" (Lacan 1998b: 60).

Here, Lacan is using the logical rule according to which it is valid to deduce the true from the false: the Real is just such a "false" entity, and as it does not exist, it must be presupposed for us to deduce the truth from it. The paradox of forbidding an impossible thing can be resolved if we link *impossibility* to *existence* and *interdiction* to *properties*. The real is impossible insofar as it cannot exist, but nonetheless it is forbidden because of its properties.

This is why the Hegelian dialectical process brings us into contact with the Real. The paradox of losing something that we never possessed – this paradox of the "loss of the loss," "the negation of the negation" – can only occur at the level of the Real. The structural parallel between the *loss of something that one never possessed* and the *interdiction of an impossible thing* is immediately clear. In both cases, the negation (the loss, the interdiction) relies on an element that is already in itself posited either as lost or as impossible. This leads to a new definition of the "negation of the negation": the point where the subject realizes that that which is forbidden to him is already in itself impossible.

Experiencing that what I lost I never had in the first place is, perhaps, a fairly rigorous definition of the final moment of analysis, of the exit from [*sortie*] the transfer, especially since the transfer is characterized by what is called "transferential" love (love for the person who is "supposed to know"). If, according to the Lacanian definition, love is "giving what one doesn't have," then in the exit from the transfer, "giving what one doesn't have" becomes the experience that I never had the thing that I lost in the first place.

Thesis-antithesis-synthesis

The logic of the dialectical process is, therefore, that of the Imaginary-Real-Symbolic. Its imaginary departure point is the complementary relationship of opposites. Then the Real of their "antagonism"[1] falls apart, the illusion of their complementarity is broken, each pole passes immediately into its opposite. This extreme tension is resolved through *symbolization*, in which the relationship of the opposites is posited as differential, the two poles are once again united, but against the background of their common lack.

The starting point – the thesis – is neither the subject (which would then oppose itself to the object) nor the immediate identity of the subject-object. Rather, it is the abstract being-in-itself of immediate objectivity. It is absolutely incorrect to think that the thesis contains the antithesis somewhere within its depths, and that, therefore, we could deduce the antithesis from the thesis. Quite the contrary, the antithesis is what the thesis *lacks* in order to accomplish its concretization. The thesis is already the abstraction, it already presupposes its mediation, it can only function in opposition to the antithesis. However, this in no way means that they are mutually fulfilling, that the relationship is a complementary one between two opposing poles, between the thesis and the antithesis, of the type "there is no . . . without . . ." (there is no man without woman, no cold without heat, no north without south, no love without hate, etc.). What Hegel calls the "unity of opposites" goes well beyond the appearance of a complementary relationship of this kind. The

1 In the framework of a "non-antagonistic" relationship, each moment receives its identity against the background of its complementary relationship to other moments (Woman is Woman in her relationship to Man, together they make a Whole, etc.), while in an "antagonistic" relationship, the relationship to the other prevents the moment in question from attaining its own identity. The other cuts, truncates, our identity. At our very core, we are already the other (the relationship between the sexes becomes "antagonistic" when a woman sees her relationships with the opposite sex as the thing that prevents her from "realizing herself as a woman"). For more on this concept of antagonism, see Laclau and Mouffe 2001).

position of an extreme is not simply the negation of the other; it is, in its abstraction of the other, the other itself. At the moment where an extreme tries to radically oppose itself to the other, it becomes that other. The most pure being is the Void, the most general will is the individual will (because it *excludes* the diversity of many individual wills), etc. This is how we end up in the "immediate exchange" between the extremes, between the alternate poles (love–hate, good–bad, anarchy–terror) that immediately pass into each other. This immediate passage takes us beyond the level of external negativity. Each of these extremes is not only the negation of the other, it is also the negation turning back in on itself, its own negation. The impasse of this "immediate exchange" between the thesis and the antithesis is resolved by the *synthesis*.

We have already said that it is lack – specifically, its abstract nature – that pushes the thesis to the antithesis. The imaginary order is defined by the complementarity of the thesis and the antithesis in an equilibrated Whole, through the mutual fulfillment of the lack in the other. What is lacking from the thesis is given to it by the antithesis and vice versa (this is what is normally thought of as the "unity of opposites"). This illusion of a complementary relationship is broken by the immediate passage from one extreme into the other. How could one of these extremes fill the lack in the other, when it itself is – in isolation from the other – the other? Relief is only offered by the synthesis. Within the synthesis, this imaginary opposition is symbolized, the thesis and antithesis are transformed into symbolic alternates. The two extremes we began with are once again "posited" (returned to their position), but this time as sublated [*aufgehoben*], "internalized," and symbolized, as elements in a signifying network. If an extreme does not provide the other with what it lacks, what can it send it, if not just *lack itself*? The thing that is holding the two extremes together is not the mutual fulfillment of a lack, but their common lack. The terms opposed by the set of signifying alternates "become one" against the background of the common lack that each one sends to the other. This is also the definition of the symbolic exchange: before anything "positive" can be exchanged, the space of the object of exchange is already occupied by this lack.

This lack is what symbolization "internalizes." Therefore, the synthesis does not function as an affirmation of the identity of extremes, an affirmation of their presupposed common foundation that would be the field in which their opposition takes place, but, on the contrary, as the *affirmation of their difference as such*. The two extremes are tied together through their difference, as each of their identities can only be formed through their differentiation from the other. The synthesis liberates difference from the "compulsion of identity," because it means that we no longer have to look for the resolution of the contradiction in the identity of the extremes. Rather, the resolution comes from the affirmation of their differential character, their identity itself being nothing more than the effect of a network of differences. The passage from one extreme to the other, contradiction in its pure form, is precisely an indication of a submission to the "compulsion of identity":

> Contradiction is nonidentity under the aspect of identity; the dialectical primary of the principle of contradiction makes the thought of unity the measure of heterogeneity. As the heterogeneous collides with its limit it exceeds itself. Dialectics is the consistent sense of nonidentity. (Adorno 1973: 5)

Specifically, the synthesis is the resolution, the "suppression," of the contradiction. The contradiction is the non-identical under the appearance of identity, and the synthesis "resolves" this contradiction not through a new encompassing unity, an even more vast identity, but simply by elevating the framework of identity, affirming the constitutive role that difference plays in identity. The traditional view is that Hegel, it is true, allowed for heterogeneity, difference, scission, etc., but did not allow them to persist because he kept them within the framework of identity. This view – which takes the form "Of course I know that (Hegel affirmed the scission, that he exploded identity), but still (he reduces difference to the framework of identity)" – is fundamentally flawed. *It is only through the synthesis that difference can truly be recognized.* And so, the "rational kernel" – if I may permit myself the use of this notorious expression – of the Hegelian triad reveals itself to be this process of the symbolization of imaginary opposites. Through this decisive passage of the antithesis/opposition, of exterior negativity, into absolute negativity, which brings us back to the initial position, we can see the passage of the immediate/external negation of a thing into its symbolization, which "posits" it once again, but this time as symbolized, founded on a particular loss, on incorporated, internalized negativity. Can we not see in this triad the very same movement that occurred in Freud's dream of Irma's injection (cf. Freud 2010: 131)? In the first phase of the dream, Freud is "playing with his patient" (Lacan 1991b: 159), there is a dual, specular, imaginary relationship between Freud and Irma. This phase ends with the irruption of the terrifying image of the back of Irma's throat:

an anxiety-provoking apparition of an image which summarises what we can call the revelation of that which is least penetrable in the real, of the real lacking any possible mediation, of the ultimate real, of the essential object which isn't an object any longer, but this something faced with which all words cease and all categories fail, the object of anxiety par excellence. (Lacan 1991b: 164)

After this encounter with the Real there is a radical shift in tone, which Lacan describes as "the coming into operation of the symbolic function" (1991b: 168), the arrival at the formula for trimethylamin. Jacques-Alain Miller was quite correct when, as a subtitle for this chapter of *Séminaire II*, he simply put: "The Imaginary, the Real and the Symbolic" (Lacan 1991b: 161).

5

Das Ungeschehenmachen: How is Lacan a Hegelian?

The three stages of the symbolic

Now that we have fleshed out the relationship between the Hegelian dialectic and the logic of the signifier, we are in a position to locate Lacan's "Hegelianism." Let's start by looking at the three successive stages in the evolution of Lacan's understanding of the Symbolic.

First we have *The Function and the Field of Speech and Language in Psychoanalysis*, which focuses on the intersubjective dimension of speech – speech as the medium of intersubjective recognition of desire. What predominates here is the theme of symbolization as historicization, as symbolic realization. Symptoms and traumatisms are blanks, empty, non-historicized spaces in the subject's symbolic universe. Analysis takes these traumatic spaces and "realizes them in the symbolic." It includes them in the symbolic universe by retroactively, after the fact, conferring their signification upon them. What we have here is a conception of language that remains basically phenomenological, similar to that of someone like Merleau-Ponty. The goal of analysis is to produce the recognition of desire in "full speech" [*parole pleine*], to integrate it into the universe of signification. In typically phenomenological manner, the order of speech is identified with the order of signification, and analysis itself functions at this level: "All analytic experience is an experience of signification" (Lacan 1991b: 325).

The second stage, exemplified by Lacan's interpretation of the Purloined Letter, is in a way complementary to the first, just as language is complementary to speech. It emphasizes that the signifying order is (that of) a closed, differential, synchronic structure. The signifying structure functions as a senseless "automatism" to which the subject is subjugated. The diachronic order of speech, of signification, is therefore regulated by the senseless signifying automatism, by a formalized differential game that produces the signifying effect. This structure that "runs the games" is concealed by the imaginary relationship – and here we are at the level of the "L schema":

> I am, of course, aware of the importance of imaginary impregnations [*Pragung*] in the partializations of the symbolic alternative that give the signifying chain its appearance. Nevertheless, I posit that it is the law specific to this chain which governs the psychoanalytic effects that are determinant for the subject – effects such as foreclosure [*Verwerfung*], repression [*Verdrangung*], and negation [*Verneinung*] itself – and I add with the appropriate emphasis that these effects follow the displacement [*Entstellung*] of the signifier so faithfully that imaginary factors, despite their inertia, figure only as shadows and reflections therein. (Lacan 2006: 11)

If the first stage was "phenomenological," this one would be "structuralist." The problem in this second stage is that the subject – as subject of the signifier, irreducible to the imaginary-me – is, fundamentally, unthinkable. On one side, we have the imaginary-me, the space of blindness and misrecognition, which is to say the *a-a'* axis. On the other hand, we have a subject who is completely subjugated to the structure, alienated entirely and without remainder, and in this sense is de-subjectified:

> The coming into operation of the symbolic function in its most radical, absolute, usage ends up abolishing the action of the individual so completely that by the same token it eliminates his tragic relation to the world. . . . At the heart of the flow of events, of the functioning of reason, the subject from the first move finds himself to be no more than a pawn, forced inside this system, and excluded from any truly dramatic, and consequently tragic, participation in the realisation of truth. (Lacan 1991b: 168)

A subject who liberated himself completely from the *a-a'* axis and who realized himself totally in the Other, and in doing so accomplished his symbolic realization, a subject without me, without imaginary blindness, would be radically de-subjectivized, reduced to a moment in the functioning of the symbolic machine, of the "structure without subject." The third stage is, of course, in no way a "synthesis" of the two previous stages, it is not a combination of the phenomenological view of speech and the structuralist view of language. The two earlier stages are already in themselves complementary, two sides of the same theoretical edifice. The third stage explodes this common edifice, this complementary relationship of the full speech of signification and the complete structure, by positing a barred, non-achieved, "*pas-tout*" Other, an Other that has a non-symbolizable, *extimate* kernel at its core. It is only from this barred Other (A) that we can grasp the subject of the signifier ($); if the Other does not have a hole, if it is a complete series, then the only possible relationship of the subject to the structure is total alienation, all-encompassing subjectivity, leaving no remainder. The fact that the Other is lacking means that there is a remainder, an inertia that cannot be integrated into the Other – the object *a* – and that the subject can avoid total alienation insofar as he posits himself as correlative to this remainder $ ◊ *a*. It is in this manner that we can conceive of a subject different from the I, a space of imaginary unfamiliarity, a subject that does not get lost in the "process without subject" of structural combination.

We can also approach this conjuncture from the perspective of desire. That the Other is barred entails an Other that is not simply an anonymous machine, the automatism of the structural combinatorial, but rather a desiring Other, an Other who lacks the object-cause of desire, an Other who wants something from the subject (*che vuoi?*). We could say that the subject of the signifier exists to the extent that this dimension of the question is insisted on by the Other; in other words, it is not a question from the subject confronted with the enigma of the Other, but rather a question coming from the Other itself.

At first glance, it may seem as if Lacan's references to Hegel are limited to the first stage, in the themes of symbolization as historicization, integration into the symbolic universe, etc. During this period, the Lacanian reading of Hegel was "mediated" by Kojève and Hyppolite. The aspects of Hegel that received the most attention were the themes of struggle and final reconciliation within the medium of intersubjective recognition of speech. Imagine that symbolic realization is accomplished, every symptom abolished, every traumatic kernel integrated into the symbolic universe. This would be the final and ideal moment in which the subject is finally liberated from imaginary opaqueness, in which all of the blanks in his history are filled in by "full speech," in which the tension between the "subject" and the "substance" are, at long last, resolved by the subject recognizing and acknowledging his desire, etc. Isn't this state of plenitude the psychoanalytical version of Hegelian "absolute knowledge": an unbarred Other, without symptom, without hole, without opaque and traumatizing kernel?

Therefore it may seem that once Lacan had introduced the idea of the barred Other, any reference to Hegel was, at the very least, relegated to the background. The barred Other specifically entails the constitutive impossibility of absolute knowledge, of the accomplished symbolization, because there is a Void, a lack in the signifier, that accompanies the movement of symbolization. To rephrase this at another level, it is because whenever meaning comes to be, a non-meaning, a non-sense, will necessarily emerge. The conceptual field of Lacan's third stage would therefore be the field of the Other who always resists complete "realization," an Other holed by the obstacle of a Real-impossible kernel whose inertia blocks dialecticalization, an obstacle that "sublates" it in and through the symbol – in short, the quintessential anti-Hegelian Other.

Das Ungeschehenmachen

Before we succumb too quickly to this seductive image of Lacan the anti-Hegelian, it would be worthwhile to describe the logic operating behind the three stages of Lacanian doctrine. There are a couple of lenses through which we could do this. For example, it is possible to demonstrate that each of these three stages corresponds to a specific determination of the end of the analytical process. (1) *Symbolic realization* is the accomplished historicization of the symptoms. (2) The experience of *symbolic castration* ("the original repression") is the dimension that gives the subject access to his desires at the level of the Other. (3) The *traversal of the phantasy* is when the object that plugs the hole in the Other falls. However, I think the best way to approach this logic is through the "death instinct," because the link between the "death instinct" and the symbolic order, while remaining a constant in Lacan's theories, articulates itself in an altogether different manner in each of the stages.

(1) In the "Hegelian-phenomenological" stage, it can be found in a variation of the Hegelian theme of the "word as murder of the thing." The symbol, the word, is not just a simple reflection, a substitute, a simple representation of the thing, it is the thing-itself. That is to say, the thing is *aufgehoben*, sublated-internalized, in its concept, which exists in the form of a word:

> Remember what Hegel said about the concept – The concept is the time of the thing. To be sure, the concept is not the thing as it is, for

the simple reason that the concept is always where the thing isn't, it is there so as to replace the thing . . . Of the thing, what is it that can be there? Neither its form, nor its reality, since, in the actual state of affairs, all the seats are taken. Hegel puts it with extreme rigor – the concept is what makes the thing be there, while, all the while, it isn't.

This identity in difference, which characterizes the relation of the concept to the thing, that is what also makes the thing a thing and the fact symbolized, as we were told just now. (Lacan 1991a: 242–3)

The "death instinct" therefore means that as soon as it is symbolized, the thing in its immediate, corporeal, reality is annihilated. The unity of the thing, the trait that makes the thing the thing, is de-centered in relation to the reality of the thing. The thing must "die" in order for its reality to reach its conceptual unity through its symbol.

(2) In the subsequent, "structuralist," stage, the "death instinct" is identified with the symbolic order itself, insofar as it follows its own laws beyond the subject's imaginary lived experience [*vecu*], which is to say, beyond the "pleasure principle." It is the mechanism that, through its automatism, breaks the equilibrium of the imaginary homeostasis. The symbolic order

isn't the libidinal order in which the ego is inscribed, along with all the drives. It tends beyond the pleasure principle, beyond the limits of life, and that is why Freud identifies it with the death instinct . . . The symbolic order is rejected by the libidinal order, which includes the whole of the domain of the imaginary, including the structure of the ego. And the death instinct is only the mask of the symbolic order. (Lacan 1991b: 326)

(3) In the third stage, Lacan emphasizes the Real as the impossible/ unsymbolizable kernel, and the "death instinct" becomes the name for what Sade called the "second death." This is the symbolic death, the annihilation of the signifying network, of the text in which reality is inscribed and through which it is historicized. This is also the name for what, in the psychotic experience, appears to be the "end of the world," the twilight, the crumbling of the symbolic universe. In other words, the "death instinct" designates the ahistorical possibility that is implied, opened, by the process of symbolization/historicization: the possibility of its own radical erasure.

The Freudian concept that best describes this act of annihilation is *das Ungeschehenmachen* – "undoing what has been done"; in short, retroactive cancellation (cf. Freud 1990: 46). And it is more than just coincidence that we find the same term in Hegel, who defines *das Ungeschehenmachen* as the supreme power of the spirit:

"Spirit . . . is lord and master over every deed and actuality, and can cast them off, and make them as if they had never happened" (1977: 406). This power to "undo" the past is only possible at the symbolic level. In the course of immediate existence the past is only the past and therefore incontrovertible. But once we are at the level of history as a text, as the network of symbolic traces, we can annihilate the past. We can therefore see the *Ungeschehenmachen*, the highest manifestation of negativity, as the Hegelian version of the "death instinct." This is not some marginal or arbitrary element in the Hegelian theoretical edifice. Rather, it designates the key moment in the dialectical process, the moment of what we call "the negation of the negation," the reversal of the "antithesis" into the "synthesis." The "reconciliation" of the synthesis is not the act of surmounting or suspending (even in a "dialectical" way) the scission by passing beyond it. It is the retroactive recognition that *there was never* any scission at all – the "synthesis" *retroactively cancels* the scission. This is how we should understand this enigmatic yet crucial sentence in Hegel's *Encyclopedia*: "The accomplishment of the infinite purpose consists therefore only in sublating the illusion that it has not yet been accomplished" (1991b: 286).

We do not accomplish the end by attaining it, but rather by having the experience that it was already attained in the very place where before we had seen only the path to its realization. As we advanced, we never seemed to reach our destination, until – all of a sudden – we had already been there the whole time. Too early suddenly turns into too late, without allowing us to determine the moment in which this passage occurred. We are therefore dealing with the structure of a missed encounter. When we were on the path, while we had still not yet arrived, truth drew us forward like a Ghost, a promise awaiting us at the end of the path. But, all of a sudden, we notice that we had always already had the truth. The paradoxical surplus that slips away in the missed encounter as the "impossibility" of the "exact right moment" is, of course, the object *a*. It is the pure semblant that pulls us toward the truth, up until the moment where it suddenly seems as if we've already overtaken the truth, that it is already behind us. It is a chimerical being that does not have "its own time," that exists only in the discrepancy between "too early" and "too late."

Crime and punishment

It seems as if, in his theoretical development, Hegel also followed this logic of the retroactive cancellation of the scission. Beginning with his Frankfurt period, Hegel's fundamental concern was overcoming, canceling, the abstract oppositions in thought determinations that came from Understanding (the subject *versus* the object, the finite *versus* the infinite, the ideal *versus* the real, freedom *versus* necessity, etc.). In Frankfurt, he saw the synthesis of these opposite determinations as Love, the force of organic, non-coercive unity, which could encompass the opposing poles. From the point of view of the mature Hegel, which begins with the moment where Hegel "became Hegel," we must nonetheless recognize that such a solution still takes place at the level of Understanding, as it sees Love as an encompassing medium that itself remains abstractly opposed to the formal determinations of Understanding. This idea that we could immerse and dissolve the fixed and abstract determinations of Understanding in an all-encompassing medium beyond Understanding, the idea according to which there is an organic Effectivity beyond Understanding, which is limited to the domain of phenomena submitted to mechanical causality, and inaccessible to it ("Love," or perhaps "Life," the other answer given by the young Hegel), is a proposition of Understanding *par excellence*. Because – to return to my initial argument – to "pass beyond" Understanding is not to limit it or to see it as the partial, abstract moment of a much vaster organic totality, but rather to experience the realization that *there is nothing that is outside of it*.

A good example of this is the status of crime, the transgression of the Law and punishment in the different stages of Hegel's thought. The Hegel of Frankfurt still saw the legal-judicial punishment of the criminal act as an external-mechanical coercion that did not lead to true reconciliation between the transgressive criminal and the community whose Law his action violated. Coercive judicial punishment is a mechanical reaction to crime that only repairs the external damage done by the crime, instead of an organic reconciliation that truly heals over the wounds. In other words, it responds to the crime by repeating the same act, this time directed against the criminal himself. The criminal resents the penalty as a reprisal from a substantial force that remains fundamentally foreign to him. After the punishment, the abyss that separated the criminal from the community has in no way been bridged.

The thesis of the mature Hegel (articulated especially in his *Philosophy of Right*) is that the judicial penalty already accomplishes the true reconciliation, the retroactive suppression of the crime. We should emphasize that the passage from the "young Hegel" to the mature Hegel did not consist in the older Hegel rejecting what had earlier appeared as the "synthesis" in order to find another form of synthesis, of reconciling opposites. Rather, it was the realization that what had at first seemed to be a coercive, external, mechanical adjudication *was already* the true synthesis. What we had originally taken to be the formal-mechanical doubling of the crime through its repetition as punishment in fact already accomplishes the reconciliation.

The fundamental question here is the *Ungeschehenmachen* of crime. The supreme power of the spirit is that it can "make it that what already happened did not happen," which is to say that, in order to suppress crime, it is not enough that the crime be resolved, repaired, repaid through some penalty; it must also be canceled retroactively. The thesis of young Hegel is precisely that the coercive-judicial penalty (fine, prison, execution) *does not accomplish* this retroactive cancellation. The criminal individual's transgression of the law is only paid back by extorting the same price from the individual ("an eye for an eye," etc.), and the crime, although formally "resolved," remains a crime, because its positivity has not been canceled out. True reconciliation does not pass through judicial penalties, but rather through Christian love and compassion, the forgiveness of sins, which liberates the criminal from his crime. But herein lies the paradox, because for the mature Hegel the judicial penalty is already the thing that effectuates the true reconciliation.

The mature Hegel begins with the point that the criminal act is not a particular act; it necessarily contains the moment of universality (insofar as it is the action of a rational and responsible being). The criminal is not just a person who breaks the universal norms of the community. At the very same time, as a rational being he, through his act, posits a new norm that presumes to have universal validity (if he steals, he posits the right to steal as a universal norm, etc.). Of course, the universal dimension, the *formal aspect* of his act, is not necessarily apparent to the criminal. He only *thinks* that he is violating a universal norm through his particular action. He is only conscious of the determined *content* of the Law he is breaking, in no way presuming to hold his act up as a universal norm. But, as Hegel says in a very concise manner, "the form of the law, its universality, pursues him and remains attached to his crime; his act becomes universal." This is why legal authorities must respond. Legal authority does not respond to crime as a particular action; it responds to crime as a criminal action attempting to establish a new universal norm that would breach the universality of the established rule of law. In this sense, punishment is reduced to a purely self-referential action; through the means of the punishment, we recognize the criminal as a rational being, we take the universal dimension of his act seriously, and we apply to him that same norm that he established through his crime. In this manner, the criminal act cancels itself out and the rule of law is reaffirmed. Therefore, the penalty does not cancel out the crime as a particular act of a contingent, empirical nature – at this level, "what is done is done." But it can retroactively cancel its pretension to universality. In other words, it retroactively makes it a crime, a particular transgression of the law's universality. Punishment cancels the crime *through the very act of positing it as crime*, as something that violated the universality of the Law and is, as such, in itself a null moment, without value, without its own consistency. The crime is posited as null as soon as it is posited as crime, as soon as we remove its universal form from it, as soon as we suppress the contradiction between its particular contents and its universal form. The punishment *rejects* the crime, as a null particular in the circle of universality.

It is this retroactive cancellation of the crime that offers us the key to the dialectic of the "beautiful soul."

The "beautiful soul"

In order to understand the figure of the "beautiful soul" in context, we must begin with Hegel's critique of Kantian ethics. According to Hegel, the fundamental feature of Kant's *Critique of Practical Reason* is the dualism between freedom and nature, between moral law (duty) and man's pathological urges. Man is, on the one hand, a phenomenal being, caught in the chain of natural causation, and, on the other, a noumenal being capable of self-determination and free action. This scission, which Kant posits as irreducible, is precisely what prevents the subject from acting, from taking action. A purely moral act is impossible; man never acts from duty alone, his pathological urges always interfere.

The "subject who is sure of himself" – the "figure of consciousness" who follows a Kantian "moral vision of the world" – breaks this vicious circle *through the act itself*; he simply takes action. Instead of the Kantian subject who experiences moral law as a transcendent, superego commandment that comes from outside of himself, that weighs heavy upon his inert nature, we have a subject for whom moral duty immediately expresses itself through natural dispositions, in whom the moral commandments and natural urges coincide, a conjunction between freedom and nature. The German term *Gewissen* – (good) consciousness – articulates this unity. The subject experiences his duty as an organic, harmonious element of his free nature. In doing his duty, he is not obeying an authority outside of himself, but rather the law of his heart. Here we have an immediate unity between knowledge and duty; you know what you must do, and your act is only the realization of your intimate convictions. This is a critique of Kant as is found in Schiller, with the emphasis on this idea of an aesthetic man for whom moral duty is in accordance with the spontaneous activity that expresses the subject's free will.

But here again, the scission re-emerges, this time between the *formal* aspect of the act and its *contents*. In the form, the subject aims at universality: he posits his conviction as universal, while awaiting recognition from the social world. He knows that the act in itself does not have any effectivity; he knows that effectivity only comes from the recognition of others, through general opinion, in other words, through its inscription in the network of symbols. The act is therefore de-centered in relation to itself; it only becomes an act once it has been acknowledged as an act. In German, the word for "act" has, besides its two main significations (taking action, actualization, effectuation; and act in the sense of being written down on paper in a notarized act), the meaning of "portrait of a naked woman" – we therefore have the full *imaginary-Real-symbolic* triad. We look at the picture of the naked woman, and become aroused; we take action; then comes the don-juanesque moment of true jouissance, we add another conquest to the list.

The aim of the acting subject is therefore the universal recognition of his act, but its particular and arbitrary contents are felt by the community as a crime. The thing that characterizes the acting consciousness is precisely this confusion of the universal and the particular, in which his individual will is posited as universal. As Hegel says, only the rock is innocent; as soon as we act we fall into sin, we impose the particular contents of our act as universal. It is in reaction to the necessarily sinful nature of the act that the "beautiful soul" emerges. Instead of acting, it talks, it expresses profound convictions that deplore the sad state of the world and its injustices. It does not want to get its hands dirty, it wants at all cost to keep a distance between itself and the prosaic world. The "beautiful soul" is a tender, aestheticized soul, too refined for the banality of the social world. We can find a form of this in Goethe's *Confessions of a Beautiful Soul*, in which a "republic of spirits" live in a small university, sealed off from the stormy outside world, preserved in purity and innocence.

Nonetheless, the Hegelian critique of the "beautiful soul" is more than just the simple criticism of talking instead of acting, of being satisfied with deploring the state of the world without changing anything about it. Complaining that he is "not adapted" to the cruel world, in fact "he is only too well adapted to it, since he assists

in its very fabrication" (Lacan 2006: 498). In the network of intersubjective relationships in which it plays the role of the passive victim,
of someone who cannot adapt to the exigencies of banal reality, *the
entirety of this network is already its creation.* The network cannot
reproduce itself without the "beautiful soul" consenting to play this
role. The appearance of a recognition of fact ("the facts are there,
they hold true to reality") hides the consent, the complicity, perhaps
even the active will to shoulder such a role and in this way permit
the deplorable situation to reproduce itself. Here we are operating at
the strictly structural level: non-activity, the role of the passive victim,
can function as a kind of activity *par excellence* to the extent that its
role is actively assumed. We can use this to make sense of the following slightly enigmatic passage from Hegel:

> Action *qua* actualization is thus the pure form of will – the simple
> conversion of a reality that merely *is* into a reality that results from
> *action*, the conversion of the bare mode of *objective* knowing [i.e.,
> knowing an object] into one of knowing *reality* as something produced
> by consciousness. (Hegel 1977: 385)

This is Hegel's fundamental insight: the true meaning of an act is
not the particular character of the act as such. The effective act is the
preconditional mode of symbolically structuring reality, the way in
which we articulate reality so that our act (or non-act, our passivity)
has a place. The "beautiful soul" presents itself as describing the sad
state of the world as if it was excluded from it, as if it was observing
from an objective distance – we could say, from the distance of metalanguage. But it forgets to include its own subjective position, the
fact that it *wants* the world to be as it is, so that it can continue to
occupy the comfortable position of the exploited victim. The entirety
of its jouissance is tied to this role, its identity as an exploited victim
gives consistency to its imaginary-me.

Take the suffering mother, for example, the "pillar of the family"
who bears her torments calmly, who sacrifices herself in silence for
the happiness of those around her. Being exploited, being the victim
of her own family, isn't that her symptom that she "loves more than
herself"? What is she afraid of? It is not of being exploited too much,
but rather that people would no longer be willing to accept her suffering. The flow of her complaints is nothing more than the inverted
form of a demand addressed to her family to accept her sacrifice. In
such a family, communication is perfect. By mercilessly exploiting the
mother, the family members return the message of her complaints to
her in their inverted form, which is to say, in their effective meaning.

This is the point that she would never want to give up. Giving up such a point entails the loss of the consistency of one's "me"; it is the point where one hopelessly cries, "I would be willing to sacrifice everything *except that!*" – everything except one's role as the victim, everything *except sacrifice itself*. What the subject must effectuate in order to rid himself of his role as the "beautiful soul" is precisely such a sacrifice of the sacrifice. It is not enough to "sacrifice everything"; one still has to renounce the subjective economy in which sacrifice leads to narcissistic jouissance.

A dual movement of this kind operates according to the logic of the "negation of the negation." The first sacrifice, the one that permits the "beautiful soul" to find its imaginary consistency in renunciation itself, functions as a simple "negation." The second, the sacrifice of the sacrifice itself, the purification of the sacrifice, effectuates a certain kind of "negation of the negation." The sacrifice of the sacrifice, the loss of the loss, is therefore far from being a simple return to full identity without loss. What it loses is its very foundation, the support that gave consistency to the loss, the framework in which the loss took on a positive signification.

Let us recall the old communist criticism of Sartre leveled during the debate surrounding "existentialism." With his theory of the subject as pure being-for-itself, negativity, emptiness freed from positive contents, Sartre certainly rejected all the bourgeois content, all the positive prejudices and limitations of bourgeois ideology. What was left over after this sacrifice of all content was precisely the pure, emptied form of the bourgeois subject. He therefore needed to make the next step: reject this form of bourgeois subjectivity itself and join the working class. This is the fundamental gesture of the "radical," "critical" intellectual. He is prepared to renounce all "bourgeois" content in order to retain the form-itself of the "free," "autonomous" subject. More specifically, he reproduces the form of the bourgeois subject through this very sacrifice of the content itself, insofar as he turns this sacrifice into the narcissistic gesture of an "autonomous" subject. In this way, the "intellectual critique" blinds itself to the fact that the "true source of Evil" is not the sacrificed contents, but the very form itself.

The duplicity of the "beautiful soul" becomes even clearer when it develops itself into the judgmental consciousness that condemns the acting consciousness by reducing action to its particular motive. Here, Hegel is especially thinking of the great men of action and the base explanations that popular opinion attributes to their acts. It is said that Caesar tried to destroy the Republic because of his lust for power, that Napoleon conquered Europe because of his grandiose ambition, etc. While it is perhaps true that Caesar, as a private individual, was driven by pathological motives of this sort, his act nonetheless realized a historical necessity, that of the passage from Republic to Empire. The judgmental conscience blinds itself to the true signification of the act. When examining the act, it isolates the act from its historical context and reduces it to an arbitrary and psychological particularity. This is a key point of the Hegelian critique. This isolation of the act from its context, this inability to see its universal signification – *it is precisely this that is true evil.* In this light, the judgmental consciousness appears even worse than the acting and sinning consciousness. Absolute evil is the innocent point of view that sees evil everywhere, much as in Henry James's *The Turn of the Screw*, in which the true evil is the governess's point of view itself, which sees the presence of evil spirits everywhere. Evil does not lie in the act, which always has a universal dimension, even if it is not known to the subject who is acting, but in the point of view that reduces the act to its particular contents. Hegel finishes Napoleon's famous quote, "no man is a hero to his valet," by adding "not because the man is no hero, but because the other is a valet."

This is why the path to reconciliation passes through the acting consciousness. Just as with all of the preceding figures in the *Phenomenology* – the opposition of the Master and the Slave, of the base consciousness and the noble consciousness, etc. – truth is on the side of the acting consciousness that introduces crimes, scission, and sin. Here Hegel brings us back to his interpretation of Christianity. The dialectic of the "beautiful soul" resolves itself in the passage to the absolute Spirit, to religion. The cancellation of sin does not occur through the condemnatory judgment of a neutral and innocent perspective, that of "metalanguage" – "Do not judge and you will not be judged!" – but through pardoning, through the forgiveness of sins. The sinful act is retroactively liberated, through the truth that it made possible through its very failure. This is what Hegel calls *das Ungeschehenmachen*. We do not simply cancel the act; rather, we just cancel out its failure, we experience the failure as positive, as "integral to the truth" – an inversion that Hegel called "the cunning of reason."

6

The "Cunning of Reason," or the True Nature of the Hegelian Teleology

Failure in Austen

Jane Austen is Hegel's only true literary complement. *Pride and Preju-dice* is the literary *Phenomenology of the Spirit*, *Mansfield Park* is the *Logic*, and *Emma* the *Encyclopaedia*. In *Pride and Prejudice*, Elizabeth and Darcy feel a mutual sympathy, even though they belong to different social classes: he is from a wealthy and noble family, she is from the shabby-genteel middling bourgeoisie. An extremely proud man, Darcy feels that the love he experiences is undignified. When he asks Elizabeth to marry him, he openly avows his disdain for the world that she belongs to, and expects her to receive his proposal as an unthinkable honor. Seeing herself being regarded with such prejudice – and victim to her own prejudice – Elizabeth experiences Darcy's offer as a humiliation and turns him down. This double failure, this twofold error, has the structure of a dual communicative movement, in which each individual receives from the other his or her own message in its inverted form. Elizabeth wants to present herself to Darcy as a cultivated young woman, full of spirit, but the message she receives from him is "you are just a vain and trivial person." Darcy wishes to present himself to her as a proud gentleman, but receives the message back from her "your pride is nothing more than despicable haughtiness." After they break off contact, a series of acci-dents leads to each learning about the other's true nature. She learns of Darcy's tender and sensitive side, he learns of Elizabeth's cultivated and refined spirit, and the story ends as it must, in marriage.

Where is the Hegelian stratagem, the "cunning of reason," here? It lies in the failure of their first encounter, in the dual misunderstanding concerning the other individual's character, which is a necessary condition for the final dénouement. We cannot access truth directly; we cannot say, "if, from the beginning, she knew his true nature and he hers, the story could have ended in marriage right away." For the sake of argument, imagine that the lovers' first encounter was a success, and that Elizabeth accepts Darcy's initial offer. What would happen in this case? Instead of two people united by true love, they would be a banal married couple – a haughty wealthy scion and a vain young girl. In trying to spare them their passage through error, we would miss the truth itself. Only through the "transference work" [*Durcharbeitung*]* of error could each of them see the other in a true light – for Darcy, to free himself from his pride, for Elizabeth, to overcome her prejudices. Elizabeth sees in Darcy's pride the mirror image of her prejudices and he, in Elizabeth's vanity, sees the mirror image of his pride. In other words, Darcy's pride is not a positive given independent of his relationship to Elizabeth, it is brought about through the perspective of her prejudices, and, vice versa, Elizabeth is only vain to Darcy's prideful eyes.

We fall prey to the teleological illusion the moment that we reduce the relationship between mutual misunderstanding and final triumph into that of a means to an end. As if the final goal (the triumph of true love) was guiding the process in advance, as if the dual misunderstanding was, ahead of time, playing the role of a means of creating love. Yes, "truth emerges out of error," but that in no way implies that this error, this fall into illusion, could be reduced to Machiavellian cunning on the part of truth, which would have used this stratagem in order to achieve its ends and its ultimate victory. It is quite literally the error itself that creates, that opens, the (still) empty space of truth. This is undoubtedly the "cunning of reason" at work, but the true problem consists in giving a precise characterization of what "cunning of reason" means.

Normally, the "cunning of reason" is reduced to a relationship of technical manipulation. Instead of acting directly on the object, we use another object as an instrument. We give the other object "free range," and through the interaction between the objects themselves, their mutual friction and erosion, the goal becomes realized, while all the while we keep a safe distance from the events. The idea is that

---

* Žižek uses the French word *perlaboration*, which is the standard translation of the Freudian term *Durcharbeitung*. Lacan himself preferred to use *travail de transfert*, which Bruce Fink translates as "transference work" (Lacan 2006: 526).

the Absolute has the same relationship to the actions of historical subjects. The Absolute is like Adam Smith's "invisible hand" of the market; each subject pursues their own personal selfish ends and it is through this activity that – unbeknownst to the actors themselves – the common interest is achieved. In history, subjects take action with the aim of accomplishing a wide variety of goals (utilitarian, religious, moral, etc.), but, in Truth, without knowing it, they are nothing more than tools in the realization of the divine plan.

The first thing we should take note of, and this is often overlooked, is that Hegel's discussion of the cunning of reason is, in general, a critique of it. More specifically, he demonstrates that the position of the subject of the "cunning of reason" is fundamentally *impossible*. The "cunning of reason" is always double, doubled in itself. For example, the worker exploits natural forces, allowing them to accomplish ends that are exterior to these forces (such as the end of the pleasure produced by the consumption of the product obtained). For him, the goal of production is the satisfaction of his needs. However, the true goal of the process of social production is not the satisfaction of individual needs, but the transformation of nature into machines and tools, which is to say the development of productive forces as "objectifications of the spirit." Hegel's thesis is therefore that *the manipulator is always already manipulated*. Unbeknownst to him, the worker who thinks that he is exploiting nature through the "cunning of reason" ends up realizing the interests of the "objective spirit."

But we did not need to wait for Hegel for the idea of the "cunning of reason" to emerge. Kant, disappointed and troubled by the outcome of the French Revolution (the terror, etc.), sought recourse to the idea of "nature's secret plan," a divine project that would guide history's development. In order to salvage the idea of the historical process's rational character, the belief that this process is guided by the "regulating idea" of an ideal state that we are progressively approaching, Kant had to posit – after the "excesses" of the French Revolution, which were affirmations of pure subjectivity – a trans-subjective Absolute that would guarantee the teleology of the historical process. This line of thinking contains an obvious paradox: the Absolute uses moral subjects; it makes use of them as unknowing means to the realization of its hidden ends. Subjects can only trust in the wisdom of the Absolute and endure their destiny, knowing that they are being sacrificed to the supreme Goal, that they are contributing to the establishment of a state in which man would no longer be the plaything of transcendental forces, but would truly be free.

We can find the same thesis in Fichte's (1889) conferences on the vocation of the Scholar. For Fichte, the Absolute governs history in the form of divine Reason. The Scholar's role is to know, at least partially, what the divine project is and to guide, in accordance with this project, the actions of un-enlightened individuals. Fichte's ideas here contain the seed of the Leninist-Stalinist conception of the Party. They saw the Party as a community of scholars ("the collective intelligence") who, because of their understanding of the divine Project (of the "necessary development of history"), could guide the activity of the masses. It might seem, at first, as if Hegel is doing the same thing when he introduces the concept of the "cunning of reason."

> This may be called the cunning of reason – that it sets the passions to work for itself, while that which develops its existence through such impulsion pays the penalty, and suffers loss. . . . individuals are sacrificed and abandoned. The Idea pays the penalty of determinate existence and of corruptibility, not from itself, but from the passions of individuals. (2001: 33)

There is nonetheless a fundamental difference between Hegel's vision of the "cunning of reason" and Fichte's conception of the Scholar's role. For Hegel, the realization of Fichte's idea in the form of the Leninist-Stalinist Party would be inconceivable and excluded a priori. Hegel would reject the idea that any force, any politico-historical actor, could legitimate its activity through the "cunning of reason," that any politico-historical subject would be capable of understanding its own role in the framework of a "divine project," of understanding the way in which its own activities were the tools of the "cunning of reason," and that therefore could posit itself in advance as the incarnation of historical Reason. In other words, such a conjunction – a subjective position that claimed to have knowledge of the Absolute and the practical-historical dimension – is impossible for Hegel. Hegel knew that a combination like this, an actor that legitimated itself as the embodiment of Reason in history, could lead only to totalitarian terror. The "cunning of reason" *only occurs after the fact*; we can only grasp it retroactively, when the subject recognizes that the true results of his act were different from his goal. It is a priori impossible to act with the knowledge of the true goal, the signification, of one's act. Action is always fundamentally a failure, it always involves some fundamental blunder. In other words, we can only act blind. Why is this? If we wish to remain Hegelian and "understand the substance as subject," which is to say, if we want to avoid falling back into traditional metaphysics (the Absolute as a transcendental substance, inaccessible to subjects, etc.), there is only one possible answer we can give. The actual goal, the "true signification" of an act, as it differs from its goal, *is only constituted after the fact, through the failure of this act.* The idea that true signification could be given in advance through divine Reason is just the teleological illusion of the "naive consciousness." Hegelian "teleology," on the other hand, is always retrospective. It is true that individuals in history are the unknowing means of the realization of Reason, of its infinite Goals. However, what individuals are "means of" is *only constituted through their activity itself.*

The Hegelian subject versus the Fichtean subject

We should therefore draw a strict distinction between the Hegelian subject and Fichte's subject. For Fichte, there is a true "violence of subjectivity" that, through its synthetic activity, wishes to abolish the autonomy of the object, which has been reduced, in the end, into an injunction to action. The fundamental relationship of the subject to the object is one of production, of the subject actively changing the object.

Two divergent interpretations of German idealism that are as different as Heidegger's and Marx's overlap when they place the foundation of the Hegelian "work of the concept" in the *concept of work.* Both argue that the Hegelian dialectic is fundamentally a metaphysics of labor, the articulation of a technical-productive relationship to objectivity. For Marxism, there is a "mystification," an "idealist absolutization" of social labor (cf., e.g., Adorno 1993). Heidegger's position, as defined in his *Letter on Humanism* (1993), is that the concept of work is the key to understanding *The Phenomenology of the Spirit.* From this perspective, the Hegelian "reconciliation" becomes, *vulgari eloquentia,* "Fichte on steroids," as if the Hegelian dialectic could succeed where Fichte fell short, as if in Hegelian "absolute idealism" the subject would finally be able to "devour," to internalize the object, to abolish the remainder, that un-mediatable surplus that Fichte's "subjective idealism" was unable to do away with.

My goal, of course, is to show the exact opposite. There is a radical difference between Fichte and Hegel. Work is not the fundamental character of the Hegelian dialectic. It would be futile to search for the matrix of the dialectical process in the process of work, in the externalization-objectification of the subject in its product. Nor should we look for the matrix of "reconciliation" in the act of recognizing oneself in one's own product and appropriating for oneself the alienated result of one's labor. For Hegel, the act is fundamentally tragic; it never attains its goal. Through "reconciliation," the subject recognizes that, through the very failure of his act, he has realized a different end, the "endless end." Such a retroactive structure radically excludes any progressive or evolutionary framework.

Even though the standard view of this pairing is that it is the ultimate proof of the evolutionary nature of the dialectical process, Hegel's radical anti-evolutionism is clearly visible in the conceptual pairing *in itself/for itself* (the progressive development of the in-itself into the for-itself). In-itself as the opposite of for-itself is both (1) the possible, that which only exists as potential, as internal possibility, the opposite of realized – which is that which has been externalized, actualized; and (2) realization in the objective sense, in its raw external given form, the opposite of subjective mediation, internalization, self-examination. In this sense, in-itself is realization that has not yet attained the conceptual level.

Advancing these two aspects simultaneously subverts the traditional view of the dialectical process as a gradual, progressive realization of the object's internal potential through its spontaneous self-development. Hegel is very clear on this point: in an object, its internal potential for self-development and the pressure that is exerted upon the object by an external force are *strictly co-relative*, they are the two sides of the same conjunction. The potential object must also be present in an external realization under the form of a heteronymous constraint. For example (and this example comes from Hegel himself), saying that the student is, at the beginning of the educational process, the one who has the potential to know, the one who will realize his creative potential through the framework of this process, means that his internal potential must be, from the beginning, present in some external realization in the form of the authority of the Master who exerts pressure on the student. Today, we might also add to this the tragic example of the working class as potential revolutionary subject in itself. Saying that the revolutionary character in itself, in its potential in the working class, exists, is strictly equivalent to saying that this possibility has already been actualized, present, realized in the Party, which knew it in advance and therefore put pressure on the working class to direct it toward the realization of its potential. This is how the Party is legitimated in its role as educator-leader, how it gets the right to guide the working class according to its potential, imbuing it with its "historical mission."

The counterargument to this theory is that, despite all this, the dialectical process still consists in a gradual progression toward an increasingly concrete, mediated truth. Each successive stage is the "truth" of the stage that preceded it; progress is nevertheless still being made. Let us take the first passage of the Hegelian system – the passage from being to void – and try to determine the exact meaning of the proposition that the void, the "nothing," is the truth of being. First, we posit being as the subject (in the grammatical sense), then we try to attribute some or other predicate to it, determining it in some or other way. But every attempt fails. There is nothing we can say about being, there is no predicate that we can attribute to it. The void, the "nothing," as the "truth" of being, is only this impossibility given substance, realized. It is essential to recognize the way in which impossibility is realized in each (Hegelian) passage from one moment to the subsequent moment as the "truth" of the first moment. We are never dealing with a simple descent toward an increasingly deep and concrete essence. The logic of the passage is always that of a reflexive realization of the failure, the impossibility, of the passage itself. Take moment X. If we attempt to determine it more "deeply," by uncovering its hidden essence, we will find that we cannot. The next moment, then, is the realization of this failure. In trying to reach the hidden truth of X, to determine the essence that was supposedly hidden behind its appearance, we miss this truth – *and this failure is the truth of X.*

Let us return to the Hegelian critique of Zeno's argument that movement does not exist. By showing the contradictory character of movement, Zeno wants to prove the existence of calm, immobile, self-identical Being beyond the false appearance of movement. However, if this Being is in itself empty, Zeno can only describe the movement itself of movement's self-sublation. This is why Heraclitus' movement is the "truth" of the Eleatic Being. The passage to Being beyond the appearance of movement fails; all that remains is the movement itself of this passage, the reflexive, self-referential movement of movement's self-sublation.

The "reconciliation"

The *Witz* about Rabinovitch, Christ's death, and the closure and dissolution of the unconscious in transference all draw on the same basic matrix, one which illustrates the manner in which truth emerges out of failure, in which failure makes itself an immanent constituent of truth. In order to understand the logic of this, we must completely reject the classical view of the Hegelian process according to which there is, first, a positive point of departure – the thesis – followed by the negation, the scission, the thesis reversing itself into the antithesis, and finally, at a higher level, the thesis comes to include the antithesis once again. The synthesis is not a return to the initial thesis; in a certain sense, it is only through the synthesis that we *get rid of*, that we *free* ourselves from, the perspective of the thesis.

Let us return to the *Witz* about Rabinovitch. In this *Witz*, the "synthesis" is *exactly the same as the antithesis*; it is the bureaucrat's argument itself ("Soviet power is eternal and indestructible"). The only thing we have to do is notice that the counterargument to the initial argument is already the true argument for emigration. The whole passage from the antithesis to the synthesis can be reduced to this change in perspective. The same thing is true with the death of Christ. The "thesis" is Christ's earthly mission – the liberation of the Jews. The "antithesis" is its defeat, which, nonetheless, only looks like a failure from the perspective of the thesis. The "synthesis" repeats the "antithesis" (the defeat of Christ's mission on Earth, his death on the cross), but from another perspective, one in which it appears as a triumph, the accomplishment of Christ's true mission: the reconciliation of man and God, the finite and the infinite. The process is once again the same in the case of transference as the "enaction of the reality of the unconscious" (Lacan 1998a: 136). The "end of analysis" can, essentially, be reduced to a simple change in perspective, the experience of the way in which the transfer – the retreat, the closure, of the unconscious – simultaneously realizes its enactment. The "return to the thesis" in the synthesis is therefore not the return to the same thesis – the thesis that was negated by the antithesis – but rather it is the antithesis itself that becomes, so to speak, *its own thesis*.

In a certain sense, "nothing happens" in the dialectical process. The passage from one stage to the next always implies that "this was already the case." We do not pass from the thesis to the antithesis by developing the thesis, by demonstrating the way in which the thesis presupposes the antithesis. Rather, the whole passage consists in the recognition that the thesis *is already* in itself its own antithesis, its own contradiction. Being, when we try to determine it, to understand it, "as is," in its own specific contents, is already the void. In the same way, we do not pass from the antithesis to the synthesis by attempting to understand the way in which the thesis and the antithesis are both part of the same totality, in a way in which they would mutually imply and complete each other. The antithesis is a reflexive concept: the true antithesis is not the antithesis as the contradiction of the synthesis, but the *antithesis between antithesis and synthesis itself*. We remain inside the antithesis for as long as we believe that "something is missing from it," that its two poles should be unified by an additional synthesis. We "overcome" the antithesis when we recognize that nothing is missing from it, that the antithesis itself was already the synthesis that we were searching for outside of it.

We can therefore say that "dis-alienation" – the "reconciliation" of the subject with the alienated substance – *changes nothing* besides the subject's perspective. Far from "appropriating the alienated substantial content," far from recognizing the content as "his own product," the subject simply notices that he is already inside the substance because of the very trait that he had thought excluded him from it, that the distance that seemed to separate him from the substantial Other was a distance from the self, a gap inside the Other. Through this lens, we can see how Hegelian "dis-alienation" radically differs from Marx's. Marx's view of "dis-alienation" is in line with Fichte's "productivist" perspective of a subject who produces his own world, who posits objectivity as the objectification of this world, a world from which his own product alienates itself, twisting itself into a strange force. "Dis-alienation" is therefore understood as the act through which the subject casts off the illusion of an autonomous objective world, recognizing his own product and appropriating its contents. From this perspective, Hegelian "reconciliation" looks like "hidden positivism" (Marx). It is easy to show that nothing changes in "dis-alienation" of the Hegelian kind; the realization remains the same as it was before. But this view has already missed the key point of Hegelian "reconciliation." That "nothing changes" is precisely what Hegel is trying to say. In other words, the thing that changes radically in Hegelian "reconciliation" is the mode in which reality is symbolized. To say that, during such a change, "reality remains as it was" implies the idea of a reality that is simply external to the symbolic, which is to say, an understanding of the symbolic as the means to designate pre-existing facts.

Hegel does not "cancel out," he does not "abolish," the scission into which Fichtean philosophy had fallen. Hegel does not "overcome" the obstacle of inert objectivity, the obstacle that, for Fichte, continued to resist subjectifying internalization. The entire Hegelian operation can be reduced to the retrospective recognition that the obstacle was not an obstacle, that what had seemed to Fichte to be an "obstacle" to the movement of subjectification was in fact its necessary condition. The un-dialecticizable remainder that seemed to block the full realization of the subject reveals itself to be its objectual correlate. The subject must recognize this inert surplus as its *Dasein*, it must realize that the non-integrated object is only the realization of the void, the empty space of the subject.

Thus, our proposition remains the same as Fichte's: "the inert object marks the limit that blocks the subject's full realization." All that we have to do is just take the speculative meaning of this and change the emphasis ever so slightly: the subject himself is nothing more than the void, the blockage, his own impossibility, and this is why the inert, non-subjectified object, because it embodies this blockage, functions as the subject's *Dasein*, its objectual correlate. The subject, pure negativity, the absolute movement of mediation, can only attain being-for-itself, effective existence, by embodying itself once again in an absolutely inert, non-subjective moment.

"The spirit is a bone"

At the level of the immediate, of "Understanding" and "representation" [*Vorstellung*], this proposition certainly seems to be an extreme variant of vulgar materialism. We reduce the spirit – the subject, pure negativity, the most mobile and flexible element – into a rigid, frozen, dead object, total inertia, an absolutely non-dialectical presence. Therefore, our first reaction is that of the Soviet bureaucrat in the *Witz* about Rabinovitch. We are indignant, the proposition "the spirit is a bone" seems senseless; it produces in us the feeling of a radical, intolerable contradiction, the image of a grotesque incongruity, an extreme negative relationship. And it is precisely this response – just as in Rabinovitch's case – that is its speculative truth, because *this negativity, this unsustainable discord, is subjectivity itself*, it is the only possible way of presenting subjectivity's negativity. We *succeed* in transmitting the dimension of subjectivity *through the means of the failure itself*, through its radical insufficiency, through the absolute non-correspondence of the predicate to the subject. The "speculative proposition" is thus a proposition whose terms are not comparable.

The proposition "the spirit is a bone," the equivalence of two absolutely non-comparable terms – the pure negative movement of the subject and the total inertia of the frozen, rigid object – is it not something along the lines of a Hegelian version of the phantasy: $ \$ \lozenge a $? In order to show this with certainty, we need only to understand this proposition within its specific context: the passage from physiognomy to phrenology in *The Phenomenology of the Spirit*. Physiognomy – the language of the body, the expression of the subject's internality through gestures and facial expression – is still linguistic, signifying, *representation*. A physical expression (a gesture,

a grimace) represents, signifies, the internality of the subject.
The final result of physiognomy is its *failure*: each signifying representation betrays and displaces the subject. There is no signifier
that belongs to the subject. The passage from physiognomy to phrenology functions precisely in the same way as the passage from
representation to *presence*. The skull, unlike gestures and facial
expressions, is not a sign, not an expression of an internality, it does
not represent anything. It is, in its own inertia, the immediate presence of the spirit:

> In physiognomy . . . Spirit is supposed to be known in its *own* outer
> aspect, as in a being which is the *utterance* of Spirit – the visible invis-
> ibility of its essence. . . . In the determination yet to be considered
> [that of phrenology], however, the outer aspect is lastly a wholly
> *immobile* reality which is not in its own self a speaking sign but, sepa-
> rated from self-conscious movement, presents itself on its own account
> and is a mere Thing. (Hegel 1977: 195)

Take the bone, the skull. Here is an object that, through its *presence*, fills the emptiness, the impossible signifying *representation*
of the subject. It is – to put it in Lacanian terms – the realization
of lack. It is the thing that fills the place where the signifier is lacking,
the phantasmic object that fills the lack in the Other. We might
say that Hegel's "idealist" wager was his belief that it might be
possible to dialecticize the inertia of the phantasy object through
the movement of *Aufhebung*, the reversal of the lacking signifier
into the signifier of lacking. We know that the signifier of this
Aufhebung is the phallus, and – this is the greatest surprise of all
from Hegel – at the end of the section on phrenology, Hegel himself
uses the phallic metaphor to designate the relationship between the
two levels on which the proposition "the spirit is a bone" can be
read: the traditional reading of "picture-thinking" and the speculative reading.

> The depth which Spirit brings forth from within – but only so far as
> its picture-thinking consciousness where it lets it remain – and the
> ignorance of this consciousness about what it really is saying are the
> same conjunction of the high and the low which, in the living being,
> Nature naively expresses when it combines the organ of its highest
> fulfillment, the organ of generation, with the organ of urination.
> The infinite judgment, qua infinite, would be the fulfillment of life
> that comprehends itself; the consciousness of the infinite judgment
> that remains at the level of picture-thinking behaves as urination.
> (Hegel 1977: 210)

"Wealth is the self"

When a "figure of consciousness" appears in *The Phenomenology of the Spirit*, the question we must always ask is: where does it repeat itself, where is the ulterior, richer, more "concrete" figure who, insofar as it is a repetition of the original figure, might offer us the key to understanding it (cf. Labarrière 1968)? For example, the passage from physiognomy to phrenology is taken up again in the chapter on the alienated Spirit, in the form of the passage from the "language of flattery" to Wealth.

The "language of flattery" is the middle term in the triad *Noble Consciousness – Language of Flattery – Wealth*. The noble consciousness is in the position of extreme alienation. It posits all its contents in the common Good, which is incarnated by the State. The noble consciousness serves the State with a sincere and total devotion and acts accordingly. It does not speak: its language is limited to a few "counsels" concerning the common Good. Here, this Good is a thoroughly substantial entity, but in the passage to the next stage of development, it subjectivizes itself. Instead of the substantial State, we have a Monarch who can say "I am the State." This subjectivation of the State entails a radical change in the way the State is served: *"the heroism of silent service becomes the heroism of flattery"* (Hegel 1977: 310; italics mine). The medium of the activity of consciousness passes from action to language, in the form of flattery addressed to the Royal person who embodies the State.

The obvious historical backdrop for this passage is the transition from medieval feudalism, with its notions of honor, loyal service, etc., to absolute monarchy. This is much more than a simple corruption, a degeneration from silent and devoted service into hypocritical flattery. The paradoxical expression "the heroism of flattery" should not be taken as the ironic juxtaposition of two contradictory notions; rather, Hegel means heroism in the full sense of the word. We have to understand the concept of "heroic flattery" in the same register as the idea of "voluntary servitude," because it leads to the same theoretical impasse: how can "flattery," normally seen as a non-ethical activity *par excellence*, a pursuit of the "pathological" interests of gain and pleasure, obtain an ethical status, the status of a duty that goes "beyond the pleasure principle"?

The key to this enigma, according to Hegel, is the role played by language. Of course, language is the medium itself of the path of consciousness in the *Phenomenology*, to the point that we could define each step of this path, each "figure of the consciousness," by a specific linguistic modality. Starting at the very beginning, in "sensible certainty," the dialectical movement is put in motion by the discord between what the consciousness "wants to say" and what it actually says. However, the "language of flattery" presents us with an exception to this series. It is only here that language does not reduce itself to the medium of the process, but as such becomes, in its very form, what is at stake in the struggle; "here it has for its content the form itself, the form which language itself is, and is authoritative as *language*. It is the power of speech, as that which performs what has to be performed" (Hegel 1977: 307).

This is why we should not seek to understand "flattery" at the psychological level, as hypocritical and greedy adulation. What it represents is, instead, the dimension of a type of *alienation that belongs to language as such*. It is the very form of language that introduces this radical alienation. The noble consciousness betrays the sincerity of its internal convictions *as soon as it begins to speak*. As soon as we speak, truth is on the side of the universal, of what we "actually say," and the "sincerity" of our personal sentiments comes to be "pathological" in the Kantian sense, radically non-ethical, coming from the domain of the pleasure principle. The subject can believe that the flattery he utters is simply feigned and nothing more. He can think that flattery is only an external rite that has nothing to do with his personal and sincere convictions. The problem is that as soon as he thinks he is being insincere, he is already the victim of his own insincerity, given that he does not realize that his true place lies in this empty externality. What he thought was his most personal conviction was nothing more than the vanity of his null subjectivity. To put it in more "modern" terms: the "truth" of what I say is tied to the "performative" function of speech, to the way in which it affirms (creates) the social bond, not to the psychological "sincerity" of what I said. The "heroism of flattery" takes this paradox to its extreme. Its message is: "While I am aware that what I'm saying is a complete disavowal of my most personal convictions, I know that this form that has been emptied of all sincerity is truer than my convictions, and in this sense, I am sincere in my desire to give up my convictions."

This is how "flattering the Monarch against one's own convictions" can be an ethical act. You submit yourself to a constraint that destabilizes your narcissistic homeostasis, you "externalize" yourself completely. By speaking the empty words that deny your personal convictions, you heroically give up the thing that is most precious to you: your "sense of honor," your moral consistency. Flattery radically hollows out "personality." What's left is the empty form of the subject, the subject as that empty form. We can find an altogether parallel logic in the passage from the Leninist-revolutionary consciousness to the Stalinist post-revolution consciousness. Here again, after the revolution, loyal service to the Cause necessarily turns into the "heroism of flattering" the Leader, the subject who supposedly embodies revolutionary power. Here again, the truly heroic dimension of this flattery consists in the fact that, in the name of loyalty to the Cause, one is willing to sacrifice honesty and even sincerity itself – adding to it the additional coercion that one is ready to *admit to this insincerity itself* and announce that one is a "traitor." Ernesto Laclau was absolutely right when he said that it is not enough to say that "Stalinism" was a fundamentally linguistic phenomenon, we must go so far as to reverse this proposition and say that, in a previously unnoticed sense, *language itself is already a "Stalinist phenomenon."* In the Stalinist rite, in the empty flattery that holds that community together, in the neutral, completely de-psychologized voice that "confesses," is the realization, in its purest form that has so far existed, of a dimension that marks perhaps the essential feature of language. There is no need to return to pre-Socratic foundations in order to "penetrate into the origins of language"; *The History of the Communist Party of the Soviet Union (Bolsheviks): Short Course* is sufficient.

Where is the objectual correlate of this completely "emptied" subject? The Hegelian response: in the money that he gains in exchange for his flattery. At this level, the proposition "the wealth is the Self" performs the same operation as "the spirit is a bone." In both cases we have a proposition that at first appears senseless, an equation whose terms cannot be compared. In both cases, this passage has the same logical structure: the subject, who loses himself completely in the linguistic medium (the language of gestures and facial expressions; the language of flattery), finds his objectual correlate in the inertia of a non-linguistic object (the skull, money). The paradox, the obvious senselessness of the idea that money, an inert, external, passive object that I can hold in my hand, would be the immediate incarnation of the self, is no less difficult to accept than the proposition that the skull would be the immediate realization of the spirit. Their difference lies in the different starting points of the dialectical movement. If we begin with language in the sense of the body's gestures and facial expressions, the objectual correlate of the subject is that which, at this level, presents the point of total inertia – the bone, the skull. But if you start with language in the sense of the medium for social relationships of domination, the objectual correlate that offers itself is money as social power in its material form.

7

"The Suprasensible is the Phenomenon as Phenomenon," or How Hegel Goes Beyond the Kantian Thing-in-Itself

Kant and McCullough

It is a commonplace, common-sense truth that we must be wary of excessive, overly radicalized, absolute Good because it can suddenly transform itself into Evil. Even moderate religious doctrine warns us that the Devil's subtlest temptation is inducing us into doing evil in the name of Good itself, that an exclusive obsession with the Good can lead to hatred of the worldly and the secular (cf. Umberto Eco's *The Name of the Rose*). For the most part, however, such wisdom obscures a far more unsettling converse truth: Evil itself, when radicalized, elevated to the point of a "non-pathological" (in the Kantian sense) attitude, a "principled" attitude beyond possible costs or benefits, becomes an ethical position, becomes Good. At the end of Mozart's *Don Giovanni*, the count's statue comes to save him. All he must do is repent and renounce his escapades, and he will be spared the torments of Hell. Even though he knows what awaits him, Don Giovanni turns down the offer that would have saved him. He does not deviate from his Evil path, even though this choice is senseless from the point of view of the pleasure principle. By refusing to repent, he affirms his Evilness as a properly ethical position, more than a simple greedy search for pleasure.

This is what Kant, the philosopher of unconditional Duty, the greatest obsessive in the history of philosophy, missed. But what eluded Kant is something that our contemporary vulgar sentimental literature, our *kitsch*, knows well. There is nothing surprising about

this, if we remember that it is precisely in the universe of this kind
of literature that the tradition of courtly love has survived, a tradition
whose defining trait is that it posits love of the Lady as the supreme
Duty. Let us take an exemplary instance of the genre, *An Indecent
Obsession* by Colleen McCullough (which is unreadable, and therefore was published in France as part of the *"J'ai Lu"* [literally, "I
have read" – trans] collection). The book takes place near the end of
World War II, in a small hospital in the Pacific where a nurse takes
care of shell-shocked soldiers. She is torn between her professional
duty and her love for one of her patients. At the end of the book,
she makes up her mind as to what she truly wants, renounces love,
and returns to her duty. At first glance, this seems to be moralism of
the most insipid sort; duty wins out over romantic passion, "pathological" love is renounced in the name of duty, and so forth. However,
the description of her motives for this renunciation is slightly more
nuanced. From the final paragraphs of the novel:

> She had a duty here . . . This wasn't just a job – her heart was in it,
> fathoms deep in it! This was what she truly wanted . . . without any
> fear, understanding herself at last. And understanding that duty, the
> most indecent of all obsessions, was only another name for love.
> (McCullough 1981: 324)

What we have here is a true Hegelian dialectical turn: the opposition of love and duty is "sublated *[aufgehoben]*" when one experiences duty itself as "another name for love." Through this reversal
– the "negation of the negation" – duty, which at first appeared to
be the negation of love, coincides with the supreme Love that abolishes all the other "pathological" loves. Or, in Lacanian terms, it
functions as a "quilting point" in relation to the other "ordinary"
loves. The tension between duty and love, between the purity of duty
and the indecency, the obscene pathology of romantic passion,
resolves itself in the moment when we experience the radically
obscene, indecent character of duty itself. In the French version the
final sentence of the novel is mistranslated in a telling way. Duty is
referred to as *"la plus tyrannique des obsessions"* ["the most tyran-
nical of all obsessions"], when in fact, it is "the most indecent of all
obsessions."

The key here is the shift in the location of "indecent obsession"
with regard to the opposition between duty and love. At the beginning, duty appears as pure and universal, the opposite of pathological, particular, indecent romantic passion. But then, duty itself is
revealed to be *the most indecent of all obsessions*. This is the Hegelian

logic of the "reconciliation" between the Universal and the Particular. The most radical, absolute particular is the Universal itself, insofar as its relationship to the Particular is one of negative exclusion, which is to say, it opposes the Particular and excludes the richness of its concrete contents. This is how we must understand the Lacanian thesis that Good is only the mask for radical, absolute Evil, concealing the "indecent obsession" behind *das Ding*, the horrible-obscene Thing. Behind Good lies radical Evil; Supreme Good is just another name for an Evil that does not have a particular, "pathological" status. To the extent that it obsesses us in an indecent, obscene manner, *das Ding* makes it possible for us to detach ourselves, to liberate ourselves from our "pathological" attachments to worldly, particular objects. The "Good" is just a way of maintaining distance from the evil Thing, a distance that makes it bearable.

This is what Kant, unlike our contemporary *kitsch* literature, misunderstood. He did not see the other side, the obscene, indecent side of Duty itself. And this is why he was only able to evoke the concept of *das Ding* in its negative form, as an incomprehensible (im)possibility. In his treatise on negative magnitudes, for example, he discusses the difference between logical contradiction and real opposition. For Kant, contradiction is a logical relationship that does not exist in reality, while in cases of real opposition, both poles are *positive*, which is to say that their relationship is not the relationship of a thing to its lack, but rather two existing phenomena in opposition to each other. For example – and this example is not random insofar as it bears directly on what is in question here, the pleasure principle – pleasure and displeasure.

> Consider the following question: Is displeasure simply the lack of pleasure? Or is displeasure a ground of the deprivation of pleasure? And in this case, displeasure, while being indeed something positive in itself and not merely the contradictory opposite of pleasure, is opposed to pleasure in the real sense of the term. (Kant 1992: 219)

Therefore, pleasure and pain, the two poles of a real opposition, are positive phenomena; one is negative only in relation to the other, while Good and Evil are contradictory, their relationship is of a + to a 0. This is why Evil is not a positive entity, it is only the lack, the absence of the Good. It would be an absurdity to attempt to understand a contradiction's negative pole as something positive, and therefore "to think of a special sort of thing and to call such things negative things" (Kant 1992: 214). But *das Ding* is, in its Lacanian conceptualization, just such a "negative thing," a paradoxical Thing that is only the positivization of a Lack, a hole in the symbolic Other. *Das Ding* as "Evil incarnate" is an object irreducible to the pleasure principle, to the opposition between pleasure and pain. In other words, it is, in a strict sense, a "non-pathological" object. This paradox would be unthinkable for the Kant at his "critical" stage, and this why we must think about Kant "with Sade."

The *ne explétif*

It follows from this that there is a fundamental incompatibility between the Lacanian Real and the Kantian "Thing-in-itself," and that it is a mistake to try to interpret *das Ding*, the Lacanian Thing, the non-symbolizable kernel of the Real, through the lens of the Thing-in-itself. The Lacanian Real is not a non-symbolizable surplus that will always elude us. Rather, it appears in the form of a trauma-tizing *encounter*; we stumble upon it where we had thought we were only dealing with misleading "appearances." Such an encounter – a paradoxical junction in which "appearance" itself unknowingly touches upon the truth – was unthinkable for Kant, and it is why we must read him "alongside Sade." The true aim of Kant's "obsessive" economy is precisely the avoidance of this traumatic encounter with the Real. At first, Kant's approach, which limits the field of possible experience to phenomena, excluding the "Thing-in-itself," appears to represent a quest for truth, a fear of being taken in too quickly by phenomena, of mistaking them for the "Thing-in-itself." However, as Hegel said, the content of this fear of error, of confusing the phe-nomena and the "Thing-in-itself," is its opposite, the fear of truth itself. It contains a desire to avoid, at all costs, the "encounter with the truth."

> If the fear of falling into error sets up a mistrust of Science, which in the absence of such scruples gets on with the work itself, and actually cognizes something, it is hard to see why we should not turn round and mistrust this very mistrust. Should we not be concerned as to whether this fear of error is not just the error itself? (Hegel 1977: 47)

The relationship between appearance and truth is therefore dialec-tical. The most radical illusion is not the act of mistaking misleading appearance for truth, for the "thing itself," but rather the refusal to recognize the truth because you claim that you are only dealing with appearance, illusion, fiction. In other words, the "*ne*" [not] in "*peur de ne pas être sujet à l'erreur*" ["I worry, might I not be prone to error?"] is not purely *explétif*.* Or, if it is, it is insofar as the symptom of a full semantic negation, betraying the subject's true desire. The Kantian subject "wants to say" that his intention is to avoid error, but in fact, he is actually afraid of *"ne plus être sujet à l'erreur"* ["not being prone to error"], of touching upon the truth.

The Hegelian idea that the principal mistake is the actual fear of mistakes and that therefore the fear of mistakes conceals its opposite (fear of the truth) brings to mind the infinite precautions and infinite deferment that are characteristic of the obsessive subject. Understanding the parallels with the obsessive economy allows us to reject the mistaken view according to which this fear of the truth comes from the worry that the truth might be, in all its richness, "too strong," too bright for our eyes, that it would be impossible for us to look directly into the brilliant light of truth. But this is not the case; behind the fear of truth is the fear of the Void at the heart of truth, rooted in a premonition that the truth is already in itself *"pas-tout,"* holed – a relationship to the truth that is just like the obsessive's relationship to jouissance. By establishing a whole series of rules, obstacles, detours, etc., the obsessive attempts to delay the encounter with the Thing that embodies jouissance – seemingly because he thinks the experience of jouissance would be too strong, too traumatic for him, but actually because he is afraid that jouissance would not satisfy him, that the encounter with the Thing would be a horrible letdown. The surplus is therefore only the form in which lack appears; fleeing from the Thing that would give us too much jouissance betrays our premonition that the Thing would be disappointing.

"The suprasensible is the phenomenon as phenomenon"

In his chapter "Force and Understanding" in *The Phenomenology of the Spirit* – the chapter in which the consciousness passes into the consciousness-of-self – Hegel undermines the very foundation of Kant's obsessive economy by stating the following: the essence that we search for is nothing more than appearance as appearance. By implying that there is something behind itself, something that is manifested through it, that it conceals a truth while also giving us a clue as to this truth, the phenomenon simultaneously conceals and reveals the essence hidden behind its curtain. But what is it that is

---

* In French grammar, the *ne explétif* is an optional double negative that retains the negativity of a single negative.

actually hiding behind the phenomenon? Simply the fact that there is nothing to hide. The thing that is concealed is the act of dissimulation, which in fact dissimulates nothing. The thing that must be hidden is the fact that the suprasensible – the essence that we thought we could glimpse – is nothing more than the phenomenon as phenomenon.

Is the suprasensible then just a pure illusion of the consciousness, similar to a simple optical illusion? Is it that "we" see that there is nothing behind the curtain, while the consciousness falls into error? For Hegel we should never contrast the state of things as "we" see them "correctly" and the viewpoint of the errant consciousness. If there is an illusion, we cannot subtract it from the thing, for it is at the very heart of it. If there is only a Void behind the phenomenon, then this is where the subject constitutes itself, from the basis of its own misrecognition. The illusion that there is something hidden behind the curtain is itself reflexive; the thing hidden behind the phenomenon is the very possibility itself of this illusion. There is nothing behind the curtain except the subject's belief in the existence or presence of some thing. In order for the illusion to be "false," it must find itself in an empty space behind the curtain. It opened a space where it was possible, an empty space that it filled (with what we call "the sacred," for example) and where illusory reality could construct itself. "We" can see there is nothing there where the conscience thought it saw something, but our knowledge can only be produced by this illusion, our knowledge is a moment inside it. When we have dissolved the illusion, there remains the empty space where it was possible – there is nothing beyond the phenomenon except this emptiness, and this emptiness is the subject. In order to grasp the phenomenon as phenomenon, the subject already had to pass outside of it, but there all that he will find is his own passage.

Normally, this argument of Hegel's is just seen as ontologically elevating the subject to the position of the substantial Essence of the totality of being. First, the consciousness thinks that behind the curtain of phenomena there is a hidden, transcendental Essence. Then, when the consciousness passes into the consciousness-of-self, it experiences that the Essence behind phenomena, their animating force, is the subject himself. Such a reading identifies the Subject immediately as the Essence behind the curtain, and so omits the way in which Hegel saw the passage from the consciousness to the consciousness-of-self as an experience of a radical failure. The subject (the consciousness) wants to penetrate into the secret behind the curtain, but his effort fails because there is nothing behind the curtain, *a nothingness that is the subject.* Lacan is saying precisely the same thing when he states that the subject (of the signifier) and the (phantasmic) object are correlative, even identical. The subject is the empty space, the nothingness behind the curtain, and the object is the inert, non-dialecticizable content that fills this void. The entirety of the subject's *Dasein* is given to him by the phantasy object that fills this void. This Hegelian formulation is similar step-by-step to Lacan's apologue in *Seminar XI*:

> In the classical tale of Zeuxis and Parrhasios, Zeuxis has the advantage of having made grapes that attracted the birds. The stress is placed not on the fact that these grapes were in any way perfect grapes, but on the fact that the eye of the birds was taken in by them. This is proved by the fact that his friend Parrhasios triumphs over him for having painted on the wall a veil, a veil so lifelike that Zeuxis, turning toward him said, *Well, and now show us what you have painted behind it.* By this he showed that what was at issue was certainly deceiving the eye [*tromper l'oeil*]. A triumph of the gaze over the eye. (Lacan 1998a: 103)

We can trick animals with an appearance that imitates reality and replaces it. But to trick a human being, to deceive in a uniquely human way, one imitates the dissimulation of reality. What is hidden is the act of hiding that seems to hide something. There is nothing behind the curtain except the subject who has already passed behind the curtain:

> It is manifest that behind the so-called curtain which is supposed to conceal the inner world, there is nothing to be seen unless *we* go behind it ourselves, as much in order that we may see, as that there may be something behind there which can be seen. (Hegel 1977: 103)

This is how we should understand the Hegelian distinction between the substance and the subject. The substance is the positive, transcendental Essence, supposedly concealed behind the curtain of phenomena. "Grasping the substance as subject" means to experience that the so-called "curtain of phenomena" only hides the fact that there is nothing to hide – and that this nothingness behind the curtain is the subject. In other words, appearance at the level of the substance is indeed misleading; it offers us the false image of a substantial Essence. Whereas at the level of the subject, appearance is misleading precisely because it feigns being misleading, it pretends that there is something to hide, it conceals the fact that there is nothing to conceal; it does not pretend to be telling the truth when it is really lying, it pretends to be lying when it is in fact telling the truth. In short, it deceives us by assuming the form of deception. Like in the famous story of the two Jews, in which one lies by telling the truth (about the destination of his trip), a phenomenon can tell the truth precisely by presenting itself as a lie. In his commentary on the apologue, Lacan gives the example of Plato's criticism of the illusion of painting:

> The point is not that painting gives an illusory equivalence to the object, even if Plato seems to be saying this . . . The picture does not compete with appearance, it competes with what Plato designates for us beyond appearance as being the Idea. It is because this picture is the appearance that says it is that which gives the appearance that Plato attacks painting, as if it were an activity competing with his own. (Lacan 1998a: 112)

For Plato, the true danger was appearance that presents itself as appearance, because this is nothing less – and Hegel knew this – than the Idea. This is the secret that philosophy must hide in order to preserve its consistency. And Hegel, working at the highest level of the metaphysical tradition, gives us a glimpse of this secret – in this way, he was an important precursor to psychoanalysis.

8

Two Hegelian *Witz*, Which Help Us Understand Why Absolute Knowledge Is Divisive

The signifying reflection

Let us wrap up the first section of this book with the following quite Hegelian *Witz* that provides an excellent example of the way in which the truth can emerge from misunderstanding, how truth is the same thing as the path to itself. A Pole and a Jew are sitting in the same carriage in a train. Something is bothering the Pole and he keeps fidgeting in his seat. Finally, he can't hold it in any longer and blurts out: "Tell me how it is that you Jews are able to get so rich by bleeding people down to their last cent?" The Jew answers: "Okay, I'll tell you, but I won't do it for free. Give me five zlotys." After pocketing the coins, he begins: "First, you have to take a dead fish, cut off its head, and pour its guts into a glass of water. Then, when the moon is full, you bury this glass in a graveyard." "And," the Pole asks greedily, "if I do that I'll be rich?" "Not so fast," the Jew replies; "there is more to it, but if you want to hear the rest you'll need to give me five more zlotys." The money is exchanged and the Jew continues his story, soon asks for more money, etc., up until the Pole finally explodes: "You cheat! You think I'm not on to you? There's no secret, you just want to take all my money!" The Jew calmly replies: "There you go, now you understand how the Jews . . ."

Every aspect of this little story is worth interpreting, starting with the very beginning. The fact that the Pole can't stop looking over at the Jew means that he is already in the process of transferring onto the Jew; for him the Jew embodies the subject who supposedly knows (the secret of how to extract every last cent from people). The fundamental lesson is that ultimately the Jew *did not trick* the Pole: he kept his word, he fulfilled his part of the deal by showing him how Jews, etc., etc.

The decisive twist takes place in the gap between the moment in which the Pole gets angry and the Jew gives his final answer. When the Pole explodes, he is already speaking the truth, he just doesn't know it yet. He sees how the Jew took his money from him, but he only considers this to be some kind of Jewish trick. To put this in topological terms, he does not yet see that he's already passed onto the other surface of the Möbius strip, that the trick itself contains the answer to the initial question, given that the reason he paid the Jew was precisely to teach him the way in which Jews . . . The mistake lies in the Pole's perspective; he was waiting for the Jew's secret to be revealed at the end of the story. He thought that the story the Jew was telling was just a path toward the final secret. His fixation on the hidden Secret, the final point of the narrative chain, blinded him as to the true secret, which was the way in which he was tricked by the Jew's story about said secret.

The Jew's "secret" lies in the Pole's desire, and therefore our own desire; it lies in the fact that the Jew knows how to make use of our desires. This is why the conclusion of this little story corresponds perfectly to the final moment of analysis, the exit from the transfer and the traversal of the phantasy, the two stages of which are split between the final two moments of the joke's denouement. The Pole's explosion of anger marks the point where he exits the transfer, where he realizes that "there is no secret" and thus the Jew ceases to be the "subject who supposedly knows." The Jew's final comment articulates the traversal of the phantasy. Isn't the "secret" that causes us to follow the Jew's story so attentively the object *a*, the chimerical "thing" of phantasy that provokes our desire, all while being retroactively posited by the desire itself? In this sense, the traversal of the phantasy coincides precisely with the experience that the object, the pure semblant, does nothing more than positivize the hole in our desire. In addition, this story is also a perfect illustration of the unique and irreplaceable role of money in the analytical process. If the Pole was not paying the Jew for his story, he would not reach the level of anger necessary for him to exit from the transfer. It is puzzling that, as a general rule, we do not recognize the structure of this *Witz* in another, much more famous, story. I am talking, of course, about the *Witz* of the entrance to the Law in Chapter IX of Kafka's *The Trial* and its final reversal when the man from the country who is waiting asks the guard:

"Everyone seeks the Law," the man says, "so how is it that in all these years no one apart from me has asked to be let in?" The doorkeeper realizes that the man is nearing his end, and so, in order to be audible to his fading hearing, he bellows at him, "No one else could be granted entry here, because this entrance was intended for you alone. I shall now go and shut it." (Kafka 2009b: 155)

This reversal is quite analogous to the twist at the end of the story of the Pole and the Jew. The subject finally understands that he was included in the game from the beginning, that the door was already designed for him alone – in the same way that in the story of the Pole and the Jew, the point of the Jew's story is, ultimately, just to catch the Pole's desire. And, I should add, it is the same as in the story from *Arabian Nights* I mentioned earlier in which the hero's accidental entrance to the cave turns out to have been long-awaited by the wise men. We could even rework Kafka's story about the entrance to the Law in a way that would make it all the more similar to the *Witz* of the Pole and the Jew. Let us imagine that, after a long wait, the man from the country suddenly exploded in anger and started to scream at the guard: "You dirty liar! Why are you pretending to guard the entrance to unknown secrets, when you yourself know that there is not a single secret behind that Door, because that entrance was designed for me alone, it serves only to capture my desire?" – to which the guard would calmly reply: "There you go! You've finally discovered the true secret of the entrance to the Law."

In these two cases, the logic of the final twist is strictly Hegelian, functioning similarly to what Hegel called the "sublation of the bad infinity." Both cases start out the same way: the subject is confronted with an inaccessible, transcendental, substantial truth, a forbidden secret that is infinitely deferred. In one case there is the inaccessible Heart of the Law that lies beyond the infinite series of entrances, in the other there is the inaccessible final answer to the question of how Jews manage to get people to give them all their money down to their last cent (because it is clear from the narrative that the Jew could keep going forever). In both stories, the denouement, the solution, is the same – instead of finally succeeding in lifting the final curtain and unveiling the ultimate secret, the Heart of the Law/the way in which the Jews extract people's money, the subject realizes that he was included in the game from the very beginning, that his exclusion from the Secret and his desire to learn the Secret were already included in the very way the Secret operated.

This reveals the dimension of a certain type of reflexivity that is missed by the classical philosophical conception of reflexivity.

Philosophical reflexivity consists in the mediating movement through which the One comes to include its alterity, the Subject appropriates the substantial content opposed to it by positing itself as the unity of itself and its other. But this idea of the positivation of impossibility necessarily implies a whole different kind of reflexive reversal, whose key moment occurs when the subject recognizes that the impossibility of appropriating the Heart of the Other is a positive condition for the definition of his own status as subject. This twist constitutes a radical change in perspective. It is this very *failure* – the frustration of the subject's attempt to appropriate the opposed substantial contents in order to penetrate into the Heart of the Other – that *includes* the subject in the substance, in the Other. This reflexive shift is exactly what we see at the end of Kafka's "parable" about the Doors of the Law: the man finally understands that the Door that supposedly hid an inaccessible substantial content *was destined for him alone*, that from the very beginning the unreachable Other of the Law was addressed to him, that it had accounted for him from the outset.

The other's lack

It would therefore be a mistake to think that the dialectical relationship between Knowledge and Truth is a progressive approach guided by knowledge of the Truth, in which the subject recognizes the "falseness" and insufficiency of some figure of his knowledge, and so progresses to another figure that is closer to the Truth, etc., until finally Knowledge and Truth come together in Absolute Knowledge. In such a perspective, Truth is a substantial entity, an in-Itself, and the dialectical process takes the form of simple asymptotic progress, a gradual approach to the Truth, something along the lines of Victor Hugo's famous quote: "Science is asymptotic to truth. Ever approaching but never touching it." The Hegelian conjunction of the truth with the path toward the truth implies, on the contrary, *that we are always already in contact with the truth*. When knowledge changes, truth itself must change, which is to say that when knowledge does not correspond to the truth, we don't simply need to accommodate the truth, but in fact transform the two poles – the insufficiency of knowledge, its lack in relation to the truth, indicates that there is always a lack, an incompleteness at the very core of truth itself.

We must therefore toss out the traditional conception of the dialectical process as moved forward by particular, limited, and "unilateral" elements that push it toward a final totality. The truth at which we arrive is not "whole," the question always remains open, it simply becomes a question we ask of the Other. This is the perspective from which we should understand Lacan's statement that Hegel was "the most sublime hysteric"; the hysteric asks questions because he wants to "burrow a hole in the Other," he experiences his own desire as if it were the Other's desire. The hysterical subject is above all the subject who asks himself a question while at the same time presupposing that the Other has the answer, that the Other holds the key. In the dialectical process, this question asked of the Other is resolved through a reflexive turn in which the question begins to function as *its own answer*.

To illustrate this, let's take the following example of Adorno's (1970): it is impossible today to give a single definition of society, there is always going to be an endless number of definitions that are more or less contradictory, even exclusive (for example, those who see society as an organic Whole that transcends individuals and those who think of society as a link between atomized individuals – "organicism" versus "individualism"). It may seem at first as if these contradictions block us from understanding society "in-itself," but this presupposes that there is a Societal "thing-in-itself" that we could only approach through a multitude of partial, relative conceptions, never being able to truly touch it. The dialectical turn takes place when the contradiction itself becomes the answer; the different definitions of society no longer serve as obstacles; rather, they come to be seen as elements of the "thing itself," indicators of actual societal contradictions. The antagonism of society as an organic Whole opposed to atomized individuals is not simply gnoseological, it is *the fundamental antagonism that constitutes the very object that we wished to know.* This is the key to the Hegelian strategy: the "very inappropriateness" itself (in our case, the contradictory definitions) "would flush out the secret" (Lacan 2006: 695). Through the dialectical turn, what had at first seemed to be an obstacle becomes the very indication that we have reached the truth. We are immersed in the thing through that which had earlier seemed to conceal it, which implies that the "thing itself" is holed, constituted around a lack. Examples of this kind of paradoxical logic, in which the problem functions as its own solution, are numerous in Lacan's works. Besides the obvious *"Subversion of the Subject and the Dialectic of Desire in the Freudian Unconscious,"* let's take two examples of Lacan's replies to his critics. In "Science and the Truth," Lacan comments on the confusion of Laplanche and Leclaire on the subject of the problem of the "double inscription," and says that they "could have read its solution in their own split over how to approach the problem" (Lacan

2006: 734). And in *Encore*, Lacan's reply to Nancy and Lacoue-Labarthe's criticism of the impasse in his theory of the signifier:

> Beginning with what distinguishes me from Saussure, and what made me, as they say, distort him, we proceed, little by little, to the impasse I designate concerning analytic discourse's approach to truth and its paradoxes. . . . It is as if it were precisely upon reaching the impasse to which my discourse was designed to lead them that they considered their work done. (Lacan 1998b: 65)

In both cases, Lacan takes the same approach, drawing attention to an error in perspective. What his critics saw as a problem, a dead end, an impasse, a contradiction, was already in itself the solution. I am even tempted to see here the basic form of Lacanian refutation of criticism: your formulation of the problem already contains its own solution. It is here, rather than in his explicit references to Hegel, that we can find Lacan's "Hegelian" side!

We can find the logic of a question that functions as its own answer in the *Witz* about Rabinovitch. At first it seems we have a problem: our initial position is invalidated by our adversary's objection, but then comes the turn, and this objection reveals itself to be our true argument. Hegel himself, in his *Philosophy of History*, quotes the French witticism: "In rejecting the truth, one ends up embracing it" [*la verité, en la repoussant, on l'embrasse*], which implies a paradoxical space where the very heart of the "thing itself" joins up with its own externality. A very rudimentary form of this structure can be found in the famous Hegelian quip that the secrets of Egypt are also secrets for the Egyptians themselves; the solution to the enigma comes from splitting it, relocating the same enigma in the Other. The solution to this question consists in understanding it as a question that the Other asks herself. It is through the very thing that initially seemed to exclude us from the Other – our question through which we came to see the Other as enigmatic, inaccessible, transcendent – that brings us together with the Other, because this question is the Other's question, *because the substance is the subject* (let us not forget that the thing that defines the subject is the very question itself).

Would it not therefore be possible to base Hegelian "dis-alienation" on Lacanian *separation*? Lacan defined separation as the superimposition of two lacks (cf. Lacan 1998a: 214); when the subject encounters the lack in the Other, he responds with a pre-existing lack, his own lack. In the process of alienation, the subject is confronted with a full, substantial Other, in whose depths there supposedly lies a "secret," an unreachable treasure. "Dis-alienation," therefore, has nothing to do with appropriating this secret; the subject never finally pierces into the Other's hidden core – far from it, the subject simply experiences that this "hidden treasure" (*agalma*, the object-cause of desire) *is already missing from the Other herself*. "Dis-alienation" can be reduced to the act through which the subject perceives that the Other's substantial secret is also a secret for the Other, in other words, the experience of a *separation* between the Other and its "secret," *the object little a*.

The symbolic act

If the field of truth was not "*pas-tout*," if the Other was not incomplete, we could not "understand the substance as subject," and the subject would only be an epiphenomenon, a secondary moment caught up in the advance of substantial truth. The subject is inside substance precisely because it is its constitutive hole, it *is* the Void, the impossibility around which the field of substantial truth structures itself. The answer to the questions, "Why are error and illusion immanent to truth? Why does truth emerge out of misrecognition?" is therefore quite simple: *because the substance is already the subject*. The substance is always already subjectivized; substantial truth is the same thing as the path to itself, which passes through "subjective" illusions. And so there is another answer to the question of why error is immanent to truth: *because there is no metalanguage*. The idea that we could take our own error into account from the outset, put it in its proper place, and thus keep a safe distance from it is the supreme mistake of the belief in the existence of a metalanguage. It is the illusion that even though one is taken in by an illusion, one might still be able to observe this process from an "objective" distance. By trying not to identify oneself with error, one makes the greatest error and misses the truth, because truth itself is constituted through error. In other words, to return to the Hegelian proposition that the fear of error is error itself: true evil is not the evil object, but the perspective that perceives it as evil.

This logic of error as integral to truth can be found in Rosa Luxemburg's description of the dialectic of the revolutionary process. Arguing with Edouard Bernstein about the revisionist fear of seizing power "too early," "prematurely," before the "objective situation" on the ground was fully ripe, she replied that initial seizures of power are *necessarily* "premature." The only way for the proletariat to arrive at its "maturity," to reach the "opportune" moment of seizing power, was to form itself, to train itself for this seizure of power, and the only way to do this was precisely through these "premature" attempts. If we wait for the "opportune moment," we will never reach it, because the "opportune moment" – which cannot arrive if the revolutionary subjects have not yet reached the subjective condition of "maturity" – can only arrive through a series of "pre-mature" attempts. The opposition to seizing power *"pre-maturely"* reveals itself to be an opposition to seizing power *in general, as such*; let us recall Robespierre's famous quote about revisionists, that they want "revolution without revolution" (cf. Luxemburg 2011).

Under closer inspection, we can see that the decisive thrust of Rosa Luxemburg's argument is precisely that a metalanguage of the revolutionary process could never exist. The revolutionary subject does not "direct" the revolutionary process from an objective distance, as she herself is constituted through this process, and it is because revolutionary timing passes through this subjectivity that "a timely revolution" can only come after failed, "premature" attempts. Rosa Luxemburg's position is that of the hysteric confronted with the obsessive metalanguage of revisionism; in her view, one must leap into action, even prematurely, in order to reach, through this very error, the correct path. One must be taken in by one's own desire, even if this desire is impossible, in order for something to actually happen.

This is why the propositions "we must grasp the substance as subject," "there is no metalanguage," and "truth emerges from error" are just variations on the same theme. We cannot say: "Although we accept the necessity of premature revolutions, we should not have any illusions about it, we should remain clear-eyed to the fact that they are already doomed to fail." The idea that we could simultaneously act and remain at the distance of an "objective" viewpoint from which we could – even during the act itself – become conscious of its "objective signification" (that it is destined to fail), ignores the way in which the "subjective illusion" of the actors is part of the "objective" process itself. This is why the revolution must repeat itself: the "signification" of the premature attempts is literally to be found in their defeat, or, in Hegel's words, "in general, a political revolution is sanctioned by popular opinion when it repeats itself."

Hegel's theory of historical repetition (developed in his *Philosophy of History*) is basically just this; "repetition realizes and confirms something that initially seemed only contingent and possible." Hegel uses Caesar's death as an example of this theory at work. When Caesar was consolidating his personal power, he was acting "objectively" (in itself) in accordance with the historical truth that "the Republic could no longer be decisive, and that this decisiveness could only come from an individual will." However, the Republic was still formally in power (for-itself, in the "public opinion") – to paraphrase the Freudian dream of the father who did not yet know that he was dead, the Republic "was only alive because it had forgotten that it was already dead." From the "viewpoint" of someone who still believed in the Republic, Caesar's actions appeared arbitrary, accidental, it seemed as if "we only have to dispose of this one individual, and the Republic will spontaneously return." However, it was precisely the conspirators against Caesar who – in accordance with the "cunning of reason" – confirmed Caesar's truth. The final result of Caesar's death was the reign of Augustus, the first Caesar. In this way, the truth emerged out of failure itself: "While it failed in its immediate aim, Caesar's murder fulfilled the role that history had cunningly assigned to it, revealing historical truth by trying to deny it" (Assoun 1975: 68).

The full scope of historical repetition can be found here, in the passage from Caesar – the name of an individual – to Caesar – the title of the Roman Emperor. The murder of Caesar – the historical individual – ended up resulting in the establishment of *Caesarism*; Caesar-the-person is repeated as Caesar-the-title. What then is the reason, the "motive" of this repetition? Assoun does a good job of developing the dual operation of Hegelian repetition, which simultaneously signifies the passage from contingency to necessity and the passage from unconscious substance to consciousness. In other words, from the in-itself to the for-itself: "an event that only happens once seems by definition *as if it could have not happened*" (Assoun 1975: 69–70). However, it still seems as if Assoun interprets this conjunction a little too "mechanically," as if the fact that an event repeated itself simply means that there are "two instances of a general law" (Assoun 1975: 70), which convinces "public opinion" that the event was inevitable. Assoun's interpretation is, essentially, that the end of the Republic – together with the rise of imperial power – was an objective inevitability that was recognized as such once it had repeated itself. However, Assoun's own formulation actually goes beyond this simplistic interpretation: "It is by recognizing a previously experienced event that the historical consciousness comes to understand the necessity of the generating process" (Assoun 1975: 70).

Taken literally, this means that it is the signifying network in which the event is inscribed that changes between the "original" and the repetition. The first time, the event was experienced as a contingent trauma, as the irruption of the non-symbolized. It was only through its repetition that it gained "recognition," which here can only mean "realized in the symbolic." This recognition-through-repetition necessarily presupposes (just as it did in Freud's analysis of Moses) a crime, the act of murder; Caesar must die as an "empirical" person in order for his historical necessity to be realized as the *title* of imperial power, precisely because the "necessity" in question is *symbolic* necessity.

Therefore, it is not simply that people "need time to understand," that the initial form in which the event occurs is too "traumatic"; the *misunderstanding* of its initial occurrence is "integral" to its symbolic necessity, it is a basic and essential component of its *recognition*. To give the standard formulation: the first murder (the "patricide" of Caesar) gives rise to "guilt," which is what "gives force" to the repetition. The event does not repeat itself because of some "objective" necessity "independent of our subjective will" and therefore "irresistible" – rather, it is the "guilt" itself that opens this symbolic debt and therefore gives rise to the repetitive compulsion. This repetition announces the entrance of the law, of the Name-of-the-Father in the place of the assassinated father. Through its repetition, the repeated event retroactively receives its law. In other words, we can conceptualize the Hegelian repetition as precisely this passage from *lawless* to *lawlike* (cf. J.-A. Miller 1978), as the quintessential interpretive gesture (Lacan says somewhere that interpretation always takes place under the sign of the Name-of-the-Father); the symbolic "appropriation" of the traumatic event.

Hegel has therefore already succeeded in describing the constitutive delay of the interpretive gesture. Interpretation only comes through repetition; an event cannot already be lawlike the first time it occurs. We can see an analogy to the necessity of repetition in the famous passage from the preface to the *Philosophy of Right* in which Hegel writes that the owl of Minerva only spreads its wings at twilight. Contrary to the Marxist critique, which saw this as a sign of the impotence of the *post festum* interpretive position, we must understand this delay as integral to the "objective" process itself. The fact that "opinion" saw Caesar's act as accidental, and not the manifestation of historical necessity, is not just an example of the "delay of the consciousness in regard to effectivity." Historical necessity itself, missed by "opinion" on its first appearance, mistakenly seen as arbitrary, *is only constituted, only realized, through this first mistake.*

There is a crucial distinction between this Hegelian position and the Marxist dialectic of the revolutionary process. For Rosa Luxemburg, the failure of the premature attempts creates the conditions necessary for the final victory, whereas, for Hegel, the dialectical reversal consists in a shift in perspective through which *failure as such* comes to appear as a victory – the symbolic act, the act as symbolic *succeeds in its very failure*. The Hegelian proposition that "the true beginning only arrives at the end" should therefore be taken literally. The act – the "thesis" – is necessarily "premature"; it is a "hypothesis" that is condemned to failure, and the dialectical reversal occurs when the failure of this "thesis" – the "antithesis" – is revealed to be the true "thesis." The "synthesis" is the "signification" of the thesis that emerges through its failure. And so, after all, Goethe was right in his criticism of Writing. At the beginning there is the act, the act implies a constitutive failure, it misses, it "falls short," and the original gesture of *symbolization* is to posit this pure waste as something positive, to experience this loss as a movement that opens a free space, that "lets be."

Take the traditional criticism according to which the Hegelian dialectic reduces the process to its logical skeleton, omitting the contingency of the delays and outpacings – all the inertia of reality that spoils and troubles the dialectical game, which is to say, that does not let itself be taken in by the movement of the *Aufhebung*. This critique completely misses the point; the back and forth of delay and overshooting is included in the dialectical process, and not simply at an accidental, non-essential, level, but as its central element. The dialectical process always takes the paradoxical form of delay/overshooting, the form of reversing a "not-yet" into an "always-already," a "too soon" into an "afterwards" – its true motor is the structural impossibility of the "right time," the irreducible delay between the thing and its "proper moment." By definition, the initial moment, the "thesis," arrives too early to achieve its full identity, and it only realizes itself – it only becomes "itself" after the fact, retroactively – when it is repeated by the "synthesis."

". . . that integral void that we also call the sacred"

Let me be precise. It is not that we should see the connection between the failure of the act and symbolization in a way that reduces the latter to some kind of supposed "imaginary compensation" along the lines of: "When the act, the active intervention in reality, fails, we try to compensate for this loss through a symbolic restitution, attributing a profound signification to events. For example, the powerless victim of natural forces makes them divine, turns them into personified spiritual forces. . . ." Such a quick passage from the act to its "profound signification" misses the intermediate step particular to symbolization, the moment in which the loss, before it flips itself into an "imaginary compensation" and is given its "profound signification," becomes in itself a positive gesture. We can pin this down precisely as the distinction between *the* Symbolic [*le symbolique*] in a strict sense, and what we call "symbolic signification" [*la symbolique*].

In the standard view, one passes directly from reality to "symbolic signification"; a thing is either itself, identical in itself in its raw, inert presence, or it has a "symbolic signification." Where is the Symbolic in all this? In order to locate it, we must make the crucial distinction between "symbolic signification" and *the very place it occupies*, the empty space that is filled by signification. The Symbolic is above all a space, a space that was initially empty, but that gradually came to be filled by a tangle of "symbolic significations." The crucial feature of the Lacanian conception of the symbolic is this logical priority, the fact that the (empty) space pre-dates the elements that come to fill it. Before it could become a tangle of "symbols" carrying any kind of "signification," the Symbolic was a differential network structured around an empty, traumatizing space. Lacan designated this as the space of *das Ding*, the "sacred" space of impossible jouissance. Using Heidegger's vase as an example, Lacan showed how *das Ding* is above all an empty space surrounded by signifying articulation – an empty space that can be filled with whatever we want, even Jungian "archetypes." Hegel already emphasized the primacy of the "sacred" as an empty space in relation to its contents:

> In this *complete void*, which is even called the holy of holies, there must yet be something, we must fill it up with reveries, appearances, produced by the consciousness itself . . . since even reveries are better than its own emptiness. (Hegel 1977: 88)

This is why the Hegelian "loss of the loss" is in no way a return to full, lossless, identity. Far from it, the "loss of the loss" is precisely the moment when the loss stops being the loss of "something" and becomes the inauguration of an empty space in which the object ("something") can survive, the moment when the empty space is recognized as pre-dating its contents – the loss opens the space for the arrival of the object. In the "loss of the loss," the loss remains a loss; it is not "abolished/canceled" in the ordinary sense of the term. The recuperated "positivity" is that of the loss as loss, the experience of the loss as a "positive" – perhaps even "productive" – condition.

Would it not be possible to determine the final moment of the analytical process, the pass, as the experience of the positive character of the loss, of the initial emptiness filled by the dazzling and fascinating phantasy object – experiencing the realization that the object as such is fundamentally the positivization of an emptiness? Isn't this experience of the primacy of the place over the phantasy object the traversal of the phantasy, the moment in which, to quote Mallarmé, "nothing takes place except the place"?

This is why it is so important to completely differentiate the pass from "resignation," from "giving up"; from this perspective, analysis would be finished when the analysand "acquiesced to his symbolic castration," resigning himself to the fact that radical Loss is part of the condition of the being-of-language [*parlêtre*]. This kind of interpretation turns Lacan into some kind of "wise guru" who preaches "total renunciation." It may initially seem as if there is a lot of evidence for this interpretation. Isn't the Phantasy fundamentally the Phantasy of the sexual rapport finally become possible, finally fully realizable? And isn't the end of the analysis, the traversal of the Phantasy, simply experiencing the realization of the impossibility of the sexual rapport, and therefore the irreconcilably blocked, knotted, failed nature of the "human condition"? But nothing of the kind is true. If we posit as the fundamental ethical principle of analysis "not to give up on one's desire" – from which it follows that the symptom is, as Jacques-Alain Miller pointed out, precisely a specific mode of "giving up one's desire" – we must determine the pass as the moment in which the subject takes on his own desire in its pure, "non-pathological," form, beyond its historicalness/hystericalness. The best example of a "post-analytic" subject is not the dubious figure of a "wise guru," but rather Oedipus at Colonus, a grumpy old man who asks for everything, who does not want to give up anything. If the traversal of the phantasy is tied to the experience of some kind of lack, *this lack is the Other's* and not that of the subject himself. In the pass, the subject undergoes the realization that the *agalma*, the "hidden treasure," is already missing from the Other, the object separates itself from the *I* – the signifying trait in the Other. After the subject has been placed in relation to the object *a*,

> the experience of the fundamental phantasy becomes the drive. What, then, does he who has passed through the experience of this opaque relation to the origin, to the drive, become? How can a subject who has traversed the radical phantasy experience the drive? This is the beyond of analysis, and has never been approached. Up to now, it has been approachable only at the level of the analyst, in as much as it would be required of him to have specifically traversed the cycle of the analytic experience in its totality. (Lacan 1998a: 273)

Isn't the incessant drive of Hegelian "Absolute Knowledge [AK]" ["*savoir absolu [SA]*"], the infinitely repeated journey down the already traveled path, the ultimate example of how to "live one's drive" once history/hysteria are gone? It is no surprise, then, to see Lacan, in Chapter XIV of *Seminar XI*, articulating the circuit of drive in terms that directly evoke the Hegelian distinction between the "finite" end and the "infinite" end. Lacan makes use of a distinction in the English language between *aim* and *goal* (cf. 1998a: 179). The circuit of drive can be determined specifically as the back and forth between *aim* and *goal*. Drive is, initially, a path toward a particular goal, and then it becomes the experience that its true goal is the same thing as the path itself, that its "goal is nothing more than turning around in circles" (1998a: 179). In short, the true end (the "infinite," the *aim*) realizes itself through the continual failure of the realization of the "finite" end (the *goal*). In the very failure of the stated goal of our activity, our true aim is always already realized.

How "Absolute Knowledge" is divisive

AK is in no way a position of "total knowledge," a position from which, at long last, the subject could finally "know everything." We must take into account the exact place at which the idea of AK emerges, the end of the *Phenomenology of Spirit*, the point when the consciousness "de-fetishizes" itself and thus gains the ability to access true knowledge, knowledge instead of truth, and therefore "science" in the Hegelian sense. As such, AK is just a "scilicet," a "you can know" that opens the space for the development of science (logic, etc.). What does the fetish represent at its core? An object that fills the constitutive lack in the Other, the empty space of the "original repression," the place where the signifier must be missing in order for the signifying network to articulate itself. In this sense, "de-fetishization" is equivalent to the experience of the constitutive lack in the Other, the Other as barred. Perhaps de-fetishization is even more difficult to accomplish because the fetish reverses the traditional relationship between the "sign" and the "thing." We normally understand the "sign" as something that represents, replaces, the missing object. When the fetish is an object, it is a thing that replaces the missing "sign." It is easy to detect absence, the structure of co-referential signifiers, where we thought there was the full presence of a thing, but it is much harder to detect the inert presence of an object in the place where we thought there were only "signs," an interplay of representations referring back to each other, nothing more than traces.

This is why we must take care to differentiate Lacan from any so-called "poststructuralist" tradition whose objective is to "deconstruct" the "metaphysics of presence," to deny the possibility of full presence, to see only the traces of absence, to dissolve fixed identity into a cluster of references and traces . . . Lacan is actually much closer to Kafka than to the poststructuralists. It has become a cliché to see Kafka as the "writer of absence" who described a world whose structure remained religious, but where the central space reserved for God is empty. But this is not where it ends; it remains to be shown how this Absence itself conceals an inert, nightmarish presence, an obscene superego object, the "Supremely-Evil-Being."

It is from this perspective that we must reinterpret the two features of AK that initially seem to possess a certain kind of "idealistic" resonance: AK as the "abolition of the object," in which it does away with objectivity as outside the subject and opposed to it, and AK as the abolition of the Other, removing the dependence of the subject on an instance that is external and de-centered. Hegelian "sublation of the Other" is in no way equivalent to a fusion of the subject with its other, in which the subject appropriates the substantial contents. Rather, we should understand it as a specifically Hegelian way of saying "the Other does not exist" (Lacan), that it does not exist as Guarantor of truth, the Other of the Other, and that therefore we must posit a lack in the Other, that the Other is barred. The subject must recognize that his place is in this hole at the heart of the substantial Other. The subject is internal to the substantial Other because he is identified with the blockage, the "impossibility" of arriving at a closed self-identity. And the "abolition of the object" only represents the other side of this; it is not a fusion between the subject and the object into a subject-object, but only a radical change in the status of the object – it no longer masks nor fills the hole in the Other. This is the post-phantasy relationship to the object: the object is "abolished," "suppressed," it loses its fascinating aura. The thing that earlier had dazzled us with its charm is revealed to be a disgusting and viscous piece of trash; we look at the gift we were given and it is "changed inexplicably into a gift of shit" (Lacan 1998a: 268).

In his discussion of Joyce, Lacan emphasized that he was perfectly correct to refuse analysis (a condition that a wealthy American patron attempted to place on him in exchange for financial support). He did not need it because through the practice of his art he had already reached the subjective position that corresponds to the final moment of analysis, as we can see from – to take just one example – his famous play on the words *letter/litter*, the transformation of the object of desire into shit, the post-phantasy relationship to the object (Jacques-Alain Miller). In the field of philosophy, Hegelian AK – and perhaps only Hegelian AK – refers to the same subjective position of the traversal of the phantasy, of the post-phantasy relationship to the object, the experience of the lack in the Other. Why only Hegelian AK? Well, look at the so-called "post-Hegelian inversions." Whether it's Marx or Schelling, aren't they all essentially just attempts to escape the unbearableness of Hegel's approach? The price of these "inversions" seems to be a reading of Hegel that completely misses the dimension of his thought that involves the traversal of the phantasy and the lack in the Other. For them, AK became the culminating moment of "idealistic panlogicism," which we can easily disprove by examining the "process of effective life."

Traditionally, AK is seen as the phantasy of a full discourse without rupture or discord, an Identity that could encompass all divisions. My reading, however, which shows the way in which AK is the *traversal* of the phantasy, holds the exact opposite. The distinctive feature of AK is not that Identity is finally achieved in the place where, for the "finite consciousness," there had been only scission (between subject and object, knowledge and truth, etc.), but rather it is the experience of a distance, a *separation* where the "finite consciousness" had seen only fusion, that the object *a* and the Other were one and the same. AK, far from filling the lack felt by the "finite consciousness" separated from the Absolute, merely relocates it to the Other itself. The twist operated by AK concerns the status of lacking. The "finite," "alienated" consciousness suffers from the loss of the object, and so "dis-alienation" simply consists in the experience that the object *was lost from the beginning*, and that any given object only fills the hole in that loss. The "loss of the loss" is the point where the subject finally perceives that the loss preceded the object. Over the course of the dialectical process, the subject always continues to lose that which he never possessed, in that he always keeps falling prey to the necessary illusion that "in the past, he had possessed it." The illusion that AK is the name for a final harmony between subject and object, knowledge and truth – which is to say, that it designates the moment when absolute identity abolishes all difference and fills the lack – is based on an error in perspective that is altogether analogous to the idea that the end of the analytical process, the irruption of the non-rapport, appears as its very opposite, as the creation of a fully realized sexual genital rapport:

> But what did Freud expect of the experience if not a formula for the sexual relation? He hoped to find it inscribed in the unconscious; hence

his despair at not finding it. And after Freud, what happened? In attempting to solve the question of the end of analysis, analysts have again and again proposed formulas for the sexual relation. To cast the end of analysis in the event of a possible sexual relation has necessarily led them to rub out the castration complex – with the genital eraser.

Lacan, on the other hand, is true to Freud when he states that there is no sexual relation. This formula preserves the irreducibility of what Freud designated as castration, but it also suggests that the question of the end of analysis cannot be posed in terms of the sexual relation which does not exist.

The question of the end of analysis cannot be solved if such a solution requires the sexual relation. It can only be solved on the basis of its absence.

It is a fact that psychoanalysis does not bring about the sexual relation. For Freud this was cause for despair. Eager to redress this state of affairs, the post-Freudians have been attempting to elaborate a genital formula. Lacan brings these attempts to a close. The end of the analytic process cannot be tied to the emergence of the sexual relation. It depends rather on the emergence of the sexual un-relation.

The question of the end of analysis thereby finds a solution in a way that was previously inconceivable. The solution appears on the side of the object – the object dismissed as pre-genital by the post-Freudian trend.

It is not the object that obstructs the emergence of the sexual relation, as the expectation of its eventual coming might lead one to believe. On the contrary, the object is that which stops up the relation that does not exist, thereby giving it the consistency of the fantasy. Inasmuch as the end of analysis supposes the advent of an absence, it depends on breaking through the fantasy and on the separation of the object. (J.-A. Miller 1988)

Therefore, the massive presence of the pre-genital object – the object that, through its inert phantasy presence, appears to block the achievement of a full, mature, genital, sexual rapport – obscures the fundamental blockage, the emptiness of the impossible sexual rapport. Far from masking another presence, it only blinds us, through its own presence, to the *space* that it has filled. Where does this error in perspective come from? From the fact that *the void is strictly co-substantial with the very movement of its own dissimulation.* It's true that the phantasy *masks* the emptiness of "there is no sexual rapport," but at the same time it *serves* as this void. The phantasy object masks the *open, self-supported,* emptiness.

The same thing goes for the Hegelian object, the objectual fetish-figure: far from being a "premature" figure of a true dialectical synthesis, it conceals, through its "non-dialectical," "unmediated" presence, the impossibility of a final Synthesis of subject and object. In other words, the error in perspective consists in thinking that the end of the dialectical process consists in the subject finally *obtaining* what he was looking for. This is an error in perspective because the Hegelian solution is not that the subject will never be able to possess the thing that he was searching for, but that he *already had it*, in the form of its loss. Gérard Miller's description of the difference between Marxism and psychoanalysis ("In Marxism, man knows what he wants but does not have it, in psychoanalysis, man does not know what he wants and has always had it") applies well to the distance between Hegel and Marxism as well, particularly the way in which Marxism ignores the dialectical reversal of the impasse into the pass. Saying that the pass is the final moment of the analytical process in no way means that the impasse has finally been resolved (that the transfer has closed off the unconscious, for example), that its obstacles have been overcome. Rather, the pass is just the retroactive experience that the impasse itself was already its own "resolution." In other words, the pass is *exactly the same thing as the impasse* (the impossibility of the sexual rapport), in the same way that – as I said earlier – the synthesis is exactly the same thing as the antithesis. The only thing that changes is the subject's position, his "perspective."

However, there is a definition of AK in Lacan's first seminars that seems to directly contradict the one I have just given. He lays out AK as the impossible ideal of attaining the complete closure of the field of discourse:

> Absolute knowledge is this moment in which the totality of discourse closes in on itself in a perfect non-contradiction up to and including the fact that it posits, explains and justifies itself. We are some way yet from this ideal! (Lacan 1991a: 264)

But this Lacan, who had not yet arrived at the concept of the lack in the Other, could not yet see the way in which this idea functioned in Hegel's thought. At this early juncture, Lacan's main focus was symbolization-historicization, the symbolic realization of the traumatic kernel that had not yet been integrated into the symbolic universe of the subject. For Lacan at this stage, the ideal endpoint of analysis was therefore the accomplished symbolization that would reintegrate all the traumatic ruptures into the symbolic field – an ideal embodied in Hegelian AK, but whose true nature is Kantian. This conception saw AK as a type of regulatory idea that would guide the "symbolic realization of the subject" (Lacan 1991b: 321).

That is the ideal of analysis, which, of course, remains virtual. There is never a subject without an ego, a fully realized subject, but that in fact is what one must aim to obtain from the subject in analysis. (Lacan 1991b: 246)

We must counter this view by insisting on the key fact that Hegelian AK *has nothing to do with any ideal of any kind.* The reversal operated by AK comes about when we realize that the field of the Other is already "closed" in its very discord. In other words, because the subject is barred it must be posited as the correlate of the inert remainder that blocks its full symbolic realization, its full subjectivization: $\$ \lozenge a$.

This is why, in the matheme for Absolute Knowledge [*SA*], both terms must be barred, because it is the conjunction of $\$$ and $Å$.

Book II

Post-Hegelian Impasses

9

The Secret of the Commodity Form: Why is Marx the Inventor of the Symptom?

Marx, Freud: the analysis of form

There is a fundamental *parallel* between Marx and Freud's interpretive approaches, especially in the way in which each sought out their respective "secrets," the secret of commodity and the secret of dreams. In both cases, they guard us against the blindness that comes from a fetishistic fascination with some hidden "content" behind the form – the "secret" that we uncover through analysis is not the content concealed by the form (dream form, commodity form); on the contrary, it is *the form itself*. A theoretical analysis of the form of the dream is not an explanation of its "hidden core," of the latent thought buried within it; its purpose is, rather, to answer the question: why did the thought latent in the dream take on this particular form, why did it transpose itself into the form of a dream? The same goes for our analysis of commodity. It is not that we must penetrate into the "hidden core" of commodity – that its value is determined by the quantity of labor expended producing it – but rather that we must seek to explain why labor took the form of commodity value, why it was only able to affirm its social character through the commodity form of its product.

We are all familiar with the common accusation that Freudian dream interpretation is "pansexual." Hans-Jürgen Eysenck in particular, a harsh critic of psychoanalysis, drew attention to what he saw as a fundamental contradiction in Freud's approach to dreams. According to Freud, the desire articulated in a dream is – at least in theory – supposed to be a desire that is at the same time both unconscious and sexual in nature. However, this doesn't even apply to most of the examples Freud himself gives, including the dream that he used to introduce the concept of dream logic, his dream of Irma's injection. The thought latent in this dream was Freud's attempt to rationalize away the guilt he felt about the failure of Irma's medical treatment by thinking "it wasn't my fault, there were so many reasons for what happened. . . ." However, the "desire," the signification of the dream was neither sexual in nature (it was mostly a problem of professional ethics) nor unconscious (this worry had troubled Freud at a very conscious level and was therefore a self-examination of his own conscience).

There is a fundamental theoretical error in this line of criticism: it conflates the unconscious desire at work behind the dream with the "latent thought," the signification, of the dream. However, as Freud emphasized in several places, *there is nothing unconscious about the "thought latent in the dream" in itself*, it is an altogether "normal" thought that can be articulated by the syntax of ordinary language. Topologically, it belongs to the "conscious/preconscious" system. Ordinarily, the subject is conscious of it – perhaps even excessively so; it might gnaw away at him constantly. Under certain conditions, this thought can be ejected from the conscious and pulled into the unconscious, which is to say, submitted to the laws of the "primary process," translated into the "language of the unconscious." The relationship between the "latent thought" and what is called the "manifest contents" of the dream – the dream's text, the dream in its literal phenomenality – is therefore the relationship between an altogether "normal," conscious-preconscious, thought and the translation of that thought into the "rebus" of the unconscious, the "primary process." The essence of the dream is not the "latent thought," but the *mechanism* (the mechanism of the displacement, the condensation, the figuration of the contents of the words and symbols, etc.) that gives it its *dream form*. This has been systematically misunderstood; if we look for the "dream's secret" in the latent content hidden by the manifest text, we will be disappointed, as we will only find a perfectly "ordinary" thought whose nature is, for the most part, non-sexual and which, to top it off, has nothing unconscious about it.

This "ordinary," conscious-preconscious thought is repressed – drawn into the unconscious – not simply because it seems "disagreeable/uncomfortable" to the consciousness, but because of a "short-circuit" between it and another already repressed desire, which is always already unconscious, *a desire that in itself has absolutely nothing to do with the "thought latent in the dream."*

A "normal train of thought" – normal and therefore capable of being expressed in "daily," "public" language, in the syntax of the "secondary process" – "a normal train of thought is only submitted to abnormal treatment of the sort we have been describing [such as dreaming or hysteria]" – in other words, it is only submitted to the workings of dream, the mechanisms of the "primary process" – "if an unconscious wish, derived from infancy and in a state of repression, has been transferred onto it" (Freud 2010: 594). And, if this unconscious desire cannot be reduced to "a normal train of thought," it is, from the very beginning, continually repressed – this is the "original repression." Its "origin" is not in the "normal" language of everyday communication, in the syntax of the conscious-preconscious, its only space is in the mechanisms of the "primary process." Therefore, we must not reduce – as Habermas did, for example (cf. Habermas 1971) – the work of interpretation to the re-translation of the "thought latent in the dream" into "normal," "everyday" language, because the structure is always *ternary*, there are always three moments: the *manifest* text of the dream, the content or thought *latent* in the dream AND the *unconscious desire* that articulates itself in the dream. This desire latches onto the dream in the gap between latent thought and the manifest text. It is not "even more hidden, stowed away even deeper"; it is – in relation to the latent thought – significantly closer to the surface. It consists entirely in the mechanism of signification, the processes that operate upon the latent thought, its only space is the *form* of the dream.

This is the fundamental paradox of dreaming: the unconscious desire, the thing that is supposedly the most obscure, articulates itself precisely through the process of obscuring the dream's "kernel," its latent thought, this process that disguises the core-content by translating it into the rebus of dream. Here is the key passage from Freud:

> I used at one time to find it extraordinarily difficult to accustom readers to the distinction between the manifest content of dreams and the latent dream-thoughts. Again and again arguments and objections would be brought up based upon some uninterpreted dream in the form in which it had been retained in the memory, and the need to interpret it would be ignored. But now that analysts at least have become reconciled to replacing the manifest dream by the meaning revealed by its interpretation, many of them have become guilty of falling into another confusion which they cling to with equal obstinacy. They seek to find the essence of dreams in their latent content and in so doing, they overlook the distinction between the latent dream-thoughts and the dream-work. At bottom, dreams are nothing other than a particular *form* of thinking, made possible by the conditions of

the state of sleep. It is the *dream-work* which creates that form, and it alone is the essence of dreaming – the explanation of its peculiar nature. (2010: 241–2)

Freud's argument here has two stages. *First*, he argues that we must break down our initial impression that dreaming is nothing more than meaningless confusion, a disturbance conditioned by physiological processes that have nothing to do with any kind of signification whatsoever. In other words, we must first take the *hermeneutic* step; we must recognize that dreams must be approached as signifying phenomena, as something that transmits a repressed message that could be uncovered through the interpretive procedure. *Then*, we must free ourselves from our fascination with the signifying kernel, the content concealed behind the form of the dream – the dream's "hidden meaning" – and refocus our attention on the form of the dream itself, on the "transference work" of the latent thought through the mechanism of "dream-work."

This same two-stage analysis can be found in Marx's discussion of the "secret of the commodity form." According to Marx, first we must do away with the appearance that a commodity's value is arbitrary, the result of an accidental relationship, say, supply and demand. We must take the essential step toward the "meaning" hidden behind the commodity form, the meaning "expressed" in this form; we must pierce into the "secret" of the value of commodity:

> The determination of the magnitude of value by labour-time is therefore a secret hidden under the apparent movements in the relative values of commodities. Its discovery destroys the semblance of the merely accidental determination of the magnitude of the value of the products of labour, but by no means abolishes that determination's material form. (Marx 1992: 168)

However, as Marx writes, there is a "but" – simply arriving at the secret *is not enough*. The classical bourgeois political economy has already arrived at the "secret" of the commodity form; its limitation is that it remains blinded by its fascination with the "hidden meaning" of the commodity form, remaining fixated on work as the true source of wealth. In other words, the bourgeois political economy is only interested in the content hidden behind the commodity form, and this is why it cannot explain the true secret – not the secret *behind* the form, but the *secret of the form itself*. The bourgeois political economy lacks an exact determination of the "secret of the magnitude of value," and so the commodity remains enigmatic, mysterious – and we see the same thing happen with dreams. Dreaming remains an enigmatic phenomenon even after we have explained its hidden meaning, the thought latent within it. The thing that remains unexplained is quite simply the form-itself of the dream, the process through which the "hidden meaning" came to disguise itself in this particular way.

We therefore must take another – absolutely decisive – step and analyze the genesis of the commodity form itself, not just reducing the form to its essence, to its secret contents, but examining the process – analogous to the "dream-work" – through which the hidden content takes this form, because, as Marx said: "Whence, then, arises the enigmatic character of this product of labour as soon as it assumes the form of a commodity? Clearly from this form itself" (Marx 1992: 164). The classical political economy is unable to make this crucial step toward the genesis of the form, and this is its fundamental shortcoming:

> Political economy has indeed analysed value and its magnitude, however incompletely, and has uncovered the content concealed within these forms. But it has never once asked the question why this content has assumed that particular form, that is to say, why labour is expressed in value, and why the measurement of labour by its duration is expressed in the magnitude of the value of the product. (Marx 1992: 173–4)

The commodity form in the unconscious

What is it about the Marxist analysis of the commodity form that makes it so fascinating? It's the fact that his analysis supplied the matrix that made all the later "fetishistic reversals" possible. It is as if his discussion of the commodity form revealed the basic mechanism in its pure form, a mechanism that is essential to the functioning of phenomena that appear on the surface to have nothing in common with the field of political economy (law, religion, etc.). There is much more in the commodity form than simply the commodity form, and its power to fascinate comes from this "surplus." Alfred Sohn-Rethel, one of the "fellow travelers" of "critical social theory," is certainly the thinker who went the furthest in describing the universal scope of the commodity form. His fundamental thesis was that "in the innermost core of commodity structure there was to be found the 'transcendental subject'" (Sohn-Rethel 1978: xiii). The commodity form prefigured the anatomy, the skeleton, of the transcendental

Kantian subject, the transcendental network of categories that constitute the a priori framework of "objective" scientific knowledge. This is the paradox of the commodity form. As a worldly – "pathological" in the Kantian sense – phenomenon, it offers us the solution to the most fundamental question in the theory of knowledge: how could it be possible for there to be universally valid objective knowledge?

After a series of meticulous analyses, Sohn-Rethel came to the following conclusion: the categorical apparatus presupposed by scientific procedure (of Newtonian science), the conceptual lens through which it approaches nature, is already present in social effectivity, it is already at work in the act of commodity exchange. Before thought arrived at pure *abstraction*, abstraction was already at work in the social effectivity of the market. The exchange of commodities involves a dual abstraction: the abstraction of the changeable nature of commodity during the act of exchange and the abstraction of its concrete, particular, empirical, tangible determination. In an exchange, a commodity is posited as undifferentiated despite its specific qualities; once its specific nature, its "use value," has been abstracted, a commodity has "the same value" as another commodity. Even before we arrived at the idea of a purely *quantitative* determination – the *sine qua non* of modern natural science – pure quantity was already at work in the form of money, the commodity that made it possible to measure the value of all the other commodities, whatever their specific qualitative determinations might be. Well before physics articulated the concept of a purely abstract *movement* that occurred in geometric space, independent of any qualitative determinations, everyday acts of exchange had already realized just such a "pure" abstract movement, movement that was unaffected by the concrete-tangible qualities of the object in motion: the transfer of property. Sohn-Rethel then demonstrated the same thing in regard to the relation between substance and accidence, in regard to the notion of causality in Newtonian science . . . In short, for the whole run of categories of pure reason.

This is why the transcendental subject, the foundation for all a priori categories, ends up faced with the very worrisome fact that its formal genesis came out of a worldly, "pathological," process. This is a scandal, an "impossible" non-sequitur from the transcendental perspective, given that the formal-transcendental a priori is, by definition, independent of all contents. And this scandal corresponds perfectly to the "scandalous" character of the Freudian unconscious, which is similarly unbearable for the transcendental-philosophical point of view. In fact, if we closely examine the "ontological" status of what Sohn-Rethel called the "real abstraction" ["*reale Abstraktion*"] (the act of abstraction contained within the practice of commodity exchange), the parallel between this status and that of the unconscious – that signifying chain that exists "on an Other Stage" – becomes abundantly clear: *the "real abstraction" is the unconscious of the transcendental subject*, the very thing that provides the foundation for objective-universal scientific knowledge.

On the one hand, there is nothing "real" about "real abstraction" in the sense of actual properties of things; the determination of "value" is not part of the object-commodity in the way that the particular properties that make up its "use value" (form, color, taste, etc.) are. As Sohn-Rethel emphasized, "real abstraction" has the character of a *postulate* implied by the real world practice of exchange; its nature is that of an "as if" ["*als ob*"]. In the act of exchange, individuals act *as if* the commodity is not subject to physical changes during the act, *as if* it only existed at the level of the "consciousness," even though the participants "know full well" that "this is not true." This postulate is even more evident when we examine the materiality of money. We *know* full well that currency is subject to wear and tear, that its physical form changes with time, but nonetheless, in the social *reality* of the market, we *treat* it as "immutable substance, a substance over which time has no power, and which stands in antithetic contrast to any matter found in nature" (Sohn-Rethel 1978: 59). This brings to mind the fetishist disavowal, "Of course I know, but still. . . ." We should therefore add to the list of the most common examples of this formulation – "of course I know that my mother does not have a phallus, but still . . ."; "of course I know that Jews are people like the rest of us, but still . . ." – the example of money.

Here we are touching upon a problem that Marx did not resolve, that of *the materiality of money*. Not the "empirical," "tangible" materiality of money, but its *sublime* materiality, its other body that is "indestructible and not created," that exists beyond the degradation of the physical body – money's body is just like that of the Sadien victim who endures every torture only to emerge immaculately beautiful (cf. Riha 1986). The immaterial corporality of a "body without body" is the definition itself of the sublime object, and it is in this sense alone that we can make the argument that money is a "pre-phallic," "anal" object – as long as we do not forget that the postulated existence of this sublime body depends upon the symbolic order. The indestructible "body without body" that cannot be worn down by use presupposes a guarantee from a symbolic Authority.

Its weight and metallic purity are guaranteed by the issuing authority so that, if by wear and tear of circulation it has lost in weight, full replacement is provided. Its physical matter has visibly become a mere carrier of its social function. A coin, therefore, is a thing which conforms to the postulates of the exchange abstraction and is supposed, among other things, to consist of an immutable substance, a substance over which time has no power, and which stands in antithetic contrast to any matter found in nature. (Sohn-Rethel 1978: 59)

If, then, "real abstraction" does not operate at the level of "reality," of the object's existing properties, it is nonetheless not a "thought abstraction," a process that takes place "inside" the thinking subject. Unlike an "internal" process, the abstraction of the act of exchange is irreducibly external, de-centered, or, to use Sohn-Rethel's rather succinct formulation: "The abstraction of exchange is not thought, but it has the *form* of thought" (1970: 98). Here we have a possible definition of the unconscious: a form of thought whose "ontological" status is not that of thought, which is to say, one that remains irreducibly external to thought – an Other Stage outside of thought, where the form of thought has already been articulated beforehand. As a formal order, the Symbolic is precisely such a *third way* in relation to the dual empirical reality of the "external/internal" of subjective lived experience. Sohn-Rethel was therefore quite right to criticize Althusser for giving abstraction the status of thought, and thus reducing it to a process that can only occur at the level of knowledge and rejecting the category of "real abstraction" as epistemological confusion. "Real abstraction" was unthinkable for Althusser because it exploded his fundamental epistemological distinction between the "real object" and the "object of knowledge" by introducing a third option: the form prior to thought and external to thinking; simply put, the symbolic.

Now we are in a position to specify what exactly it is about Sohn-Rethel's arguments that are unbearable for philosophical thought – the thing that is "scandalous" about his approach. He made the circle of philosophical thought confront an external space where its form has been already "pre-established." Philosophical thought found itself faced with a worrisome experience similar to the Eastern proverb "you are that"; here, in the external practice of exchange, is your true place, this is the stage on which your truth was performed before you became conscious of it. The confrontation with this place is therefore unbearable for the Philosopher, because the Philosopher's position *defines* itself by not seeing this space. It cannot become aware of this space without falling apart, without losing its consistency.

This does not mean that, unlike the philosophical-theoretical consciousness, the "practical" consciousness – the consciousness of the subjects involved in the act of exchange – does not involve a similar constitutive misrecognition. This consciousness "practices" its own blindness. The individual involved in carrying out the act of exchange proceeds in the manner of a "practical solipsist." In the act of exchange he fails to see the socio-synthetic function of exchange, the level of "real abstraction" at which private production is socialized through the marketplace. This failure is the *sine qua non* of the successful completion of the act of exchange; if the participants were to become aware of the "real abstraction," "effective" exchange would no longer be possible:

> Exchange as a synthetic social form of commerce blinds itself . . . Here, socialization can only occur if it is not perceived. Consciousness would require a reflection that would be incompatible with the act of exchange; the observation of the process of socialization would cut its cord. This ignorance of reality is part of its very essence. (Sohn-Rethel 1970: 119)

This misrecognition brings out the scission in the consciousness between the "practical" consciousness and the "theoretical" consciousness. The owner who participates in the act of exchange proceeds in the manner of a "practical solipsist." He blinds himself to the universal socio-synthetic dimension of his act by reducing it to a relation between atomized monads encountering each other in the marketplace. The repressed, *social*, dimension of his act then appears in the form of its opposite: universal reason oriented toward the observation of *nature* (the network of the categories of "pure reason" as the conceptual framework for the natural sciences).

Here we encounter the relationship between "being" and "knowledge" that characterizes the Freudian conception of the unconscious. There is a paradoxical "being" that is not "independent of the consciousness" (the standard definition for materialist realism: an objective process that operates according to its immanent necessity, "independently of what subjects think about it"), but is nonetheless not an entity that depends on the consciousness nor one that exists only as the object of a consciousness (*esse-percipi*: the formula for subjective idealism), but *an entity whose existence implies a lack of knowledge*. Its given form is itself the result of a blunder; its "ontological" consistency rests entirely on a misunderstanding. This is, perhaps, a potential definition of the imaginary order. For example, as soon as the subject "knows too much about" the imaginary-Me, it vanishes, dissipates, loses its consistency. The full presence of the

Imaginary gets its consistency from the fact that somewhere there is a "forbidden zone," a zone of lethal knowledge.

Marx, inventor of the symptom

Lacan's thesis that Marx invented the symptom refers to the way in which the latter problematized commodity fetishization. He did so by uncovering a fissure, an asymmetry, a "pathological" imbalance, that subverts the universality of bourgeois "rights and duties." This imbalance, far from showing that this universalism was "insufficiently implemented," that there was a remainder that had to be abolished through further radicalization, in fact functions as its constitutive moment. In a strict sense, the "symptom" is an exceptional element of this very kind, one that subverts the Universal of which it is a part.

Marx's theoretical approach, his "critique of ideology," is fundamentally symptom-based; it consists in seeking out the "point of rupture" ["_point d'écrasement_"] (J.-A. Miller 1967) that is _different_ from an ideological field and at the same time _necessary_ for this field in order for it to achieve totality, for its circle to be closed. The logic of the exception is integral to Marx's theoretical approach. Each ideological universality – of freedom, justice, or equality, for example – is "false," it necessarily contains a specific case that breaks its unity, that exposes its fallibility. Freedom is a universal concept that contains quite a number of subspecies (freedom of speech and of conscience, freedom of the press and of trade, etc.). However, there is, by structural necessity, a particular freedom that subverts the universal concept of freedom: the freedom of labor, of the worker to freely sell his labor in the free market. This freedom is the opposite itself of effective freedom, because through the free sale of his labor, the worker _loses_ his freedom. The effective content of this free act of sale is subjugation to Capital. And it is precisely this paradoxical liberty, the form-itself of slavery, that completes the field, that closes the circle of bourgeois freedoms. The same thing is true with the ideal of the marketplace: fair, equivalent exchange. Each commodity must be paid for in full, but there is a paradoxical commodity – which is, of course, labor once again – that is exploited precisely because it has been paid for in full. The exploitation of labor is not that it is not paid its full due; the exchange between the capitalist and the worker is – in principle, at least – a perfectly fair, equivalent exchange in which the worker is paid the full price for his labor. The sleight of hand consists in the fact that "labor" is a paradoxical commodity whose use – the work itself – produces a surplus of value in relation to its own value, and it is this surplus value that the capitalist appropriates. We therefore have another ideological universality, that of the fair, equivalent exchange, and a paradoxical exchange – of labor for wages – that, *precisely because it is equivalent*, is the form itself of exploitation.

We could also formulate this question using the now infamous description, the "dialectic of quantity and quality." Suppose we have a quality, a property, a universal trait. As soon as we wish to understand, to unify, to totalize every case of a universality, the whole quantity of a quality, or, to put it in a logician's terms, the full extension of a concept, there will necessarily be "at least One" paradoxical element that – precisely because it is internal – subverts and destroys the universality of the quality in question. When, in pre-capitalist society, the production of commodities was not universal, when natural production predominated, the owners of the means of production were still, in theory, producers themselves. This is artisanal production, in which the owner himself works and sells his products on the market. At this level of development there is no exploitation – in principle at least, if we leave aside the exploitation of apprentices, etc. – and market exchange is equivalent, each commodity is paid its full value. However, as soon as market production begins to *universalize*, as soon as it begins to become the predominant model in the economic framework of society, there is a "qualitative leap." A new and paradoxical commodity starts to appear in the marketplace: labor, workers who are not themselves owners of the means of production and who must, as a result, sell not the *products* of their labor but *their labor itself* in order to survive. With the arrival of this new commodity, equivalent exchange becomes its own negation, it inverts itself into the form itself of exploitation, of the appropriation of surplus value. The "qualitative" development itself, the universalization of the production of commodities, therefore produces a "new quality" and leads to the appearance of a new commodity that functions as the internal negation of the universal principle of the equivalent exchange of commodities. The *utopia* of "petit-bourgeois" socialism is precisely the belief in the possibility of a society in which relationships of exchange are universalized, marketplace production predominates, but nonetheless workers remain owners of the means of production. An economy that has universalized the production of commodities but that does so without exploitation is, precisely, *a universality without symptom*, without the paradoxical exception that serves the role of its internal negation.

This is also the Marxist critique of Hegel, of the Hegelian idea of a rational totality. As soon as you try to grasp the existing social order as a rational totality, you must add a paradoxical social element that, while being internal to this rational totality, functions as its symptom and subverts the principle's universal totality. In the society of Marx's era, the irrational element of the societal structure was, of course, the proletariat, which functioned as the "unreason of reason itself" (Marx), as the moment in which universal reason encountered its own unreason. (For more on the proletariat as "symptom," cf. also Naveau 1983). When Lacan attributes the discovery of the symptom to Marx, he is even more specific. Lacan argues that the discovery comes in Marx's conceptualization of the passage from feudalism to capitalism: "The origin of the notion of the symptom is not to be sought in Hippocrates, but in Marx, in the liaison that he makes the first between capitalism and what? – the good old days, what one calls the feudal time" (Lacan n.d.: 33).

In order to understand this link, we must begin with its theoretical underpinning: the Marxist concept of commodity fetishism.

Fetish and commodity

The fetishistic character of commodity consists in the fact that: "the definite social relation between men themselves which assumes here, for them, the fantastic form of a relation between things" (Marx 1992: 165). The *value* of a commodity is, in truth, just the representation of a certain type of network of social relationships between the producers of various commodities. This value gets its form as a "quasi-natural" property from another commodity-thing, money; we say that the value of a commodity is such and such an amount of money. The key moment in the process of fetishization is not the infamous replacement of humans with things ("a relationship between men takes on the form of a relationship between things"); instead, it can be found in a particular mistake that touches on the relationship between the structured network and one of its elements. Something that is actually a structural effect (of the network of relationships among elements) appears as if it were an immediate property of an element, a property it would possess independent of its relationship to other elements. Such a mistake can arise from relationships "between things" as well as "between people." Marx says this explicitly about simple expressions of value. Commodity A can only express its value in relation to another commodity, B, which thereby becomes its equivalent. Because of the value relationship, "the physical body" – which is to say the existing properties, the use value – "of commodity B becomes a mirror for the value of commodity A" (Marx 1992: 144). Marx expands on this idea in a footnote:

> In a certain sense, a man is in the same situation as a commodity. As he neither enters into the world in possession of a mirror, nor as a Fichtean philosopher who can say "I am I," a man first sees and recognizes himself in another man. Peter only relates to himself as a man through his relation to another man, Paul, in whom he recognizes his likeness. With this, however, Paul also becomes from head to toe, in his physical form as Paul, the form of appearance of the species man for Peter. (Marx 1992: 144)

In a way, this little aside prefigures the Lacanian mirror stage. The I can only achieve its own unity, its own identity, when its self is reflected in another, because this other person offers me an image of my own unity. Marx then follows up on this parallel: the other commodity, B, is only equivalent to the extent that A approaches it as the form in which its own value appears; it is only equivalent inside this rapport. But it appears – and this is the key effect of *fetishism* – it appears as if the exact opposite is true. A appears to develop a relationship to B as if B's property of being-an-equivalent was not a "determination of reflection" (Marx) of A, as if B was *already in itself* an equivalent. The property of being an equivalent seems to belong to it even outside its relationship with A, just another of its existing, "natural" properties that constitute its use value. Marx again offers a quite interesting aside:

> Determinations of reflection [*Reflexionsbestimmungen*] of this kind are altogether very curious. For instance, one man is king only because other men stand in the relation of subjects to him. They, on the other hand, imagine that they are subjects because he is king. (Marx 1992: 149)

"Being-king" is an effect of the network of social relationships between the "king" and his "subjects," and – and here is the effect of the fetish – insofar as you are caught up *in* these social ties, you fall victim to a mistake and your understanding of the relationship flips. You think that you're a subject, you act like a subject toward the king, as if the king was already, in himself, outside his relationship to his subjects, king, as if "being-king" was a natural property of the royal person. This, of course, reminds me of Lacan's famous statement that the insane person is not just the beggar who thinks he is king, but also the king who thinks he is king, which is to say, who identifies his self immediately with the designation "king."

There is therefore a parallel, a deep similarity, between the two modes of fetishism, and now the key question becomes: what is the relationship between these two levels? In fact, this relationship is not a simple parallel. We cannot say that in societies in which market production predominates – which is to say, basically, capitalist societies – "what goes for commodities goes for people as well." In fact, just the opposite is true. While commodity fetishism is the rule in capitalist society, in capitalism relationships among people are non-fetishistic, they are relationships between "free" actors, each of whom acts according to his or her own self-interest. The predominant and determining type of relationship is not that of domination and servitude, but rather a contract between free subjects who are equal in the eyes of the law, modeled directly on market exchange. Two subjects encounter one another, and their relationship is unencumbered by any yoke of domination or servitude, of veneration for the Master, of the Master's patriarchal obligations toward the servant. When I meet you, it is as if we are two people whose behavior is determined through and through by "selfish" interest, each of us acting like a good utility-maximizer. You have no mystical aura; I only see you as a partner who, just like myself, follows his own self-interest, and you are only interesting to me because you have something – a good, a commodity – that can satisfy my needs.

Thus, the two forms of fetishism are *incompatible*. Where commodity fetishism rules there is a total de-fetishization of "relationships among people," and, on the other hand, in places where the fetishism of "human relationships" is the norm – which is to say, in pre-capitalist societies – commodity fetishism has not yet developed because "natural" production rather than market production predominates. Let me call the fetishism that exists between people by its true name: it is, as Marx says, "relationships of domination and servitude," and more specifically the Hegelian relationship of the Slave to the Master. It is as if the retreat of the Master caused by capitalism was in fact only a *relocation*, as if the de-fetishization of interpersonal relationships was paid for by the fetishization of "relationships among things." The decisive social relationships, those of production, are not immediately visible in the way that the interpersonal relationship of Master and Slave (lord to serf, etc.) are. They disguise themselves – to use Marx's extremely precise description – as "social relationships between things, products of labor," which is to say, as commodities.

This is why the discovery of the symptom comes in Marx's conceptualization of the passage from feudalism to capitalism. With the establishment of bourgeois society, relationships of domination and servitude became *repressed*. In capitalism it appears as if, in theory, there are free subjects, whose interpersonal relationships are free of any fetishism. The repressed truth – that of the continued existence of domination and servitude – breaks through in a symptom that subverts the picture presented by ideology of equality, freedom, etc. The symptom through which the truth of social relationships irrupts is the "social relationship of things." The decisive social relationships, those of exploitation, cannot be found through analyzing interpersonal relationships. We must look toward the "social relationships of things," unlike feudal society, in which:

> Whatever we may think, then, of the different roles in which men confront each other in such a society, the social relationships between individuals in the performance of their labour appear at all events as their own personal relations, and are not disguised as social relations between things, between the products of labour. (Marx 1992: 170)

That the social relationships of people, instead of neatly announcing themselves as personal relationships, disguise themselves as social relationships among things – this is a beautiful definition of the symptom, this is capitalism's "hysteria of conversion."

The "subjects who supposedly . . ."

We must not let ourselves be distracted by the fact that the opposition between "people" and "things" may initially seem "naive" and "humanist." Marx's reasoning is precisely so subversive because of the way in which he makes use of this distinction, which can be summarized in the following way: in capitalist society, relationships among "people" are transparent and de-mythologized, individuals are liberated from "naive" beliefs, from all obscurantist prejudices. They all act as rational-utilitarian subjects, in other words, it is the *"things" themselves that believe for them*, and this belief is embodied, materialized, in the "social relationships of things." This is similar to Tibetan prayer wheels; I turn the wheel (or better yet, if I act through the "cunning of reason" and build a windmill that turns it on its own) and thus the thing itself prays for me. More precisely, I pray through it. The thing acts as an intermediary, while "I myself" can go and do whatever I please; I can go off and indulge in the filthiest fantasies. To put this in Stalinist terms, it doesn't matter what I do, because *objectively I'm praying*.

On the topic of the paradoxical possibility of delegating one's belief to another, I am tempted to bring up the Lacanian thesis about the fundamentally anti-psychological nature of psychoanalysis. "Emotions" themselves already follow a certain logic, and they can be transposed, combined, delegated, etc. without undermining their "sincerity" or "authenticity." Not only can I delegate belief to the other, but also the most "spontaneous" emotions, like, for example, laughter or crying. On the subject of the role of the Chorus in ancient tragedy, Lacan remarked:

> When you go to the theater in the evening, you are preoccupied by the affairs of the day, by the pen that you lost, by the check that you will have to sign the next day. You shouldn't give yourselves too much credit. Your emotions are taken charge of by the healthy order displayed on the stage. The Chorus takes care of them. . . . Therefore, you don't have to worry; even if you don't feel anything, the Chorus will feel in your stead. (Lacan 1997a: 252)

The Chorus feels terror and pity for us, for us spectators, so that we can watch the spectacle even if we are tired, or preoccupied with our daily concerns. By placing the Chorus in the position of an intermediary, we can still "objectively" feel the appropriate emotions. In so-called primitive societies, we can find an analogous phenomenon in the form of paid criers, women who are paid to cry at funerals. Through these women, one honors the obligations of being in mourning through the other, so that we can focus on more important and lucrative affairs, such as how the inheritance will be divided. And this phenomenon does not cease to exist after the so-called "primitive stage of social development." Think, for a moment, about the television shows where "canned" laughter is part of the show. After the supposedly hilarious jokes or gags there is a burst of laughter or applause – this is certainly the modern-day equivalent of the ancient Chorus; this is "living antiquity." What's the point of this laughter? The first answer – that it reminds us that we have to laugh, it compels us to laugh – is not sufficient, although it does present an interesting paradox in the sense that laughter could be some kind of duty. The only appropriate answer is that the *other laughs for us*. This, of course, involves the assumption that our position, the position of "our-selves," was already in advance the position of the Other – otherwise, how could we explain the efficacy of such a substitution? In this manner, we were "objectively" quite amused, even though in reality, silent and tired, we just sat there staring at the screen.

Marx is much more subversive here than most contemporary critics. Take Umberto Eco, for example. In *The Name of the Rose*, the hidden secret at the center of the monastery's labyrinth is revealed to be a supposedly lost section of Aristotle's *Poetics* on comedy. The lesson seems clear: the foundation of totalitarianism is blind belief and fanaticism, the supreme Evil is the obsessive fascination with the Good, which we must subvert through the liberating distance of laughter: laughter, which undermines every fixed, dogmatic proposition. There is no idea more ill suited to contemporary "real, post-Stalin, socialism" than this. The reigning ideology in this system is the very fact that no one "takes it seriously" (except a few dissidents who criticize power for not following its own rules), the cynical ironic distance is a *sine qua non* component of the way in which it functions. The famous carnavalesque "liberating laughter" is through and through on the side of power.

The question that we must now ask about an ideological conjuncture like this is: in what way is belief – a necessary condition for the establishment of a social order – at work here despite what I've said so far? In order to answer this, we must first introduce the idea of the subject who supposedly believes, the correlate of the subject who supposedly knows (cf. Mocnik 1986). In order to pin down exactly who this subject is, let me give an example characteristic of contemporary socialist countries, where there is always a shortage of something – toilet paper, for example. At first, stores are well stocked with toilet paper. Then, a rumor starts to spread that there will be a shortage of toilet paper, and everyone rushes out to buy some, and, in the end, there is no more toilet paper on the shelves. This may seem to be a simple case of a self-fulfilling prophecy, but the mechanism at work is actually slightly more complicated than that. Each person's reasoning goes as follows: "I know that there is no actual shortage of toilet paper, but there are people out there who are dumb enough to believe that there is and, as a result, they're going to go buy it all up. Therefore, even though there's no actual shortage, I should go out and buy some toilet paper right away."

Each person's actions are based on those of another subject who supposedly believes, and this other who supposedly believes "directly," "naively," *has an effect even if he does not exist in the real world*. In a social group, anyone can play this role for the others. Even if no existing individual actually fits the description of the subject who supposedly believes, this does not stop this subject from triggering a series of effects in social reality, including, for example, an actual shortage of toilet paper. This is the paradox of an object that, even though it does not exist, still has properties. This is a new version of "too clever by half"; the true fool is the person who is too smart to buy into the rumors and continues to stick to the true fact that there is a sufficient supply of toilet paper. In the end, he will wind up paperless.

I cannot overemphasize how important the category of the subject who supposedly believes is for a certain kind of psychoanalytical practice. I am tempted to say that the main difference between true Freudian analysis and "revisionist" methods is that in the latter the analyst plays for the analysand the role of the subject who supposedly believes, instead of embodying the subject who supposedly knows. To wit, the analysand's reasoning goes as follows: "I need analysis to help with my psychological problems, but I don't believe in the maternal phallus, castration, or any of that nonsense. But, the analyst, he believes, and perhaps, despite everything, he might be able to help me because he believes." The lesson we can draw from this about society is that belief, far from being "internal" and "intimate," is always materialized in our "effective" activity. It is around our belief that the phantasy that governs social effectivity is articulated.

Take the example of Kafka. We are told that in the "irrational" world of his novels, Kafka depicted modern bureaucracy in an "exaggerated," "fantastical," and "subjective" manner. But this ignores the key fact that this "exaggeration" is precisely the place where the phantasy at work in the libidinal operational of "real world" bureaucracy itself is inscribed. The so-called "Kafkaesque universe" is not a "fantastical image of social reality," but, on the contrary, it is the staged representation of the phantasy that is already at work at the heart of social reality itself. Of course we know that bureaucracy is not all-powerful, but our "effective" conduct is already regulated by a belief in its omnipotence. Unlike the standard "ideological critiques" that seek to deduce an ideology out of the conjunction of actual social relationships, the analytic approach aims to find the ideological phantasy that presides over actual society. What we call "social reality" is an ethical construct that bases itself on an *as if* (we act *as if* we believed that bureaucracy was all-powerful, *as if* the President represented the Will of the People, *as if* the Party embodied the objective interests of the working class, etc.). If this belief (we must keep in mind that there is absolutely nothing "psychological" about it; it is materialized in the "objective," "real" way society operates) is lost, the texture of society itself dissolves.

But the subject who supposedly believes is only the first of three subjects that we can construct using the model of the subject who supposedly knows. After the subject who supposedly believes comes the *subject who is supposedly jouissant* (cf. Dolar 1986), the other as possessing a jouissance that is unlimited, unbearable, traumatic. Jacques-Alain Miller already emphasized the way in which this logic operates inside racism. The thing that worries us about the other (the Jew, the Arab) is fundamentally his particular mode of organizing jouissance ("they enjoy themselves too loudly, their food smells unpleasant . . ."). Or it is Woman who appears to the obsessive as possessing an overflowing, self-destructive jouissance. The obsessive will then behave in such a way so as to save her from her own jouissance, even if it comes at the cost of her destruction. And finally, there is the *subject who supposedly desires*. We assume that the other "knows how to desire," that she knows how to get around the fundamental impasse of human desire. The parallels between this and the basic structure of hysteria are obvious. If the obsessive is traumatized by the other's unbearable jouissance, the hysteric needs the other in order to organize his desire. It is in this very specific sense that we should interpret Lacan's statement that "the hysteric's desire is the other's desire," i.e., the other who, for the hysteric, embodies the subject who supposedly desires. The question we must ask about the hysteric is not "What is the object of his desire?" but, rather, "Where does his desire come from?" "What is the other subject through which he organizes his desire?" In the case of Freud's patient Dora, it is clear that for her, Madame K is the other who embodies "knowing how to desire."

I should emphasize that, in this triad, the subject who supposedly knows retains its place as the keystone of the basic matrix, the other three are only derivatives whose function is specifically to obscure the radical dimension of the implications of supposed knowledge.

10

Ideology Between the Dream and the Phantasy: A First Attempt at Defining "Totalitarianism"

The Real in ideology

In Seminar XI, Lacan references the famous paradox of Choang-tsu [*Tchouang-tseu*], who, after having dreamed that he was a butterfly, wondered upon awaking whether he might not be a butterfly dreaming of being Choang-tsu. According to Lacan, he had good reasons to ask himself this question – first of all because "it proves he is not mad, he does not regard himself as absolutely identical with Choang-tsu" and, second, because:

> In fact, it is when he was the butterfly that he apprehended one of the roots of his identity – that he was, and is, in his essence, that butterfly who paints himself with his own colours – and it is because of this that, in the last resort, he is Choang-tsu. (Lacan 1998a: 76)

The first reason comes from the fact that the symbolic network that determines the subject's identity is external to the subject; Choang-tsu is Choang-tsu because that is who he is "for others," because this is the identity bestowed upon him by the intersubjective network to which he belongs. He would be crazy if he thought that others treated him like Choang-tsu because that's who he already was in himself, independent of the symbolic network. The truth of the subject is decided externally, the subject "in himself" is nothing, emptiness without consistency. However, is simply reducing the subject to emptiness, "dissolving" him into the symbolic network, all that we can say here? Is the entirety of the subject's "content" reducible to what he is "for others," to the symbolic determinations, the "titles" and "mandates," that have been placed upon him? Despite everything, the subject has a way of giving consistency to his identity outside of "titles," of symbolic determinations that situate him in the universal symbolic network, a means of presentifying his *Dasein* in its "pathological" character, in its absolute particularity: the phantasy. In the phantasy object, the subject "grasps some root of his identity." By seeing himself as a "butterfly who dreams of being Choang-tsu," Choang-tsu was therefore correct; "the butterfly" is the object that constitutes the framework, the skeleton of his phantasy identity. The Choang-tsu-butterfly relationship would be written $ \lozenge a$. In the dream that we call socio-symbolic "reality," he is Choang-tsu, but in the Real of his desire, he is the butterfly, his entire determinate existence consists in "butterfly-being."

Initially, Choang-tsu's paradox seems to just symmetrically invert the so-called "normal" relationship between wakefulness and dreaming. Instead of Choang-tsu who dreams about being a butterfly, we have a butterfly that dreams about being Choang-tsu. But, as Lacan emphasizes, this appearance of symmetry is misleading. While awake, Choang-tsu can take himself for Choang-tsu who is a butterfly in his dreams, but when he is a butterfly, he cannot ask himself "whether, when he is Choang-tsu awake, he is not the butterfly that he is dreaming of being" (Lacan 1998a: 76), which is to say, he cannot see himself as the butterfly who dreams of being Choang-tsu. The mistake cannot be two-sided, symmetrical, because if that were the case we would end up with a nonsensical situation like the one described by Alphonse Allais. Two lovers, Raoul and Marguerite, promise to meet each other at a masked ball. At the ball, they think that they've recognized each other and slip off to a secluded corner where they take off their masks and – surprise! – "they both cry out in shock when neither one recognizes the other. He is not Raoul and she is not Marguerite." (We can find the same paradox in certain works of science fiction that are narrated from the point of view of a hero who gradually learns that all the people around him are not humans but robots that look like humans – the final twist comes when the hero realizes that *he himself* is just an android.)

Psychoanalysis is therefore quite different from the theory of a "universalized dream," which holds that "all of reality is just an illusion." Rather, psychoanalysis insists on there being a remainder, a rock, a "solid kernel" that escapes the universal ephemerality of appearances. The only major difference between psychoanalysis and the "naive realism" that trusts in the "hard realities of facts" is that, according to analytic theory, the "solid core" arrives in dreams. It is only while dreaming that we approach the Real, the traumatic Thing that is the object-cause of desire, which is to say, it is only in dreams that we are on the verge of wakefulness – and the very reason that we wake up is so that we can continue dreaming, in order to avoid having to encounter the Real (cf. Lacan 1998a: Chapter V, and J.-A. Miller 1980). When we wake up, we tell ourselves "it was all just a dream," blinding ourselves to the key fact that, precisely because we are awake, we are just "the consciousness of this dream" (Lacan 1998a: 76). The same thing is true with "ideological dreaming." Our attempts to exit the dream by opening our eyes to reality will be in vain precisely because, as subjects viewed from the perspective of an "objective," "post-ideological," "disabused" gaze, one that is "freed from ideological illusions," which "sees the facts for what they are," *we are only the consciousness of the ideological dream*. The only way to escape is to confront the Real that accompanies the ideology in question. For example, it's not that we must "free ourselves of prejudice against the Jews," and "see them as they truly are" – the most effective way of unconsciously remaining a prisoner of these "prejudices" – but that we must examine ourselves and find the way in which the figure of the Jew is a reflection of an impasse in the Real of our desire.

This perspective requires us to radically redefine the concept of ideology. In the predominant Marxist perspective, ideology is an inverted "false consciousness," that obscures the actual essence of social relationships. Therefore we must search for this hidden essence, effective social relationships (the class relationships hidden behind the universalism of formal bourgeois rights, for example). However, if we understand the social field as a structure that articulates itself around its own impossibility, we are obligated to define ideology as a symbolic edifice. But the thing that it masks is not society's hidden essence, but rather the void, the impossibility around which the field of society structures itself. This is why the "critique of ideology" no longer seeks to pierce the hidden essence. Instead, it subverts the ideological edifice by denouncing the element of the edifice that plays the role of the whole's own impossibility. But in the predominant Marxist perspective, the ideological gaze is a *partial* gaze that is blind to the *totality* of social relationships, whereas, from an analytic perspective, ideology betrays a *totality that wishes to erase the traces of its own impossibility*. I need hardly mention that this difference corresponds to the one that separates the Marxist concept of fetishism from Freud's. In Marxism, the fetish masks the existing network of social relationships, whereas, for Freud, the fetish masks the lack (the "castration") around which the symbolic network articulates itself.

The fact that the Real is that which always returns in the same place leads to another, no less important, difference between the two perspectives. From the Marxist point of view, the ideological procedure is a process of false *externalization* and *universalization par excellence*, in which a conjunction that emerged out of the concrete historical constellation is posited as an eternal, universal condition, and a particular interest is posited as the universal interest. From this perspective, the point of the critical-ideological approach is to denounce this false universality, to uncover the bourgeois man in the concept of Man, to find the way in which bourgeois universal rights make capitalist exploitation possible, how the patriarchal nuclear family is a historically limited construct and in no way a universal constant, etc.

However, it seems as if, from the analytical perspective, we should change our terms and recognize that the most "cunning" ideological operation is that of *hasty historicization*. In the end, isn't the true point of the historical relativization and critique of analysis for its focus on the "patriarchal family," "oedipism," and "family-ism," that this line of criticism allows us to *avoid* the "solid kernel" of the family that these carry, the Real of the Law, the rock of castration? In other words, if hasty universalization puts forward a quasi-universal Image whose function is to blind us to its historic-symbolic determination, hasty historicization blinds us to the solid core that always returns the same through diverse historicizations/symbolizations.

This is the dimension of the Real that is missing from the Marxist theoretical edifice, centered as it is on the symptomal reading of ideological text. Let us try to pin down this lack through impasses in the Marxist concept of surplus value.

Surplus jouissance [*plus-de-jouir*] and surplus value

The proof of the solid foundation for Lacan's move to model the concept of surplus jouissance on the Marxist concept of surplus value – which is to say, the proof that Marxist surplus value does, in fact, effectively prefigure the logic of the *object little a* as surplus jouissance – is already there in the key formulation Marx gives in the third book of *Capital*, in which he attempts to pin down the historical-logical limit of capitalism: "The limit of capital is capital itself, which is to say the capitalist mode of production."

This formulation can be taken two ways. The first, standard historical-evolutionary reading sees this limit through the lens of the infamous model of the dialectic of productive forces and relationships of production as homologous to the dialectic of "content" and "form" (cf. the Preface to the *Critique of Political Economy*). This model operates like a snake that sheds its skin once it has become too tight. We posit the constant growth of productive forces (which as a rule is reduced to technical developments) as the fundamental motive force behind the development of society, as its "natural," "automatic" constant. This growth is then followed, after a delay of variable length, by a change in the relationships of production. There are therefore periods in which these relationships are well equilibrated to the forces, but then the forces develop and outgrow the framework of relationships. This framework then becomes an obstacle to their further development, until finally there is a revolution that re-equilibrates the relationships and the forces by replacing the old relationships with new ones better suited to the new situation. From this perspective, capital as its own limit simply means that the relationships of capitalist production, which had at first made the rapid development of these productive forces possible, become a hindrance to their own further development when the forces have outgrown the existing framework and require a new form of social relationships. Of course, we need only look to the passages of *Capital* in which Marx discusses the relationship between the formal and real subsuming of production to capital in order to see that he himself did not believe in such a vulgar evolutionary representation. For Marx, formal subsumption *precedes* real subsumption, which is to say, capital first subsumes the process of production as it was when it found it (artisan production, etc.), and it is only then that capital gradually begins to transform the forces of production, giving them the structure that suits it best. Unlike the above-mentioned vulgar representation, it is the *form* of the relationships of production that drives the development of the productive forces of its "content."

Here I will ask a very naive question: at what point – even if it's just a theoretical one – can we say that the relationships of capitalist production have become a barrier to the development of the forces of production? There is also the reverse of this question: when can we say that the forces of production and relationships of production are in harmony within the framework of capitalist production? A strict analysis offers us one answer, and one answer alone: *never*. It is precisely in this that capitalism differs from earlier modes of production. Previously, it was possible to talk about periods of "equilibrium," during which the processes of production and reproduction spun peacefully, and periods in which the contradiction between the forces and the relationships worsened, whereas contradiction, the forces/relationships discord, *is part of the very "concept" of capitalism itself* (in the form of the contradiction between the social mode of production and the individual mode, deprived of appropriation). It is this very contradiction that forces capitalism into a state of permanent expansive growth, incessant development of its own conditions of production. This is quite unlike earlier modes of production in which (re)production – in its "normal" state – took the form of a circular movement.

If this is the case, then the evolutionary reading of capital as its own limit is no longer sufficient. It is never the case that at a certain point the framework of relationships of production block the further development of productive forces; on the contrary, it is this immanent limit itself, this "internal contradiction," that pushes the perpetual development of capitalism ever onwards. The "normal" state of capitalism is the perpetual revolutionization of its conditions of existence. From the very outset it is "rotten," marked by contradiction, distortion, immanent disequilibrium, and it is for this very reason that it changes incessantly, that it never stops developing. Every day the fundamental, constitutive contradiction of capitalism must be resolved anew, and incessant development is the only way this can occur. Far from serving as its brakes, this limit is the motive force behind capitalist development. This is both the paradox of capitalism and its most fundamental resource: it is capable of transforming its own difficulty, its very powerlessness, into the source of its power and growth – the more it "rots," the more its internal contradiction worsens, the more it must revolutionize itself in order to survive.

And now the link between surplus value – the "cause" that drives the process of capitalist production – and surplus jouissance, the object-cause of desire, becomes clear. The paradoxical topology of the movement of capital, the fundamental barrier that resolves and reproduces itself through frenzied activity, *excessive* power as the form-itself of a fundamental *powerlessness*, the immediate passage, the intersection of the limit and the excess, of lack and surplus: aren't these all just the object-cause of desire, the surplus, the remainder that translates a constitutive lack?

Of course, Marx knew all this – and yet, in the decisive passage from the Preface to the *Critique of Political Economy*, he acts *as if he didn't*. He describes the passage-itself from capitalism to socialism in terms of the aforementioned vulgar dialectic of forces of production and relationships of production. When the forces develop past a certain point, capitalist relationships become an obstacle to their own further development, which makes it necessary for the socialist revolution to come along and put the relationships in equilibrium with the forces, to re-establish the relationships of production and make it possible for the accelerated development of the forces of production to be an end in itself. Isn't it obvious from this that Marx himself was unable to master the paradox of surplus jouissance? History has taken ironic vengeance upon this misunderstanding, because today there exists a society to which this evolutionary dialectic of forces and relationships seems to apply: "real socialism." In fact, it is already a cliché to say that "real socialism" made the process of rapid industrialization possible, but that, as soon as productive forces attained a certain level of development (the level that led to the passage to "post-industrial" society), the social relationships of "real socialism" became barriers to development.

The totalitarian phantasy, the totalitarianism of phantasy

This opens the possibility of a whole new approach to the passage from "utopian" socialism to what is called "scientific" socialism. If Marx truly discovered the symptom and developed the logic of the social symptom as the fundamental barrier in a given social order, which seems to call for its own practico-dialectical "revolutionary" dissolution, he still misunderstood the full weight of the *phantasy* in the historical process, of the inertia that does not allow itself to be dissolved dialectically and whose manifestation takes the form of the "regressive behavior of the masses" who seem to "act against their own true interests" and allow themselves to be hoodwinked by various forms of "conservative revolution." The enigmatic character of these phenomena can be found in the dumb *jouissance* they exhibit. Social theory attempts to dismiss the worrisome character of this jouissance by designating it as "mass hysteria," "devolution," "regression," "lack of consciousness," etc.

Where is the phantasy here? The purpose of the phantasy scene is to realize the sexual rapport, to dazzle us with its fascinating presence, thus concealing the impossibility of the sexual rapport. It's the same thing with the "social" phantasy, with the phantasy construction that supports the ideological field. In the end, we will always be dealing with the phantasy of a *class rapport*, a utopia in which the diverse societal groups coexist in harmonious, organic, complementary relationships. The most basic depiction of the "social" phantasy is the *social body*, which serves to avoid the rock of the impossible, the "antagonism" around which the social field structures itself. And the right wing anti-liberal ideologies that serve as the foundation for the "regressive behavior of the masses" are characterized precisely by their use of organicist metaphors; their *Leitmotiv* is society as a body, an organic totality of members that was later corrupted by the intrusion of liberal atomization.

We can already find this phantasy in so-called "utopian" socialism. Lacan said that the illusion specific to Sade's perverted phantasy was the "utopia of desire" (Lacan 2006: 775). In the sadistic scene, the scission between desire and jouissance is abolished (an impossible operation, insofar as desire is based on the interdiction of jouissance, which is to say, insofar as desire is the structural inverse of jouissance) and so is the gap that separates jouissance from pleasure – through pleasure's "negative," pain, we could supposedly reach jouissance within the very field of pleasure. The word "utopia" should also be taken in a political sense. Sade's famous "yet another effort . . ." (from the *Philosophy in the Boudoir*) should be understood as in line with "utopian socialism." Sadism is one of its most radical variations, because, from Campanella to Fournier, "utopian socialism's" project always involves a "utopia of desire," it always involves the phantasy of finally being able to dominate, to regulate, jouissance.

With the passage from "utopian" to "scientific" socialism, Marx foreclosed the dimension of phantasy. Here, the term "foreclosure" must be understood as carrying the full weight of the role it plays in Lacanian theory. It is not simple repression, but rather the exclusion, the rejection of a moment outside the symbolic field. And we know that the thing that is foreclosed from the symbolic returns in the Real – in our case, in *real socialism*. Utopian, scientific, and real socialism form a kind of triad; the utopian dimension, forbidden by "scienticism," returns in the Real – the "utopia in power," to borrow the very fitting title of Mikhail Heller and Aleksandr Nekrich's book about the Soviet Union. "Real socialism" is the price paid in blood for misunderstanding the dimension of phantasy in scientific socialism.

It may seem, however, as if talking about the "social phantasy" involves a fundamental theoretical error, given that the phantasy is strictly *non-universalizable*. It is strictly particular, "pathological" in the Kantian sense, personal – the very foundation itself of the unity of a "person" as distinct from the subject (of the signifier). The phantasy is the unique way each of us tries to finish with the Thing, to settle our score with impossible jouissance, which is to say, the way in which we use an imaginary construct in our attempt to escape the primordial impasse of the being of language, the impasse of the inconsistent Other, the hole at the heart of the Other. The realm of the Law, of rights and duties, on the contrary, doesn't just happen to be universalizable, but is universal by its very nature. It is the realm of universal equality, of equality brought about by exchange that is – in theory – equivalent. From this perspective, we can designate the object *a*, surplus jouissance, as the remainder, the excess that escapes from the network of universal exchange, and this is why the formula for the non-universalizable phantasy is written $ ◊ a, which is to say, the confrontation of the subject with the "impossible," unexchangeable remainder. This is the connection between surplus jouissance and surplus value, the excess that undoes the equivalent exchange between the capitalist and the proletarian, the surplus that the capitalist appropriates under the auspices of the equivalent exchange of capital for labor.

However, Marx was not the first to notice the dead end of equivalent exchange. Doesn't Sade's heroism stem precisely from his efforts to spread the bourgeois form of universal and equal law, of universal exchange, of rights and duties of man, into the realm of jouissance? He starts with the idea that the Revolution only went halfway because, in the domain of jouissance, it continued to be imprisoned within patriarchal, theological prejudices, which is to say that it did not reach the final goal in its project of bourgeois emancipation. However, as Lacan showed in "Kant with Sade," the formulation of a universal norm, of a "categorical imperative," that could legislate jouissance will always necessarily fail, it will always run into a dead end. We cannot legislate a right to jouissance on the model of formal bourgeois laws, which would end up being something like "to each his phantasy!"; "each person has the right to her own particular means of jouissance"; and so forth. As described by Lacan, Sade's hypothetical universal law would be something like:

> "I have the right to enjoy your body," anyone can say to me, "and I will exercise this right without any limit to the capriciousness of the exactions I may wish to satiate with your body." (Lacan 2006: 648)

The inherent limitations to a law like this are obvious. The symmetry is false, it would be impossible to consistently remain the punisher, in the end everyone would end up a victim.

How then can we refute the objection that talking about a "social phantasy" is an *in adjecto* contradiction? Far from being simply epistemological, far from being an error in our theoretical approach, this impasse *defines the thing itself*. The fundamental trait of the fabric of "totalitarian" society is precisely this loss of distance between the phantasy that provides the subject with its references for jouis-sance and the formal-universal Law that regulates social exchange. The phantasy "socializes" itself immediately, the social Law coincides with the injunction "Jouis!": it begins to operate like a superego imperative. In other words, in totalitarianism it is truly the fantasy (the phantasy) that is in power, and this is what differentiates totali-tarianism *stricto sensu* (Germany 1938–45; USSR 1934–51; Italy 1943–5) from patriarchal-autocratic *law-and-order* regimes (Salazar, Franco, Dolfuss, Mussolini up until 1943 . . .) and "normalized" real socialism. "Pure" totalitarianism is necessarily "self-destructive," it cannot stabilize itself, it can never achieve even the minimum level of homeostasis that would make it possible to reproduce itself through some equilibrated circuit. It is constantly shaken by convulsions, an immanent logic drives it to violence directed toward an enemy, be it external (the Nazi extermination of the Jews) or internal (Stalin's purges). The watchword for the post-Stalin "normalization" of the USSR was that of the "return to socialist *legality.*" They recognized that the end to the vicious circle of the purges was the reaffirmation of a Law that could introduce a necessary minimum distance from the phantasy, the need for a formal-symbolic system of rules that would not be immediately impregnated with jouissance.

This is why we can define totalitarianism as a social order in which, even though there is no law (no explicitly established law that is universally valid), anything that one does can at any moment be seen as illegal, forbidden. Positive legislation does not exist (or, if it does exist, it is completely arbitrary and non-obligatory), but despite this, one can find oneself at any moment in the position of having broken an unknown or non-existent Law. The paradox of the Inter-diction that founds the social order is that the forbidden thing is already impossible. Totalitarianism inverts this paradox by placing its subjects in the no less paradoxical position of transgressors of a non-existent law. Such a situation, in which a phantom law is con-stantly being transgressed, is a wonderful illustration of Dostoyevsky's famous statement – Lacan's version of which brings out its signifi-cance in its entirety: if God (positive law) does not exist, everything is forbidden (Lacan 1991b: 128).

11

Divine Psychosis, Political Psychosis: A Second Attempt at Defining "Totalitarianism"

"Argue . . . but obey!"

In his famous answer to the question "What is Enlightenment?" Kant tacked an unsettling qualification onto the end of the motto *Sapere aude!*, introducing a scission at the very heart of the Enlightenment: "Argue as much as you want and about whatever subject you please, but obey!" Insofar as you are an autonomous subject capable of reflection addressing an enlightened audience, you can reason freely, put any and every authority into question. But insofar as you are a "cog in the machinery" of society, you must unreservedly obey the orders of these very same authorities. In order to see how this scission is specific to the Enlightenment as such, let us return to the beginning, to the Cartesian *cogito*. The other side of universal doubt and the methodological approach is "provisional morality." Descartes lists a series of maxims regulating the conduct of ordinary life during philosophical inquiry, the first of which already lays down the rule "to obey the laws and customs of my country, adhering firmly to the faith in which, by the grace of God, I had been educated from my childhood" (Descartes 2008: 35).

The true point of this blind obedience is, of course, to make it possible for the thinker to take his distance from the contingent, "pathological" contents of social life. When you accept the rules without question, you experience their blunt inanity, their stupid senselessness ("the law is the law") – one renders unto Caesar what is Caesar's – which opens the space for you to reflect freely. Far from being a remnant of the pre-Enlightenment era, the Kantian prohibition on questioning the legitimacy of the origin of power (cf. *Doctrine of Right*) is in fact the necessary other side of the coin.

This "machine" that we must obey offers a clear parallel to Pascal's description of the automatism of "custom," that is, the symbolic rite. "Custom only has to be followed because it is custom, not because it is reasonable or just" (Pascal 2008: 110). The authority of the law is therefore an "authority without truth," a pure semblance that does not need to be true in order to function, grounded only upon the act of its own formulation. This is why we must not ask questions about the origins of the law; once we've asked this question, we have already questioned its authority, because we've asked for reasons to obey that would be different from obeying simply because it is the law. "Custom is the whole of equity for the sole reason that it is accepted. That is the mystical basis of its authority. Whoever tries to trace this authority back to its origin, destroys it" (Pascal 2008: 24).

And it was Pascal who radicalized the importance of "custom" in relation to the Enlightenment; it is an Enlightenment illusion to think that we could simply distance ourselves from the "machinery" of custom and thus carve out a free space for our internal reflection. The error consists in not realizing the way in which the internality of our reasoning depends already, unbeknownst to us, on the force of "custom," in its dead letter, in its senselessness, basically, in the fact that the signifier governs the field of the signified. "Custom provides the strongest and most firmly held proofs: it inclines the automaton, which unconsciously drags the mind with it . . . it is that which makes so many Christians, that which makes the Turks, the heathens" (Pascal 2008: 148).

However, Pascal's pre-emptive critique of the Enlightenment does not pose a problem for Kant; it only bears on the pre-critical Enlightenment belief that the opposition between "free reasoning" and "social machinery" coincides with that of theory and practice: "In theory, you can reason as much as you want, whereas in social life you must obey!" Kant, however, affirms the primacy of practical reason over pure reason, which means that our internal freedom is already subject to a far heavier and crueler Law than external social laws: the ethical imperative. The Kantian moral Law is also a necessary Law, one that can hold without being true. This is the paradox of a "transcendental fact," a fact whose theoretical truth cannot be demonstrated, but whose validity must nonetheless be presupposed in order for it to be possible for our activity to have moral meaning.

Kant therefore carried the Protestant split between external legality and internal morality all the way to the concept itself, opposing "pathological" social laws and the moral imperative. It is precisely when we distance ourselves from the field of social legality, of customs in their raw given form, that we fall under the yoke of a far more inflexible Master. As Kant says, the moral Law is the *ratio cognoscendi* of freedom. You know that you are free because you are capable of rejecting the "pathological" motives of your own activity in the name of moral Law. We never escape the Master, the Master is part of the definition-itself of human nature: "Man is an animal which, if it lives among others of its kind, requires a master" (Kant 1991: 46).

We can draw the contrast between social laws and the moral Law in a variety of different ways. Social laws structure the conditions of social *reality*, the Law contains the *Real* of an unconditional imperative that is unconcerned with the limits of the possible ("you can because you must!"). Social laws *appease*, they make the homeostasis of cohabitation possible, while the Law disrupts, constantly unsettling social equilibrium. Social laws *prohibit*, the Law *inflicts*. Social laws represent the *external* pressure of society upon an individual, while the Law is *extimate*, it is what is "in us that is more than us," a foreign body at the very heart of the subject. Here we can see clearly just how insufficient is the dominant form of social psychology, according to which morality should be understood as the "internalization of societal repression." On the contrary, social laws are a means of freeing oneself from the unbearable pressure of the moral imperative by "externalizing" it. Once the Law has been externalized, you can take your distance from it, and its worrisome power to disturb your inner equilibrium is tamed. We have laws not because they rein in our "unlimited egotism," but rather to save ourselves from the impasse of the Law.

The obscenity of the form

It is already a commonplace of Lacanian theory to interpret the Kantian imperative as the obscene injunction of the superego – but what exactly is this obscenity? Normally, Kant is criticized for his formalism, for reducing moral Law to an empty form that draws all its effective contents from the "pathological" domain of experience. We focus on the impossibility of reaching the pure form of the Law, which is to say the complete exclusion of the pathological object as a possible motive for our activity. There is always a residuum of pathological particularity that persists, that alters and sullies the pure form of the Law, and the Lacanian name for this remainder is the *object little a*.

But a critique of Kant along these lines is the exact opposite of what Lacan meant by "Kant with Sade." Far from being the pathological remainder, the *object little a,* surplus jouissance, erupts precisely at the point where the Law purifies itself of all its pathological contents, all its "material for jouissance" [*"matière à jouir"*], and becomes the empty form. Just as how, for Marx, surplus value emerges as the motive for production at the point where universal exchange value erases particular, "pathological" use value. The *object little a* is the form of the Law in its role as the cause of desire. It is the form itself, the emptiness that separates the form from the contents, the form that occupies the position of the motive. We act morally when the determining content of our activity becomes the form itself.

What is obscene about this? Perhaps it is that obscenity is precisely the fact of *getting jouissance from the form itself,* from the thing that should be the neutral form, free of any jouissance. Take the example of the authoritarian ideological edifice (of fascism) that draws its support from a purely formal imperative. We have to obey because we have to, we must not question the reasons for obeying; in other words, we must renounce all jouissance, we must sacrifice without having the right to clearly understand the meaning of this sacrifice – the sacrifice is its own end in itself, and this is where the denial of jouissance itself begins to produce a certain surplus jouissance. The intrinsically obscene character of fascism comes from the fact that its ideological form is its own end, which is to say, something that, in the end, does not serve any purpose (the Lacanian definition of jouissance); jouissance emerges directly from the form itself. A wonderful example of this is Mussolini's answer to the question: "What is the fascists' platform that would justify allowing them to rule Italy?" "Our platform is very simple: we want to rule Italy."

This is the obscene dimension of Kantian formalism that emerges in fascism – on this point, Kantian formalism resembles the attitude of the second maxim of Cartesian "provisional morality," which tells us:

> [to imitate] the example of travelers who, when they have lost their way in a forest, ought not to wander from side to side, far less remain in one place, but proceed constantly towards the same side in as straight a line as possible, without changing their direction for slight reasons, although perhaps it might be chance alone which at first determined the selection; for in this way, if they do not exactly reach the point they desire, they will come at least in the end to some place that will probably be preferable to the middle of a forest. (Descartes 2008: 25)

In this passage, it is as if Descartes was tipping the ideological game's hand, revealing its radical directionlessness; the Goal, the Direction, *doesn't matter at all*; the true endpoint of ideology is the attitude itself that ideology demands, the consistency of the ideological *form*, which is to say, the fact of walking "in as straight a line as possible." Its content, the positive reasons that ideology references in order to legitimate its injunction to obey, serve only to conceal this fact, in other words, *to blind us to the surplus jouissance of the form as such*.

This is the location of the aforementioned experience of the blunt stupidity of the law, of the senselessness of its given form. The senselessness that we experience is the senselessness of jouissance itself, the senselessness of the imperative "Jouis!" concealed in the form of ideology. The true importance of this experience is therefore not that we free ourselves from the pathological particularity of social laws, because the thing that is truly senseless is not the pathological content of the Law, but its very form when it comes to be seen as "its-own-end-in-itself."

Kant with Kafka

The fundamental feature of the superego is an impossible imperative that makes the subject guilty. The superego's injunction has no use for excuses – no invocation of our limited capacities can release us; "you can because you must!" (Kant). I've already touched on the contrapositive of this injunction, the paradox of incest: "you must not because you cannot!" – a prohibition that is superfluous because the thing it prohibits is already posited as impossible. The reference to the "objective laws of historical progress" that Stalinist bureaucracy used to legitimate its activity produces a new version of this paradox: *You must because it is objectively necessary!* – this is the paradox of an injunction that orders us to put all our might behind the realization of an inevitable process, toward a result that is "objectively necessary," that will come about independently of our will. The Stalinist "categorical imperative" – "it is your duty to realize a process governed by laws that are independent of your will!" – is taken to its extreme when we define freedom as "the understanding of necessity." In the East German *Philosophical Dictionary*, freedom is defined as the subject "freely desiring" the thing that he understands is necessary.

It is therefore the *subject* who pays the price for the totalitarian "short-circuit." The purest example of this is a person standing accused in one of the political show trials, who is confronted with an impossible choice: his confession is clearly in conflict with the "facts of the matter," the Party demands that he confesses to "false accusations." Moreover, the Party's order operates like a superego imperative, which means that it constitutes the "symbolic reality" for the subjects. Lacan repeatedly emphasized the link between the superego and the so-called "feeling of reality": "When the feeling of foreignness, strangeness, strikes somewhere, it's never on the side of the superego – it's always the ego that loses its bearings" (Lacan 1997b: 277). Doesn't this give us an answer to the question: where did the confessions in the Stalinist show trials come from? For the accused, it was as if there was no "reality" outside the superego of the Party, outside its obscene and malevolent imperative; the only alternative to this superego imperative was the void of an abominable Real, the confession that the Party demanded was the only way for them to avoid the "loss of reality." Let us take a basic example: "You are a traitor, you have betrayed the cause of the proletariat!" This "description of facts" functions as an act that, because it was declared by the Party, excludes the accused from the Party and makes him a traitor.

Therefore, if I, the accused, insist that the Party's accusation is false – if I say, for example, that in Truth I am not a traitor – I *truly* act against the Party, I *effectively oppose* its unity. At the performative level, the only way to affirm "through my actions" my adherence to the Party is to confess. Confess to what? Precisely to my exclusion, that I am in fact a traitor. The Party's order, the order given to the accused during the trials was: "If you want to be a good communist you must confess!" This order literally *divides* the subject, it operates the division between the subject of utterance and the uttering subject. For the communist accused of treason, the only manner to affirm that he is truly a communist at the level of the subject of the utterance is to utter the *statement*: "I confess, I am a traitor."

The fundamental feature of the rise of totalitarianism is therefore that the social law begins to act like a superego. It is no longer the law that prohibits and, through this prohibition, opens and sustains the field of the coexistence of "free" bourgeois subjects and their diverse pleasures – rather, it becomes "mad," it starts directly ordering jouissance. It reaches the point of transformation where the *permission* to pursue jouissance mutates into *obligatory* jouissance. The superego injunction is therefore a "you must feel *jouissance* because you can feel *jouissance!*" – one need hardly mention that this is the most effective means of blocking the subject's access to jouissance. Kafka's works contain a perfect depiction of bureaucracy in the form of an obscene, ferocious, "mad" law, a law that immediately inflicts jouissance, in short: the superego.

"That means I belong to the court," said the priest, "so why should I want anything from you? The court does not want anything from you. It receives you when you come and dismisses you when you go." (Kafka 2009b: 160)

These words, which mark the end of the conversation between K. and the priest in Chapter IX of *The Trial*, are an excellent illustration of the "malevolent neutrality" of the superego. The indifference displayed by saying "I do not want anything of you" contains a call to jouissance that is not so much deliberately concealed as it is *left unsaid*. It is as if this proposition was suspended before it arrived at its "main idea," much like President Schreber's famous interrupted sentences, as if the "positive" imperative that follows from the initial "negative" part is missing. In its full form it would be "the Court does not want anything from you – so *jouis*!" And really, in the very beginning of Kafka's two great novels, *The Trial* and *The Castle*, there are appeals to a power higher than the subject (the Law, the Count), that are examples in which "were the Law to give the order, '*Jouis!*' ['Enjoy!' or 'Come!'], the subject could only reply '*J'ouïs*' ['I hear'], in which the jouissance would no longer be anything but understood [*sous-entendue*]" (Lacan 2006: 696).

Isn't the subject's "misunderstanding," "confusion," when faced with this power caused precisely by the fact that he doesn't understand the imperative to jouissance that breathes and leaks from every pore of this "neutral" surface? Examples of the "mad," obscene side of the law can be found throughout Kafka's work. In *The Trial*, K. is in the empty courtroom where the nocturnal interrogations are held and sneaks a glance into one of the judge's lengthy tomes, immediately stumbling across "an obscene picture . . . , a naked man and woman sitting on a sofa. The artist's pornographic intention was clearly recognizable" (Kafka 2009b: 42). This is the superego: a solemn "indifference" riddled with licentiousness. The same is true in *The Castle*: the Land Surveyor K. is desperately trying to call the castle on the phone. When he's able to access the castle's network, the only thing he hears on the other end of the line is an indistinct, obscene whispering. There is therefore nothing surprising about the reaction of the teacher, whom K. has approached to help him learn about the castle; uncomfortable, the teacher looks back toward his students and whispers to K. in French: "Kindly recollect that we're in the company of innocent children" (Kafka 2009a: 12).

In the texts we can uncover the dimension of the law that is a superego injunction to jouissance. This reading allows us to do away with the idea of "Kafka as the writer of absence," according to which the inaccessible, transcendent power (the Castle, the Tribunal) occupies the space of lack, of pure absence. According to this view, Kafka's "secret" is that at the heart of the bureaucratic machinery there is emptiness, a Void. "Bureaucracy" would be a machine gone mad that "kept running on its own." But such a reading misses the way in which this absence, this empty space, is always-already filled by an *inert*, obscene, dirty, repugnant presence. The Tribunal in *The Trial* is certainly present in the form of the depraved judge who, during the nighttime interrogations, leafs through pornographic books; the Castle is present in the form of the lazy and corrupt lower-level bureaucrats. In Kafka, the idea "God is absent" leads to a dead end. The problem is quite the opposite because, in this universe, God is *too present* – through a modality, of course, but not a reassuring one: that of repugnant, obscene phenomena. The universe of Kafka is a world in which God – who had up until then remained at a substantial distance – has come too close. The exegete's theory that Kafka's universe is one of anxiety must be interpreted against the background of the Lacanian definition of anxiety: we are anxious when we are too close to *das Ding*. This is Kafka's theological lesson: the mad, obscene God, the "supremely-evil-being" (Lacan 2006: 832), is exactly the same God as the God of Supreme Good – the difference is only that we are now too close to Him.

This is why Kafka wrote that when it comes to "the origins of human nature, . . . the bureaucracy is closer than any social institution" (1977: 327). What is this "original human nature" if not the fact that from the very beginning man is a "being of language"? And what is the superego – the mode in which bureaucratic knowledge operates – if not, to borrow from Jacques-Alain Miller, the thing that presentifies the pure form of the signifier as the cause of subject's scission, which is to say, the intervention of the signifying order in all of its senselessness and deregulation?

"The Law is the Law"

> Therefore, totalitarianism grounds itself upon the final, unexplained, inexplicable mainspring upon which the existence of the law hangs. The tough thing we encounter in the analytic experience is that there is one, there is a law. And that indeed is what can never be completely brought to completion in the discourse of the law – it is the final term which explains that there is one. (Lacan 1991b: 129)

If the spirit is the Love and the letter of the Law, we have to invert Duhamel's famous quote: true love can come only from the authority of the law, specifically an irreducibly and constitutively "misunderstood," "traumatic" law – the law of a blind automatism. This is what is "scandalous" about Pascal. The experience of "faith," the most "internal" feeling, deeper and more constant than any argumentative proof, is based on some external "dead letter," on submission to a "custom" that the subject *does not understand.* In the end, in the case of belief, "the automaton unconsciously drags the mind along."

We try to cover over the fact that the "abyss" of custom is the "mystical foundation" of law through the ideological-imaginary lived experience of the law's "meaning," rationalizing its authority through appeal to justice, goodness, utility, etc. There are so many attempts to cover over the unbearable void of the signifier-without-signified, to replace it with a full signified that would guarantee the law's "Truth":

> It would therefore be a good thing if the laws and customs were obeyed because they were laws . . . But the people are not open to this doctrine. And so, as they believe that truth can be found and that it lies in laws and customs, they believe them and take their antiquity as a proof of their truth (and not simply of their authority, without truth). (Pascal 2008: 110–11)

We can find the same idea in *The Trial*, near the end of the conversation between K. and the priest:

> "I don't agree with that opinion," K. said, shaking his head. "If one accepts it, one has to take everything the doorkeeper says as the truth. But that isn't possible, as you yourself have demonstrated at great length." "No," said the priest, "one doesn't have to take everything as the truth, one just has to accept it as necessary." "A depressing opinion," said K. "It means that the world is founded on untruth." (Kafka 2009b: 159)

What we have therefore is the Law's *"necessity"/"authority" without truth.* The fact that the people believe that there is truth "in laws and customs," that they "take their antiquity as a proof of their truth (and not simply of their authority, without truth),"" is a very good description of the imaginary blindness to the senseless and traumatic form that the Law has taken, in short: the *Real* of the Law. If, then, "custom" contains the automatism of a blind and misunderstood law, why don't we identify it directly with the law, why don't we reduce it to an imaginary form in which law appears? In every ideological edifice, there is a paradoxical point that requires us to distinguish the two – as Brecht's "learning-plays" show us.

The fundamental moment in these learning-plays is *Einverständniss*, the giving of consent, when a subject consents to an obligation imposed on him by the community (generally involving sacrificing his life). As the Master explains in simpler terms to the young child in *He Said Yes* [*Der Jasager*], it is customary to ask the victim if he consents to being thrown off the cliff, but it is also customary that the victim think about it for a minute and then say yes. The pact that unites the community and the subject is fundamentally asymmetric; at a certain point the former says to the latter: "I give you the freedom to choose, provided that you make the right choice." The paradox of "voluntary servitude" is based on the constitutive short-circuit of the ideological field. Sooner or later, there will come a point where the subject is confronted with just such an impossible choice – he can freely choose between "for" and "against," but as soon as he picks wrong, he loses the right to choose. In other words, the field of ideological commandments necessarily includes a paradoxical point of "good behavior," in which commandment transforms itself into courtesy, into politeness, into a *respect for proper etiquette*.

Recently in Yugoslavia, a student completing his military service refused to sign the oath stating that he would be willing to sacrifice his life to defend the Homeland. He justified his refusal by saying that it is his decision whether or not to sign the oath, but that if any officer formally ordered him to sign, he would be happy to do so right away. His commanding officers patiently explained to him that they could not give him such an order because the whole point of the oath is the fact that he decides to sign it of his own free will, but that if he refuses to do so, he will be thrown in prison. The affair went all the way to the military tribunal where the student achieved his goal by obtaining a formal injunction ordering him to sign the oath – an "impossible" injunction, because it ordered him to make a free decision. It is not a coincidence that this paradox emerged around the question of military service, as it necessarily emerges in the place where the subject has to affirm that he fundamentally belongs to the community. Essentially, it requires a formal gesture through which the subject must freely choose to be a part of the community to which he already belongs.

Forced choice

Where in the history of philosophy do we first find this paradox of forced choice? It's already present in good old Kant, who saw choosing evil as a transcendental, a priori act. This was how he tried to make sense of a common feeling one has when faced with an evil person. One feels that this person's evilness is not simply a matter of circumstance, but that it stems from his fundamental character, that it is part of his unchanging nature. Evil seems to be an unchangeable and irrevocable trait that the person in question will never be able to change, will never be able to cast off through further moral development. Moreover, you have the impression, which at first seems contradictory, that the evil person is entirely responsible for their evilness, even though it comes from his always-already given nature. "Being evil" is not the same thing as being stupid or irritable, or any of the other traits that come from one's psychology. We always feel that Evil is a choice, a free decision for which the subject is entirely responsible. How can we resolve this contradiction between human evil's preordained, given nature and its free nature? Kant's solution is that we must think of choosing evil, deciding in favor of evil, as a transcendental, a-temporal, a priori, act. This decision does not occur at a particular place in time; rather, it is the framework itself of the person in question's development, of his practical activity.

In his treatise on freedom – the "apogee of German idealism" according to Heidegger – Schelling radicalized Kant's theory by introducing the radical distinction between freedom (which is to say, freedom of choice) and consciousness. For him, the a-temporal choice in which the subject decides to be good or evil is unconscious. One cannot help but be reminded of the Freudian claim that the unconscious is fundamentally a-temporal.

But back to Schelling's argument. Freedom is posited as the cause of evil, which is to say that evil is the result, the product, of the subject's free decision in favor of evil. However, if freedom is the cause of evil, how can we explain psychological and moral faults that do not seem to depend on our conscious will? The only possible solution is to claim that evil is a fundamental choice, one that *precedes* our conscious choices, and therefore an unconscious choice.

Schelling's solution goes against Fichte's subjective idealism, which reduced free action to action which reflects one's consciousness-of-self. Schelling starts his argument with the relatively common psychological observation: sometimes I feel responsible even in the absence of determined will on my part, a sinner without actual sin, guilty even though I didn't do anything. Psychoanalysis is quite familiar with this feeling of "irrational," excessive guilt. At first this guilt seems "inexplicable," but for analysts it masks an unconscious desire, and Schelling interprets this feeling in a quite similar way: "irrational" guilt stems from an unconscious choice, an unconscious decision in favor of evil. Everything happens as if we had already made up our minds before we awakened into consciousness. The memory of our culpability induces an anamnesis that reveals to us our own evil will, our choice to be evil that preceded our conscious decisions. Human freedom, conscious of a world in which chaos and suffering already exist, cannot question its own guilt without admitting that it is tied to its own fundamental, unconscious choice of evil. The core of Schelling's argument can be found in this really quite beautiful passage:

> In original creation, as has been shown, man is an undetermined entity (which may be mythologically presented as a condition antecedent to this life, a state of innocence and of initial bliss). He alone can determine himself. But this determination cannot occur in time; it occurs outside of time altogether and hence it coincides with the first creation even though as an act differentiated from it. Man, even though born in time, is nonetheless a creature of creation's beginning (the centrum). The act which determines man's life in time does not itself belong in time but in eternity. Moreover it does not precede life in time but occurs throughout time (untouched by it) as an act external by its own nature. Through it man's life extends to the beginning of creation, since by means of it he is also more than creature, free and himself eternal beginning. Though this idea may seem beyond the grasp of common ways of thought, there is in every man a feeling which is in accord with it, as if each man felt that he had been what he is from all eternity, and had in no sense only come to be so in time. Thus, the undeniable necessity of all actions notwithstanding, though everyone must admit, if he observes himself, that he is in no wise good or bad by accident or choice, yet a bad person, for instance, seems to himself anything but compelled (since compulsion can only be felt in becoming, not in being) but performs his acts willfully, not against his will. That Judas became a traitor to Christ, neither he nor any creature could alter; nonetheless he betrayed Christ not under compulsion but willingly and with full freedom. . . . To be sure, this free act which becomes necessity cannot occur in consciousness, insofar as it is mere self-awareness and only ideal consciousness, since the act precedes it as it precedes being and indeed produces it. But, nevertheless, it is not at all an act of which no consciousness remains to man. Thus someone, who perhaps to excuse a wrong act, says: "Well, that's the way I am," is himself well aware that he is so because of his own fault, however correct he may be in thinking that it would have been impossible for him to act differently. How often does it not happen that a man shows a tendency to evil from childhood on, from a time when, empirically viewed, we can scarcely attribute freedom and deliberation to him, so that we can anticipate that neither punishment nor teaching will move him, and who subsequently really turns out to be the twisted limb which we anticipated in the bent twig. But no one questions his responsibility,

and all are as convinced of the guilt of this person as one could be if every single act had been in his control. This common judgment of a tendency to do evil (a tendency which in its origin is entirely uncon-scious and even irresistible), as being a free deed, points to an act and thus to a life before this life. (Schelling 1992: 64–5)

Need I add that Schelling's description of original choice corresponds perfectly to the Lacanian concept of the Real; a construct, in this case an act, that never took place in reality, but that must nonetheless be presupposed in order for us to make sense of things as they are? This brings us back to the poor student; the impasse he encounters is just the same as the one present in Schelling's free act. Certainly, in the actual course of his temporal life, he never chose his Homeland, but he is treated as if he had already made this decision and shouldered the corresponding obligations, which is to say, as if his decision were a-temporal, always in the past, as if he had already chosen the thing that had been, from the very beginning, imposed upon him: the fact that he belongs to the Homeland.

This paradox of forced choice, in which the subject chooses (through a Real action that is presupposed, retroactively constructed) the very thing that is imposed upon him, this paradox of the subject who supposedly chooses, is fundamental to the subject of the signi-fier's subjugation to the communal Other. This is why the puzzled officers were correct in treating the student as if he was "crazy." There is nothing "crazy" about the paradox of forced choice; on the contrary, the "crazy" person is the person who acts *as if he really had a free choice*, as if he could truly make this decision freely, for-getting the radical consequences implied by his status as a subject. Here we have a variation on "the Other has no Other"; there is no choice of choice, the field of choice always contains a forced choice – if, at this point, we make the wrong choice, we lose the very freedom to choose itself. And the location of the barred subject is precisely the location of the impossible-void of this false choice. The subject is like the retroactive result of his own choice; the paradox of Münchhausen, who lifted himself up by his own hair, is inscribed in the very condition of being subject.

Radical evil

I have already underlined the way in which Schelling's theory is simply the radicalization of Kant. This is why Lacan was altogether correct when he located the starting point of the "movement of ideas" that culminated with Freud in Kant's philosophy, specifically in his *Critique of Practical Reason* (cf. Lacan 2006: 644–5). One of the consequences of the Kantian revolution in the domain of "practical reason," one which is usually ignored, is that for perhaps the first time in the history of ideas, Kant granted *Evil as such a properly ethical status.* With the idea of an "original evil" inscribed in a person's timeless character, evil became a matter of principle, an ethical position – ethical in the specific sense of a will that is beyond the pleasure principle (and its extension, the reality principle).

Evil was no longer simple opportunistic behavior guided only by "pathological" motivations (pleasure, profit, utility, . . .). Quite the opposite, in fact: evil became a matter of the eternal and autonomous character of the person in question, stemming from an original, a-temporal decision. Lacan's paradoxical coupling of Kant and Sade – along with the Kantian view of evil – was illustrated, in Kant's own time, by the emergence of a whole series of literary and musical figures who embody Evil as an ethical position, from Mozart's Don Giovanni to Byron's romantic heroes.

Traditionally, Good and Evil have been contrasted as pure and impure. According to a long tradition that goes back all the way to stoicism and Plato, a *good* person is one who is able to purify his will of everything that is natural, of all sensuousness, all venality, all self-serving motives, etc., whereas an *evil* individual is one who remains immersed in sensuality, prisoner of the network of the heterogeneous and heteronymous motives of lust, power, and other worldly pleasures. Schelling went against this whole tradition, arguing that an evil will possesses the same pure and chaste character, the same liberation from any natural heteronymous motive, as we find in the supposedly moral will. In the natural, immediate, spontaneous being there will always be something innocent, perhaps even good. This is why the requirement of purity, the negation of natural spontaneity, is much more clearly delineated in the evil than in the good. Schelling explicitly describes the distinction between evil, true evil, "diabolical evil," and pleasure:

> Anyone who is familiar with the mysteries of evil (which we must ignore in our hearts, but not in our heads), knows that the greatest corruption is also the most spiritual. It rids itself of everything natural, all sensuality, all licentiousness, and becomes cruelty. The most diabolical evil is far more removed from jouissance than is the good. (Schelling 1856–61: 468)

Schelling emphasizes just how terrifying the encounter with such a pure will can be. Whether it is good or evil, a pure will is always fascinating and alluring, captivating in an almost magical way. The existence of a pure will is almost miraculous, like a decision made for no reason whatsoever, one that felt no need to justify itself and only seems to base itself on – to put this in contemporary terms – the act of its own utterance. The contradiction between the pure, spiritual will and the impure will, which is bogged down in the empirical and determined by a chain of natural causes, is similar to the distinction between the *principle of identity* and the *principle of reason*. The impure, heteronymous will acts according to the principle of sufficient reason. Its actions are always triggered by some external motive (the representation of an object, a potential profit, a glimpsed pleasure). Because of this, we can place it in the chain of cause and effect, in the natural order of the "connection of things" – if we can control its causes, we can master it (this is Bentham's formula). Pure, free will, however, operates according to an "unfathomable" principle. Contemplating its existence, you get a vertiginous feeling, as if you were gazing into the vicious circle of a whirlpool, a maelstrom. In an act of pure will, it is as if the principle of sufficient reason is temporarily suspended, put into parenthesis. If we ask for the motive behind an act of pure will, the only answer that we can get is the tautology "I want to because I want to."

When a free act of pure will occurs, it is always unexpected; it is, to put it in Lacanian terms, an S1, a master-signifier. The fascinating, quasi-mystical, hypnotic power that a free act of pure will holds over humans is the same fascinating power as the master-signifier emerging from the S2 chain, breaking through the network of "knowing" about cause and effect and seeming to rely on no authority but its own. The importance of what Schelling does here is that he shows us the abyss, the traumatic, radically contingent, other side of the irruption of a new master-signifier.

Instead of being simply a relic of German Idealism, Schelling's theory of the tautology-abyss contained within the free act is still just as relevant to contemporary philosophy. Donald Davidson, for example, in his essay "How is Weakness of the Will Possible?" (1980), addresses the same problem. Davidson asks the following question: how is it possible that between two acts (*a* and *b*), someone could choose *b*, if an examination of all the relevant reasons would conclusively lead to a preference for *a*? He resolves this problem by introducing the distinction between conditional judgments that take all relevant reasons into consideration (all things considered) and unconditional judgments that cause us to act. It is inconsistent but not logically contradictory for the subject to unconditionally choose *b*, even though he knows that *a* is clearly preferable all things considered. Davidson describes the difference between S2 (the chain of sufficient reasons) and the unconditional/abyss/tautology of S1. I can act "because I want to," unconcerned with the chain of reasons. His key insight is his emphasis on the fact that this inconsistency (choosing *b* even though, all things considered, *a* is preferable) has nothing to do with the moralizing opposition between duty and egotistical interests. It is not a question of giving in to pleasure and doing *b* when our duty requires us to do *a*. In general, it is actually *a* (the preferable act, all things considered) that is mandated by the pleasure principle (and its extension, the reality principle). By choosing *a*, we choose the thing that is Good for us, while the choice of *b* could only be guided by something "beyond the pleasure principle." The only thing that we can reproach Davidson for is his inapt, incongruent, expression "the weakness of the will." In fact, it is quite the opposite; what we have here is an example of the *power* of our will, of its ability to break through the chain of sufficient reasons through an act of pure freedom, justified only by itself.

Divine prehistory

Schelling's theory of an "original evil" that is inscribed in the subject's timeless character and thus independent of contingent circumstances is simply the radicalization of Kant. Schelling's original insight was the step he took that would have been unthinkable for Kant, for whom the idea of the Absolute, of God, remained that of the Supreme Good, of Perfection lacking in nothing. The effective form of Schelling's argument was to base the possibility of human "original evil" – which is chosen a-temporally – in a lack in the Other (the Absolute) itself, in a fissure at the core of God, in the chasm between the actual, existing God who takes the form of *logos*, and the "ground" ["*Grund*"], the opaque, dark, impenetrable, Real [*das Reale*] of God, "that which, in God himself, is not yet God," his blind *drive* [*das Trieb*].

In the beginning – not in the beginning of time, the temporal beginning that coincides with the birth of the Son, of the divine Word, but rather the absolute beginning, the zero point of divine prehistory – God is absolute indifference, an undesiring desire, tranquility and beatitude, pure feminine jouissance; an unlimited, non-totalized Whole, the last stage of mystical ecstasy, pure expansion in a void that has no consistency, no foundation, and is therefore an abyss [*Un-Grund*] in the proper sense of the word. Divine prehistory begins with an initial *contraction* [*Zusammernziehung*], with its own constriction. This is how God gave Himself a solid, dense foundation, consistency as a Oneness, how He made Himself into something that exists, into a *subject*. This contraction is the supreme act of divine egoism, it is the very opposite itself of love, of pacifying calm. It is a return back onto the self, a destructive fury that annihilates everything that comes into contact with the divine One:

> This is the . . . fate of all life, that it first desires limitation, and wants to go from breadth to closeness, in order to perceive itself. After that, if it is in constriction and has felt constrained, it again desires to go back into breadth, and would like to return straightaway into the peaceful nought in which it was before. (Schelling 1942: 209)

All divine life prior to the birth of the Son, before the appearance of the Word, can be summarized by this back-and-forth between the void of limitless expansion and the force that opposes it, which contracts and limits itself, which folds back in on itself. In the course he taught from 1986 to 1987, Jacques-Alain Miller developed the thesis that, for the neo-Platonists, the initial division of the One of jouissance was – to put it in Lacanian mathemes – the division between Φ and *a*. Isn't Schelling's account of the initial division of the divine *Un-Grund* between contraction and expansion the same as the division between the Φ of phallic jouissance and the *a* of expansion, of limitless dispersion?

The verb "to contract" is ambiguous, as it can also be used to refer to disease. Pure divine will contracts its heaviness, its ground, its solid and dense consistency – it contracts them like a madness, like a divine illness. The birth of the Son is the way that the Word found to resolve this unbearable antagonism. It is with the emergence of the Word that "time begins." *Logos* distinguished the present from the past, it relegated the dark prehistory of divine rage, madness, the primitive and horrible "whirlwind" of divine drives, to the past. The *logos*, the Word of the Son, is here identified with the divine Light whose outpouring let things be, gave them their being. The arrival of the Word should therefore be understood in the sense of a primary procedure (Freudian *Bejahung* as opposed to *Verwerfung*), "which is no other than the primordial condition for something from reality to come to offer itself up to the revelation of being, or, to employ Heidegger's language, to be let-be" (Lacan 2006: 323). We could say then that this *Bejahung forecloses* the unbearable antagonism of divine madness, consigning it into an impossible-Real past, excluded by symbolization. Lacan himself emphasized that the movement of symbolization, of realization in the symbolic, always entails a certain rejection of the world of shadows, of the unrealized (cf. Lacan 1991a), just as, as Schelling said, the necessary other side of the arrival of the Word, the birth of the Son, is the rejection, the expulsion into the past of the "primitive whirlwind" of divine drives.

We should focus here on the pacifying, liberating character of the arrival of the Word. The entrance of the Symbolic, of Difference, is a relief, it is a liberation from infinite pain, from an unbearable antagonism. Divine life prior to the birth of the Son was a tension that descended into madness. It was – to put it in analytic terms – a world without an opening, before the arrival of the symbolic, a sealed world without distance, a world in which the real God, in his "terrible loneliness," was constantly choking on his own rage, a world that was *psychotic* in the full sense of the term. At this level, there is no *difference* proper – because this would imply that there was already an opposition, a symbolic articulation – only the beating, hammering, pulsing, back and forth between Nothing and One, between expansion and contraction. Schelling puts his own spin on the pantheistic formulation of God as All-One by focusing on His "nocturnal" side, which is generally as misunderstood by partisans as by critics. "Most of those who speak of the All-One see only the All; that there is a One, a subject, is something that they have not yet noticed." The One is precisely the "horrible loneliness," the "autism" of divine jouissance prior to the creation of the world.

If I may, I will risk putting forward the thesis that prior to the creation of the world, which is to say, before the birth of the Son, God was a "manic-depressive," caught in a back-and-forth from which there was no exit, no opening of any kind, an oscillation between the Nothing of the dispersion of an empty force and destructive rage, correlative to the well-known feeling of the "end of the world," the destruction of the universe. And the birth of the Son, the arrival of the Word, the creation of the world were "therapeutic." God mastered his internal antagonism, his tension, the barrier inside himself, through the externalization of conflict, by redirecting it outside, by directing his pulsing energy toward what we call a "creative goal." To the question "Why did God create the world?" Schelling replies: "It was a form of 'creative therapy' to save himself from his own madness." We must therefore admit that within the divine life there was "a moment of blindness and madness" (Marquet 1973: 500), a moment that was absolutely necessary in order for God to take on the consistency of a Oneness, of a subject, in order for Him not to lose himself in the void of limitless expansion.

Why is madness inherent to the divine life? Because the process of divine history was "a project in which God himself was engaged – if

I dare to say it – at his own risk" (Marquet 1973: 542) – to put this in more contemporary terms, it is because God does not occupy the position of metalanguage.

And all of Schelling's later work in developing a "philosophy of revelation" was only a desperate attempt to extricate himself from this position and find a way to avoid the risk of divine madness by positing that *God already possessed His own being*. God is posited as the Supreme Being whose existence was a necessary, *sine qua non*, condition of his freedom as Creator. This cancels out the short-circuit of divine madness; on the one hand we have the divine person, the God who must exist and who has the power to create, a God sheltered from the risks of creation, and on the other we have the amorphous material that awaits the intervention of the divine formative force. Therefore God is, in a strict sense, *outside of history*, he keeps himself at a distance, in a secure position from which he can intervene through *revelation*.

Why is this mythical account of "divine prehistory" relevant in our present day? At first, tying Evil and madness together like this seems like a pre-scientific understanding of things, harking back to a time when madness was considered an indication of moral corruption. However, if we read Schelling's work retrospectively, through the lens of Lacan's "return to Freud," we can see the pre-emptive outlines of the key Lacanian argument that madness rests upon freedom, upon an original choice.

> [F]ar from being an "insult" to freedom, madness is freedom's most faithful companion, following its every move like a shadow. Not only can man's being not be understood without madness, but it would not be man's being if it did not bear madness within itself as the limit of his freedom. (Lacan 2006: 144)

In other words, doesn't Schelling pre-emptively herald – beyond any Jungian obscurantist reading – Lacan's "no clinical without the ethical" ["*pas de clinique sans éthique*"]?

12

Between Two Deaths: Third, and Final, Attempt at Defining "Totalitarianism"

The second death

Sade's idea of an absolute, radical crime that would liberate the creative forces of Nature is rooted in his distinction between the two deaths, which he develops in the Pope's lengthy speech in Book V of *Juliette*. There is natural death, which is part of the natural cycle of reproduction and corruption, decomposition and recomposition, and therefore the incessant transformation of Nature. Then there is absolute death, which is the destruction, the annihilation, of this cycle itself, which would liberate Nature from its own laws and thus open a space for the creation of new forms of life *ex nihilo*. The difference between the two deaths is related to Sade's fantasies, because in his works the victim is, in a certain sense, indestructible. He can torture her and torture her, and she endures it all, suffering every torment without losing her beauty. It is as if beyond her natural, ordinary body – which is part of the cycle of reproduction and corruption – and therefore beyond natural death, she had another body, a body made from a special stuff, a body exempted from the cycle of life – a sublime body.

Today we can find examples of this very same fantasy at work in various products of "mass culture." Take cartoons, for example. Tom and Jerry, the cat and the mouse, are constantly subjected to horrible pain. The cat gets stabbed or the dynamite in his pocket explodes or he gets run over by a steamroller and is flattened like a pancake, and so forth. But in the next scene his body is as good as new and the game can start all over again – as if he had another body, one that was indestructible. Or take the example of video games in which there is a literal difference between the two deaths. Normally, the way these games work is that the player (or, more specifically, the avatar that represents the player) has several lives, often three. He is threatened by some danger, like a monster that wishes to eat him, and if the monster catches him he loses a life. But, if he reaches his goal quickly enough, he wins an extra life or two. The entire logic of these games is therefore founded on the difference between the two deaths: between the death in which I lose one of my lives and the final death in which I lose the game itself.

Lacan understood the difference between these two deaths as the difference between effective death and symbolic death, the "settling of accounts," the fulfillment of symbolic destiny. It is possible for a temporal gap to exist between the two deaths. In the case of Antigone, for example, symbolic death, the exclusion from the symbolic community of the city, precedes real death, which is what gives her person a certain kind of sublime beauty. The ghost of Hamlet's father, on the other hand, is an example of the opposite. In *Hamlet* we have a case of real death without symbolic death, before accounts have been settled, and this is why the father will return as a frightening apparition until his son settles the debt.

This space "between two deaths" is a place of sublime beauty and horrifying monsters; it is the location of *das Ding*, the object-cause of desire, the Real-traumatic kernel at the heart of the symbolic. It is opened by symbolization/historicization itself. The process of historicization contains an empty space, an ahistorical kernel around which the symbolic network articulates itself. In other words, human *history* distinguishes itself from animal *evolution* precisely because of its reference to this *ahistoric*, un-historicizable space, which is the retroactive product of symbolization itself. As soon as reality is symbolized/historicized, we distinguish it from the empty space of the Thing. It is this reference to an empty space that makes it possible for us to imagine the possibility of the total, complete annihilation of the signifying network. The "second death," the radical obliteration of the natural cycle, is only conceivable if this cycle is already symbolized/historicized, inscribed in the symbolic network. Our imagination can only grasp absolute death, the destruction of the universe, as the destruction of the symbolic universe. The "death drive" is the Freudian name for what Sade called the "second death," it is the possibility of a-history that is opened by the process of symbolization/historicization.

In the entire history of Marxism, there was probably only a single moment in which the ahistorical character of history was glimpsed, in which historical reflection was taken all the way to the point where the "death instinct" became the zero hour of history: Walter Benjamin's final work, *On the Concept of History*. Moreover, Benjamin was precisely the person who – and this too was unique in the history of Marxism – understood history as a text, as a series of events that "will have happened," which is to say whose signification will be settled after the fact, through their inscription in the symbolic network.

Benjamin: revolution as repetition

Benjamin was so exceptional precisely because he was the only one who thought to look for energy of the Revolution in the phantasy inertia of the Real. In the entirety of Marxist tradition – and I am including "critical social theory" here – phantasmic inertia has always been seen as an obstacle that hindered the revolutionary desires of the masses, manifesting itself in the "irrational" behavior of the masses, causing them to act "against their own true interests" (a fascist mob, for example). Normally it is seen as something that must be suppressed – it is seen basically as a symptom of "reactionary" jouissance that must be untangled through a clear-eyed dialectical analysis. This brings out the radical difference between Benjamin and Adorno, who was the quintessential dialectician, and helps us to define the position of Benjamin's paradoxical "internal externality" with respect to the field of "critical social theory." On one side we have Adorno, caught up in the interpretative leap, in the constant movement of reflection and self-reflection, and on the other is Benjamin, focused on the imagery of phantasy. However, his thoughts contained in *On the Concept of History*, intercalated and seeming almost to come from a different field, are not just at odds with "critical social theory," but with the evolution of Benjamin's intellectual development itself. The traditional story about how Benjamin's thinking evolved is that over time he gradually approached Marxism. *On the Concept of History* marks a clear break from any account of this sort. It was written at the very end of Benjamin's theoretical path, and it was only at this precise moment that the *theological* problematic emerged. The only way for historical materialism to achieve victory is if it "employs the services of theology" – here is Benjamin's famous first thesis:

> It is well known that an automaton once existed, which was so constructed that it could counter any move of a chess-player with a counter-move, and thereby assure itself of victory in the match. A

puppet in Turkish attire, water-pipe in mouth, sat before the chess-board, which rested on a broad table. Through a system of mirrors, the illusion was created that this table was transparent from all sides. In truth, a hunchbacked dwarf who was a master chess-player sat inside, controlling the hands of the puppet with strings. One can envision a corresponding object to this apparatus in philosophy. The puppet called "historical materialism" is always supposed to win. It can do this with no further ado against any opponent, so long as it employs the services of theology, which as everyone knows is small and ugly and must be kept out of sight. (Benjamin 2009: 2)

What is perhaps most striking here is the contradiction between the allegory as it gives itself to be read in the first part of the thesis and the interpretation of it that Benjamin gives in the second part of the thesis. In his interpretation, it is historical materialism that "employs the services of" theology, whereas, in the allegory itself, it is theology (the "hunchbacked dwarf") who pulls the strings from inside, who controls the "puppet" of historical materialism. Of course, this contradiction is none other than the difference between the allegorical figure and its final meaning, between the signifier and signified, the latter which thinks that it can "make use of" the signifier as tool, but which, through this, itself becomes more and more enmeshed in the signifier's network. In this case, the two levels overlap; the formal structure of Benjamin's allegory does not function any differently from its contents – theology in relation to historical materialism which thinks that it can simply make use of theology, but which in fact gets caught in its net – because this "theology," if I may permit myself this *Vorlust,* does a good job of representing the instance of the signifier.

But let's take this one step at a time: what was the theological dimension for Benjamin? If this following fragment from Benjamin's papers is any indication, it is a completely unique experience: "In *Eingedenken,* we discover the experience that forbids us to conceive history as thoroughly a-theological" (Walter Benjamin cited in A.E. Benjamin and Osborne 1994: 105). We cannot translate this *Eingedenken* as simple "remembrance" or "reminiscence." A more literary translation, "transposing into thought inside of something," doesn't work either. Even if it does in fact refer to a certain kind of "appropriation of the past," we cannot adequately understand *Eingedenken* if we remain within the framework of hermeneutics. Benjamin's aim is the exact opposite of the fundamental axiom of hermeneutical understanding: "a text must be interpreted within the entire context of its time." For Benjamin, it is a question of isolating a fragment of the past from the continuum of history, "thus exploding a specific life out of the epoch, or a specific work out of the life-work" (A.E. Benjamin and Osborne 1994: 19), an interpretive procedure whose contrast with the hermeneutical process is reminiscent of the Freudian distinction between interpretation *en détail* and interpretation *en masse* (cf. Freud 2010: 128).

This rejection of hermeneutics is not some lapse into pre-hermeneutic *naïveté*, it is not a question of "becoming accustomed" to the past by trying to abstract the actual position from which one is speaking. *Eingedenken* is an "interested" appropriation on the part of the oppressed class. "To articulate what is past does not mean to recognize 'how it really was'" (Benjamin 2009: 6). "The subject of historical cognition is the battling, oppressed class itself" (2009: 14). However, it would also be a mistake to think that he's advocating some sort of Nietzschean historiography in which the "interpretation is the will to power," the conqueror has the right to "write his own history," to legitimate his own "perspective," which is to say, if we tried to read Benjamin's theses as some kind of call for a struggle between the two classes, the ruling class and the lower class, around the question of "who will write history." This might be true for the ruling class, but it is not true for the underclass; there is a fundamental asymmetry between the two, which Benjamin explains by referencing two modes of temporality. There is the empty, homogeneous, and continuous time (of the dominant historiography) and the filled, discontinuous time (of historical materialism). The traditional historiographic perspective, which limits itself to only "that which actually happened," making history into a sealed, linear, homogenous course, is already a priori, in its form, the perspective of "those who have won." It sees history as the closed continuum of "progress" that resulted in the existing system of domination, all while abstracting things that are *missing* from history, that which had to be *denied* in order for us to establish "that which really happened." The dominant historiography writes a "positive" history of grand accomplishments and glorious cultural heritage, while for the historical materialist:

> What he surveys as the cultural heritage is part and parcel of a lineage [*Abkunft*: descent] which he cannot contemplate without horror. It owes its existence not only to the toil of the great geniuses, who created it, but also to the nameless drudgery of its contemporaries. There has never been a document of culture, which is not simultaneously one of barbarism. (Benjamin 2009: 7)

Contrary to this, the underclass appropriates the past to the extent that the past is "open," insofar as it already contains – through the very things that have been muffled and stifled – the horizon of the future, the "aspiration for redemption [*Erloesung*]." "The past carries a secret index with it, by which it is referred to its resurrection" (2009: 2). In order to appropriate the dimension of the past that has been stifled – the future of our own revolutionary action that, through its repetition, will retroactively liberate the past – we must break with the continuous current of historical development, making "the tiger's leap into that which has gone before" (2009: 16). It is only here that we arrive at the fundamental asymmetry between historiographic evolutionism that describes history as a continuous movement forward and historical materialism: "The historical materialist cannot do without the concept of a present which is not a transition, in which time originates and has come to a standstill" (2009: 18), and:

> Thinking involves not only the movement of thoughts but also their zero-hour [*Stillstellung*]. Where thinking suddenly halts in a constellation overflowing with tensions, there it yields a shock of the same, through which it crystallizes as a monad. The historical materialist approaches a historical object solely and alone where he encounters it as a monad. In this structure he cognizes the sign of a messianic zero-hour of events, or put differently, a revolutionary chance in the struggle for the suppressed past. (2009: 19)

This is the first surprise: for Benjamin, the unique feature of historical materialism is – contrary to the Marxist dogma – its ability to *halt* the movement of history, to *isolate* a detail from the totality of history. It is precisely this crystallization, this hardening of movement into a monad, that marks the moment at which the past has been appropriated. The monad is a given moment to which the past directly – which is to say, transversally to the continuous line of evolution – attaches itself. The monad is the true revolutionary situation understood as the repetition of past missed opportunities and the possibility of "redeeming" them at long last through revolutionary activity. The past itself is "full of the present"; when the outcome of a revolution is still unclear, it is not just its own fate that hangs in the balance, but that of all earlier attempted revolutions: "For historical materialism it is a question of holding fast to a picture of the past, just as if it had unexpectedly thrust itself, in a moment of danger, on the historical subject" (2009: 6). The danger that the defeat of a current revolution poses to the past comes from the fact that the existing revolutionary constellation functions as the condensation of past revolutionary missed opportunities that are repeated through it:

History is the object of a construction whose place is formed not in homogenous and empty time, but in that which is fulfilled in the here-and-now [*Jetztzeit*]. For Robespierre, Roman antiquity was a past charged with the here-and-now, which he exploded out of the continuum of history. The French Revolution thought of itself as a latter day Rome. (2009: 16)

For anyone familiar with Freud's claim that "the unconscious is located outside of time," it is all already there. In this "full time," in the "tiger's leap" of the present into the past, we can see Freudian "compulsive repetition." Stopping movement, the suspension of the temporal continuum that Benjamin speaks of, is exactly this "short-circuit" between old speech and present speech, in which "present speech, like the old speech, is placed within a parenthesis of time, within a form of time, if I can put it that way. The modulation of time being identical, the speech of the analyst [for Benjamin: of the historical materialist] happens to have the same value as the old speech" (Lacan 1991a: 243). In the monad, "time stops." An old constellation imposes itself onto the current constellation, through a process of pure repetition. The monad is "outside of time," not in the sense of some pre-logical archaism, but in the sense of pure synchronic significance. We should no longer search for the link between the old constellation and the present constellation in the diachronic line, but rather in an immediate paradigmatic short-circuit. The monad is the moment of discontinuity, of rupture, in which the linear course crystallizes, freezes, because in it – transversally to the linear succession of the "march of time" – it contains the direct echoes of a past that has been repressed, excluded from the line of continuity dictated by the dominant historiography. This is the true point of the "dialectic in suspense," of pure repetition in which historical movement is suspended, put in parentheses.

An appropriation of the past in which it will be "freed" by the present, and thus in some way included in it, can only be realized through a total suspension of movement, in a moment of equivalency between the past and the present – in a signifying synchrony. Now we can see what the isolation of the monad from the continuum of history really is: a signifier that has been abstracted, which puts the totality of the signification in parentheses. This bracketing is the necessary condition for the short-circuit between the past and the present. Their synchronization occurs at the level of the autonomy of the signifier. Therefore, we cannot be surprised if this "insertion [*Einschluss*] of the past into the texture of the present day" rests upon a metaphor of text, of history as text:

If one looks upon history as a text, then one can say of it what a recent author has said of literary texts – namely, that the past has left in them images comparable to those registered by a light-sensitive plate. "The future alone possesses developers strong enough to reveal the image in all its details. Many pages in Marivaux or Rousseau contain a mysterious meaning which the first readers of these texts could not fully have deciphered." (Monglond; N15a,1) (Benjamin 2003: 405)

Here, we must once again return to Lacan who – in order to explain the return of the repressed – used Wiener's metaphor of the inversion of the temporal dimension, in which we first see the square erasing itself before seeing it return as a complete square:

[W]hat we see in the return of the repressed is the effaced signal of something which only takes on its value in the future, through its symbolic realization, its integration into the history of the subject. Literally, it will only ever be a thing which, at the given moment of its occurrence, *will have been*. (Lacan 1991a: 159)

From this perspective, it is not the existing revolutionary constellation that is the "return of the repressed," a "symptom," but rather the past missed opportunities, which have been lost in the dominant interpretation of history. The constellation is an attempt to unknot, to resolve, the symptom, to "free it," which is to say, to realize in the symbolic the past missed opportunities that "will have been" only through their repetition, retroactively becoming what they were. Let us apply Lacan's formulation to Benjamin's theses: the revolution does not make the "tiger leap" into the past in order to find a foothold, but rather because the past itself that is repeated by the revolution "comes from the future" – inside it lies the open horizon of the future.

The "perspective of the last judgment"

At this point we arrive at a quite surprising parallel between Benjamin and the Stalinist understanding of history. As soon as we view history as a text, as "its own story," its own narration, as something that receives its signification retroactively – and this temporal delay and retroactive effect are inscribed in the actual event itself, which, literally, "is not" but "will have been" – we necessarily, and at the very least, implicitly, come to understand the historical process from the perspective of a "last judgment," an ultimate settling of accounts, a final point in which symbolization/historicization is achieved, the "end of history" in which each event will arrive at its definitive signification, its last meaning. Present-day history unfolds on "credit," so to speak; it is up to later developments to determine whether our current revolutionary violence will be forgiven or whether it will weigh around our necks like guilt, like an unpaid debt hanging on the heads of the following generation. Let us recall Merleau-Ponty who, in *Humanism and Terror: An Essay on the Communist Problem*, defended the Stalinist show trials because, even though the victims were undoubtedly innocent, their sacrifice would be justified by the later progress of society that they had made possible. The fundamental idea behind the "perspective of the last judgment" (the expression used by Lacan in his seminar on the ethics of psychoanalysis) is that no act falls completely flat in history, that there is no pure waste, everything that happens is inscribed somewhere, and while this mark might appear meaningless in the present day, at the moment of the last judgment it will be revealed in all its meaning. This is the idealism underlying Stalinism that, although it denies the existence of the person of God, still believes in a certain kind of Platonist sky in the form of the big Other who divides up history and keeps tabs on it in its ledger. If it were not for this bookkeeping, if historical events and actions were not inscribed in the big Other's ledger, we could not make sense of key concepts in the Stalinist discourse like "objective guilt," which is precisely guilt before the big Other of History.

Therefore, at first glance, it seems as if Benjamin and Stalinism are in agreement on the subject of the "perspective of the last judgment" – but this apparent similarity is in fact the very foundation of their disagreement. The reason they seem alike comes from the fact that Benjamin put his finger on the raw nerve of the Stalinist symbolic edifice. He was the only thinker to radically question the idea of "progress" implied by the historical Other's bookkeeping and to show – and in this he was a precursor to Lacan, who famously said that development is "merely a hypothesis of mastery" (Lacan 1998b: 55) – the uninterrupted link between progress and domination: "The concept of the progress of the human race in history is not to be separated from the concept of its progression through a homogenous and empty time" (Benjamin 2009: 15), the temporality of the ruling class.

The Stalinist perspective is that of the *victor* whose ultimate triumph is guaranteed in advance by "objective historical necessity." This is why the Stalinist view of history remains – despite all its talk of breaks, leaps, and revolutions – *evolutionist* from beginning to end. History is the continuous replacement of old masters with new ones; new victors are all "progressive" in their own time, before the inevitable development of history causes them to lose favor. Yesterday it was the capitalist who acted in concert with the necessities of progress; today it is the turn of his successors. In Stalinist bookkeeping, "objective guilt" is determined before a court of the laws of development, the objective necessity of historical progress, the continual evolution toward the final realization of the Supreme Good ("communism"). For Benjamin, on the other hand, the perspective of the "last judgment" is only meaningful if it is the perspective of those who paid the price for the series of grand historical triumphs, as the perspective of that which had to miss its goal in order for the series of grand historical acts to realize itself, as the perspective of lost hopes, of everything that left no mark on the text of history besides anonymous, senseless scribbles in the margins of those great acts whose "historical signification" is both guaranteed and imposed by the dominant historiography.

This is why, for Benjamin, revolution is not a phenomenon inscribed in the continuum of revolution, but rather a moment of "stasis," in which the continuum is broken, obliterating the texture of history up until that point, the history of the victors. All the failed attempts of the past that in the dominant text had been empty marks, devoid of meaning, will be "freed," will receive their signification. In this sense, revolution is quite strictly an act of *creation*. It announces the radical intrusion of the "death instinct," the dominant text is annihilated, a new Text is created *ex nihilo*, through which the stifled past "will have been." We can see this at work in *Antigone*. If the Stalinist perspective is that of Creon, of the Supreme Good as embodied by the Common Good of the State, Benjamin's perspective is that of Antigone. For Benjamin, revolution is a question of life and death, and, more precisely, of the second death, of the symbolic death. Revolution offers the possibility of a *liberation* that would rescue moments from the "dustbin of history" – to use a Stalinist expression – that would give meaning to the things that had been excluded from the continuum of progress, but open the possibility of an *apocalypse* (the revolution's defeat) in which the dead will be lost once again, dying their second death.

Therefore, the contrast between Benjamin's theses and Stalinism is the opposition between *creationist materialism* and *evolutionary idealism*. Lacan, in his seminar on the ethics of psychoanalysis, emphasized that evolutionism always implies the belief in a Supreme Good, the final Goal of evolution, which from the very beginning guided its development. This is why it always contains a hidden – and explicitly denied – teleology. While, on the other hand, materialism is always creationist, which is to say that it always involves *retroactive* movement. In materialism, the End is not preordained from the beginning; instead, things receive their signification after the fact, the creation of Order retroactively confers signification on the Chaos that came before it.

At first, Benjamin's position seems radically anti-Hegelian. Isn't the dialectic the most refined form of evolutionism, in which the ruptures themselves are included in the continuum of progress, in its inevitable logic? This is probably how Benjamin himself understood his position, as he refers to the point of the rupture with the historical continuum as a "dialectic in suspense," seeing it as the intrusion of a pure repetition that puts the progressive movement of *Aufhebung* in parentheses. However, I should again emphasize Hegel's radical anti-evolutionism. Absolute negativity, the "nothing" that pushes the dialectical movement forward, is precisely the intervention of the "death instinct" as the radically ahistoric "zero hour" of history. For Hegel, at the heart of historical movement there is this same ahistorical "absolute negativity." In other words, the suspension of movement is the key moment in the movement of the dialectic. Alleged "dialectical development" comes through endless repetitions of an *ex nihilo* beginning, a retroactive cancellation of the presupposed contents. Although this vulgar representation of "dialectical development," which sees it as a continuous stream of transformation in which the old dies and is replaced by the new, in which everything is always in continual movement and Nature is a dynamic process of transformation, can be found everywhere from Sade to Stalin, it has absolutely nothing to do with the Hegelian process in the true meaning of the term. However, this quasi-"dialectical" vision of Nature as an eternal path of transformation is not all there is to Stalinism – let us not forget the subjective position of the communist himself. The depictions of the communist figure that we find in Stalin's writings, which at first seem quasi-poetic and pathetic, are to be taken literally. In his writings, communists are made of sterner stuff, they are not susceptible to everyday concerns, to the passions and weaknesses of ordinary men. It is as if they possess a sublime body beyond their ordinary physical body, that they inhabit the realm "between the two deaths," that they are, in a certain sense, "walking dead," still alive and yet unaffected by passions or furies. In short, that they are the immediate embodiment of the big Other of History. Stalinism is therefore grounded on a cartoonish phantasy: behind this idea of indestructible communists, who confront every obstacle only to emerge stronger still, there is the same phantasy as the cat whose head gets blown off by dynamite but who, in the very next scene, appears once again intact and continues his pursuit of his "class enemy," the mouse. This is the key to the Stalinist "mystique of the cadres"; the cadres are "our most precious capital" (Stalin) because they possess these sublime bodies, located in the sacred realm between the two deaths.

The totalitarian body

When, at the beginning of his "solemn vow of the Bolshevik party to its leader Lenin," Stalin says: "We communists are a people of a special mould. We are made of a special stuff" (Stalin 2013: 359), we can recognize right away what the Lacanian name for this "special stuff" is: the *object little a*. Stalin's remarks take on their full weight when viewed against the background of the *fetishistic* way in which the Stalinist Party operates. The Party sees itself as the miraculous, immediate embodiment of neutral and objective knowledge, a position it would often refer to when justifying its actions – it would claim to be the only group that had access to "the knowledge of the objective laws" (cf. Zizek 1983) – Marx saw money in relationship to all other commodities as the paradoxical element that immediately embodied, in its particularity itself, the generality of a "whole," which is to say, a "singular reality, which contains in itself all existing species of the same thing":

> It is as if outside of tigers, lions, hares and all of the other real animals that together make up the different races, species, sub-species, families, etc. of the animal kingdom, there was the Animal, the individual incarnation of the whole animal kingdom. (Dognin 1977: 73)

This is the logic of the Party. Beyond classes, social groups, and subgroups, and their economic, political, and ideological organizations, which together make up the different parts of the sociohistorical universe that is governed by the objective laws of development, there is the Party, the immediate incarnation of these objective laws in the form of individuals. It is a short-circuit, a paradoxical intersection between subjective will and objective laws. This incarnation of the "objective reason of history" is the "special stuff" out of which the communists are made. This stuff is, in the end, their body, and this body undergoes a true transubstantiation, it becomes the bearer of a *different* body, the *sublime* body. It is interesting to re-read Lenin's letters to Maxim Gorky, especially those from 1913 which touch on the debate over the "construction of God [*bogograditel'stvo*]" – an idea that Gorky supported – through this perspective of the communist's sublime body. The first thing that jumps out at the

reader is a seemingly unimportant detail, of no theoretical importance: Lenin is quite literally obsessed with Gorky's health. Here are
the ends of some of his letters:

Good health! Yours, Lenin
Well, I have chattered more than enough. Write and tell me about your
health. Yours, Lenin
Did you get my last letter? Somehow we haven't had news from you
for a long time. Are you well? Yours, Lenin
I shake your hand warmly and wish you the best of luck, and most
of all health for the journey. So reply at once! Yours, Lenin. (Lenin
1971, vol. 35)

When Lenin learned about Gorky's pneumonia in the autumn of
1913, he wrote to him right away:

The news that you are being given a *new* kind of treatment by "a
Bolshevik", even if a former one, has really worried me. The saints
preserve us from comrade-doctors in general, and Bolshevik-doctors
in particular! Really and truly, in 99 cases out of 100 the comrade-
doctors are "asses", as a *good* doctor once said to me. I assure you
that you should consult (except on minor complaints) *only* first-class
men. It is terrible to try out on yourself the inventions of a Bolshevik!
The only reassuring thing is the supervision of professors in Naples, if
these professors really know their business . . . You know, if you do
go in winter, *in any case* call on some first-class doctors in *Switzerland*
and in *Vienna* – there will be no excuse for not doing so! How do you
feel now? (Lenin 1971, vol. 36: 265)

Let us set aside the reaction that reading Lenin's advice with hind-
sight cannot help but evoke (20 years later, Russia as a whole would
try out the inventions of a certain Bolshevik) and focus instead on
the question of the *field of signification* of Lenin's concern for Gorky's
well-being. At first, it may seem quite obvious and relatively innocent:
Gorky was a precious ally, and therefore Lenin had to look out for
him. But the next letter puts the whole situation in a new light: Lenin
is alarmed by Gorky's positive opinion toward the "construction of
God," which Gorky maintained had to be "adjourned," put aside for
the moment, but in no way rejected. Such views were incomprehensible to Lenin, he was extremely disagreeably surprised – from the
beginning and the end of the letter that followed:

Dear A. M., Whatever are you doing? This is simply terrible, it really
is! / Why do you do this? It's damnably disappointing. Yours, V. I.
(Lenin 1971, vol. 35: 121, 124)

And here is the post-scriptum: "P.P.S. Get as good *medical* treatment as you can, please, so that you can travel in the winter, *without colds* (it's dangerous in the winter)."

What is actually going on is even clearer in the closing to the letter after that, which was sent at the same time:

> I enclose my letter of yesterday: don't be angry that I lost my temper. Perhaps I did not understand you right? Perhaps it was as a joke that you wrote "for a time"? Perhaps you weren't serious about God-building, either? I entreat you to get the best possible treatment. (Lenin 1971, vol. 36: 266)

Here, Lenin puts things explicitly and directly: ultimately, he thinks that Gorky's ideological vacillation and confusion are results of his physical exhaustion, of his illness. This is why he does not take Gorky's arguments seriously: his final response boils down to him saying "get some rest, take better care of yourself . . . ." Lenin's attitude does not come from some kind of vulgar materialism, an immediate reduction of ideas to physical states. On the contrary, it presupposes and implies this view of the communist as a man "of a special mold." When the communist speaks and acts as a communist, it is the objective necessity of history itself that speaks and acts through his body. In other words, the spirit of a true communist cannot deviate, because this spirit is historical necessity's immediate consciousness-of-the-self. As a result, the only thing that would be capable of derailing it, of infecting it with disorder and deviation, is its own body, that fragile material vessel for the *other* body, the sublime body that is "made out of a special stuff." This motif of Power's sublime body, of the "transubstantiation" of the body of the Master, can already be found in La Boétie, who asked the famous question:

> He who thus domineers over you has only two eyes, only two hands, only one body, no more than is possessed by the least man among the infinite numbers dwelling in your cities; he has indeed nothing more than the power that you confer upon him to destroy you. Where has he acquired enough eyes to spy upon you, if you do not provide them yourselves? How can he have so many arms to beat you with, if he does not borrow them from you? The feet that trample down your cities, where does he get them if they are not your own? How does he have any power over you except through you? (2007: 52)

The answer La Boétie gives is essentially the same as Pascal's and Marx's; it is the subject himself who, by behaving toward the Master in the way that one behaves toward a Master, makes him Master. The secret of the Master, "what in the Master is more than the Master," the ungraspable X that gives him his charismatic aura, is nothing more than the inverted image of "custom," of the symbolic rite of his subjects. This is why La Boétie says that getting rid of the Master is the easiest thing in the world, all that it takes is to stop behaving toward him as one behaves toward a Master and he will automatically cease being the Master. Why, then, does the subject remain in servitude? Why does he continue to behave toward the Master in such a way as to make him Master? La Boétie locates the fundamental source of the relationship of domination in the impasse of desire: "Liberty is the only joy upon which men do not seem to insist; for surely if they really wanted it they would receive it" (2007: 51).

Freedom is the impossible point of pure performance; in order to have it, one must not desire it – such an immediate saturation would block desire completely. The "hypothesis of the Master" is a potential exit that would allow us to rescue desire; we "externalize" the blockage, the immanent impasse of desire into a "repressive" force that opposes our own will externally. This paradox is even clearer in the example of the Despot as the "caprice of the Other." In order to avoid the troublesome fact that the Other himself is already holed, blocked, marked by a fundamental impossibility, we construct the figure of an Other who *could* satisfy us, who could give us "the thing itself," "that," but who, *out of caprice alone*, does not do it (cf. Grosrichard 1998). The phantasy of the Despot is altogether analogous to the strategy of courtly love. One acts as if the sexual rapport were in fact possible, as if obstacles to it were only being raised out of capriciousness – it is impossible not to see in the Lady the figure of a capricious Despot. "What is courtly love? It is a highly refined way of making up for [*suppléer à*] the absence of the sexual relationship, by feigning that we are the ones who erect an obstacle thereto" (Lacan 1998b: 69).

If the sublime body of Power is already present in the form of the traditional, pre-bourgeois Master, what is the difference between this and the totalitarian Leader? The traditional position of the Master, who legitimates his power as coming from an extra-social authority, can be subverted by the Boétie-Pascal-Marx argument, according to which he is only a Master because we behave toward him as if he was a Master. But the totalitarian Leader knows how to get around this argument: in order to legitimate his power, *he himself directly acknowledges the Pascalian-Marxist line of argument*. He does not say to the people: "You must follow me because I am the Leader";

he says: "I am nothing, I get all of my power from you, the people, from my base, I am only the incarnation, the executor, the expression of your will." The *History of the Communist Party in the Soviet Union (Bolsheviks): Short Course* concludes with a reminder of the way in which the Party depends on the people, using language that is unmistakably incestuous:

> I think that the Bolsheviks remind us of the hero of Greek mythology, Antasus. They, like Antasus, are strong because they maintain connection with their mother, the masses, who gave birth to them, suckled them and reared them. And as long as they maintain connection with their mother, with the people, they have every chance of remaining invincible. (2013: 491)

It is as if the totalitarian Leader addresses his subjects saying: "I am not the Master because you treat me like a master," explicitly revealing the secret of the traditional Master. If then the Pascalian-Marxist argument that the Master's aura comes from the community's symbolic rites no longer applies, how can we subvert the position of the totalitarian Leader? His deception consists in the fact that the People from which he claims to draw his legitimacy *does not exist*, or, more precisely, only exists in its fetish-representation, which is to say the Party and its Leader. Here again, we have a misrecognition of the performative dimension of discourse, but in the opposite direction; it is no longer the master who is master because the people treat him like a Master, but rather the People are only the People because the Party refers to them as such and claims to embody them. In other words, the formula for totalitarian misrecognition would be: the party believes that it is a Party because it is supported by the People, that it expresses their will, and so forth, while, in truth, the people are only the People because they are embodied by the Party. The way this operates can be seen in sentences like "The People as a whole support the Party." Behind what seems like a simple observation, there is a circular definition of "the People"; a true member of "the People" is one who supports the Party, which represents the will of the People, while anyone who opposes the Party thus excludes himself from the People. This is why the proposition "The people as a whole support the Party" is irrefutable. In the universe of Stalinism, "supporting the Party" is the only trait that defines "the People." What we have is a slightly morbid variation on the joke: "My fiancée never stands me up, because if she stood me up, she would no longer be my fiancée." In this case it becomes "The people always support the Party because as soon as a member of the people opposes the Party, he is no longer a member of the People."

The final distinction between totalitarianism and what Claude Lefort calls the "democratic project" would therefore be that in the eyes of the "democratic project," *the People does not exist.*

"The People does not exist"

At first, it may seem as if the "democratic project" obscures the structural necessity of S1, of the excess, "irrational" element. Doesn't democracy rest on an illusory faith in the possibility of "rational" governance by officials elected for their abilities and know-how? But as Lefort (1985) showed, the "democratic invention" is actually even more paradoxical than it might seem. In pre-bourgeois society, the legitimacy of Power was accepted as existing at a level beyond doubt, grounded in a moment that was beyond society, whether divine and/ or natural (the divine source of Power, the hereditary title). The legitimacy of Power did not depend on the will of its subjects, its only serious concern was *usurpers* (someone who took power without the right to it, through violence or fraud). The "democratic invention" completely subverts this basis for legitimacy by saying that Power ultimately draws its legitimacy from the *people*, which is to say, the whole ensemble of the subjects of the Power, and that therefore they are the ultimate sovereigns. The paradox here is analogous to that of "natural" language as the final metalanguage of all of the metalanguages. Totalitarianism, and this is what it has in common with democracy, is also only possible if the extra-societal foundation of power has been demolished. It does not draw its legitimacy from some extra-societal body, but by granting an element of society itself (class, race, or even religion in the form of a force in society) the role of the immediate embodiment of the universal interests of Society.

The superficial idea that the passage to democracy only involved a small change at the heart of the same basic framework (instead of the Monarch who draws his legitimacy from an extra-societal point, the ultimate foundation of sovereignty now rests with the People) is therefore misleading because it misses the fundamentally paradoxical nature of having the People – the whole ensemble of the *subjects* of Power – in the role of the foundation of sovereignty. Because the People cannot function immediately as its own Power, the space of Power becomes a place that is fundamentally and irre- ducibly *empty*:

> The legitimacy of power is based on the people; but the image of popular sovereignty is linked to the image of an empty place, impossible to occupy, such that those who exercise public authority can never claim to appropriate it. (Lefort 1985: 279)

To quote Saint-Just – and in this, at least, he showed himself to be the exact opposite of a "precursor to totalitarianism" – "One cannot rule innocently" [*"on ne peut point régner innocement"*]. That no one can claim the right to occupy the place of Power is embedded in the very nature of democracy. The person who ends up occupying this place can do no more than fill the void of a fundamental "impossibility"; he will always remain a place-holder for the impossible Sovereign. In other words, the foundation of democracy is that "the People does not exist"; it does not exist in the form of a People-as-One, as a positive totality. The only moment in which "the people" actually exists is during an election, when the entire social network dissolves and is reduced to a dispersed collection of "citizens," of atomized individuals. "The people" as the source of supreme Sovereignty is, in this sense, a purely negative entity: it reminds the person in power that he is only occupying the empty position of the impossible Sovereign. In a democracy, "the people" is just a limit, a boundary, that prevents the person in power from overidentifying with the place of Power, whereas totalitarianism could be defined as a certain kind of turning point in which the People take shape and become a positive entity – at the price, of course, of embodying the "empirical" people in a transcendent object, in the totalitarian object (the Party, for example), which would supposedly represent the "true interests of the people." Lefort already noted the dual character of the substantial, unique, fully formed body of the People in totalitarianism: "The movement towards pure internality (a substantial society, a People-as-One) is accompanied by a movement towards pure externality (power that is distanced from the population, the holder of Power-as-One" (Lefort 1981: 157). The fact that we call the countries in which real socialism exists "people's democracies" is therefore more than simply an exercise in cynicism on the part of the totalitarian authorities. In these countries, Power is exercised in the name of the People as a positive, existing entity, which means that the person wielding Power no longer occupies a necessarily empty position – *the Party can once again "rule innocently."*

Understanding the "emptiness" of the position of power illustrates the true rupture that the "invention of democracy" represents in the history of institutions. "Democratic society" can be defined as a society that has an institutional structure whose "normal," "regular" cycle of reproduction includes a moment when symbolic ties disappear, and therefore when the Real erupts: elections. Lefort interprets elections (or, at least, the "bourgeois" elections that take place in "formal democracy") as the act of dissolving the social edifice. For him, their key feature is the very thing decried by contemporary Marxist critiques: the fact that one participates in elections not as the member of a concrete social organism, but as an abstracted, atomized individual, a pure and unqualified One. In a certain sense, at the moment of an election, the entire hierarchical network of social relationships is suspended, put into parentheses. "Society" as an organic unity ceases to exist, becoming instead a contingent collection of individuals, of abstract units, and the final outcome comes down to the purely quantitative mechanism of counting votes, which often comes down to the dumb luck of an unanticipated (or manipulated) event. A scandal breaking a few days before an election, for example, can add the crucial "half a percentage point" to one side and therefore determine the orientation of a country for years to come.

It is in vain that societies try to conceal the fundamentally "irrational" character of so-called "formal democracy"; when elections occur, society is placed in the hands of pure chance. Democracy is only possible if we consent to taking the risk of placing society in the hands of "irrational" chance. This is how we should understand Winston Churchill's famous quote that democracy is the worst form of government, except for all the others that have been tried. It is true that democracy makes all kinds of manipulations possible, but as soon as we try to eliminate the possibility of these aberrations, we find we have lost democracy itself – a fine example of the truly Hegelian paradox of Universality that can only realize itself in its diverse impure, corrupt, deformed iterations. If we wish to grasp Universality in its pure intactness, we end up with its very opposite. Even though, "in reality," there are only "exceptions" and "deformations," the universal idea of "democracy" is a "necessary fiction," a symbolic fact without which "effective" democracy, in its many particular forms, could not reproduce itself. Here Hegel ends up paradoxically close to Bentham, whose *Theory of Fictions* is often cited by Lacan. The Hegelian "universal" is a "fiction" that "exists nowhere in reality" (there are only exceptions), but which "reality" nonetheless requires in order to achieve its symbolic consistency.

"Effective democracy" will therefore transform into non-democracy if we try to exclude the possibility of any "manipulation." If we pre-emptively "verify" the candidates, or draw a distinction between the "actual interests of the people" and contingent public opinion, which is prey to demagoguery and all sorts of other machinations, we end up with the "organized democracy" of "real socialism," in which the "true elections" take place before the elections and in which the act of voting only has value as a plebiscite. The key feature of the "organized democracy" of "real socialism" is precisely the fact that it excludes the eruption of the Real that is fundamental to "bourgeois" elections, the moment in which the social edifice is "dispersed" into a numerical collection of atomized individuals.

13

The Quilting Point of Ideology: Or Why Lacan is Not a "Poststructuralist"

The "arbitrariness" of the signifier

The fundamental insight that a Lacanian theory of ideology offers is an understanding of the gap between reality and the modes of its symbolization. But what exactly does it mean to say that symbolization is fundamentally contingent?

Let me begin with what it does not mean. First and foremost, it does not mean what is often called "the arbitrariness of the sign"; both "table" and "Tisch" are arbitrary signs designating a table, and so forth. As Lacan emphasizes (cf. Lacan 1998b: 29), an accusation of "arbitrariness" of this kind is the discourse of a Master. By making this claim, one puts oneself in an external position beyond language, from which one could hold up signs and *compare them to* their real or ideal referent in order to demonstrate the arbitrariness of the sign in relationship to the content it designates. As a first approach, we could say that the contingency of symbolization is the very opposite itself of this manner of conceptualizing the arbitrariness of the sign. As soon as we speak we are caught up in the abyss of a vicious circle; a signifier always refers to other signifiers. "The Other has no Other" – there is no ultimate guarantor that provides a solid ground for the interplay of signification. In short, the signifier is "arbitrary" precisely because we *cannot exit from it* and leave it behind; we cannot cross the line that separates it from reality; we cannot take a position outside of it from which we could observe it; there is no external vantage point that would allow us to "relativize" it.

Nor is the gap between reality and the way in which it is symbolized the distance between a symbolic determination and the concrete richness of the "reality" designated by the determination, some surplus of reality's "richness" that would overflow from the abstract network of symbolic determinations. Any attempt to emphasize the "richness" of the concrete as opposed to the abstract nature of symbolic determinations will always miss the fundamental mechanism of symbolization, the "quilting point." The "quilting point" turns the symbolic trait's *lack* in relation to the richness of "reality" into a sign of its *supremacy* over "reality." This may initially seem counterintuitive, so let me give an example of how this works in reference to the example of the role played by the figure of the "Jew" in Nazi ideology. We are always quick to emphasize the difference between the ideological stereotype of the Jew (a demonic being, the incarnation of Evil, a cancer within the societal body, etc.) and our daily experience of our neighbor, Mr Blumenstein, a fine fellow whose kids play with ours and who often likes to sit and while away the time talking in the late afternoon. This daily lived experience is supposed to offer an inarguable refutation that would supposedly cause the ideological edifice to collapse. From this perspective, experience constitutes a reality that ideology would never be able to cancel out without leaving behind a remainder. However, the distance between the ideological stereotype of the Jew and the level of daily experience is not actually a limit or even an obstacle to the full power of the anti-Semitic project; in fact, *it is already included in advance in the way anti-Semitism operates*. This dissonance functions as further, even more damning, proof of Jewish depravity – "You have to be very careful with Jews, it isn't always easy to spot them because they can take on the appearance of ordinary people. They will act like normal folks in order to hide their true corrupt nature!" The scission, the dissonance between their Jewish character and their misleading appearance is therefore part of this Jewish character itself, further confirmation of Jewish hypocrisy. The "Jew" is a paradoxical figure who can only exist in the shadows, whose fundamental trait is that he conceals his true nature.

This gives us a clue as to the successful operation of a "quilting point." An element that, taken at face value, refutes the thesis (for example, the daily experience of my Jewish neighbor in contrast to the stereotype of the Jew – the demonic incarnation of Evil), begins to function as proof of its opposite; it becomes further confirmation of the very thesis it would have seemed to refute. If one's "everyday experiences" seem to get in the way of the effectiveness of one's ideology, this just indicates that the ideology in question has not been particularly successful. This is why one cannot weaken the effectiveness of anti-Semitism by bringing up examples of the non-ideological reality of Jews, by saying: "But just look at the Jews, they're friendly and hard-working people." If anti-Semitism works, such a reminder does nothing but *reinforce* one's anxiety about the "elusive" Jew.

What then is the gap between reality and the symbolic? It lies in the fact that the manner in which reality is symbolized, in which a "quilting point" structures and totalizes the symbolic universe, is neither inscribed in reality nor prescribed by it. There is no necessity such that we could look at reality and then deduce the mode of its symbolization. The division is not between "words" and "things," but rather between, on the one hand, "things" themselves as elements of a symbolic reality, included in the field of signification, and, on the other, reality outside the symbolic. The way in which the "thing" is symbolized is radically contingent and external to the "nature" of the thing.

In order to show what this gap really looks like, let us examine the conception of the "revolutionary situation" that predominates in the Marxist tradition. Social reality is always complicated and the actors caught up in a melee are blind as to their true role: they hold a multitude of illusions that prevent them from seeing the situation clearly. But out of all this confusion emerges the revolutionary situation, in which social reality finally becomes self-transparent, in which, suddenly – to use the expression that is often employed at such a juncture – "the circumstances themselves begin to speak." The masks are removed, the gap between being and signification is finally abolished, the revolutionary agent (the working class) needs only shoulder its true condition and realize the goal inscribed immediately within it. Here, it is useful to ask whether it is not the greatest "ideological illusion" of all to think that we could abolish the distance between being and its "illusory," "ideological" meaning, that there could be a conjunction between reality and meaning as articulated by the "existing conditions" themselves, rather than the empty and chimerical subject. In other words, isn't the feeling that "the circumstances themselves begin to speak" the ideological effect *par excellence*? Isn't the impression that our language could immediately become "the language of real life" (to borrow an expression of Marx's from *The German Ideology*) an indication that we have fallen into an "ideological trap"? We are truly in the clutches of an ideology when we no longer experience it as an "ideology," as opposed to "reality," but as "the language of reality itself." The goal of the "critique of ideology" is simply to reveal the way in which this feeling that "the circumstances themselves have begun to speak" comes out of a series of symbolic operations that are "fabricated" and contingent through and through.

The "open" and contingent nature of the process of symbolization becomes even clearer in situations of crisis when the symbolic edifice that had provided society with its ideological coherency falls apart. In these situations, it is up to a fundamentally contingent symbolic operation to determine what kind of discourse will be able to serve as the "quilting point" for the social field and thus take on a hegemonic role. Let us take the example analyzed by Gérard Miller (1975) of France in 1940, in the aftermath of its shocking military defeat. The country is in total disarray, total confusion, in shock after having encountered the impossible-Real ("How could such a thing have happened to us?"). It was Pétain's discourse that was able to make the situation understandable, "legible," by situating it within the context of a narrative, and therefore bringing about its symbolization-historicization. According to Pétain, the true enemy was not Germany; France's collapse was the necessary consequence of Judeo-liberal decadence, of "democrascum" ["*democrassouille*"], which had corroded the natural unity of the People. The military catastrophe was therefore, even in its very horror, a welcome development, an opportunity to reintroduce order to society, to unite the French People behind an authoritarian-patriarchal State. The whole situation subtly became legible again, "everything once again had meaning"; it seemed as if Pétain had uncovered the signification inscribed in the actual events themselves, that the "circumstances themselves began to speak."

The mythical revolutionary moment in which symbolization would overlap perfectly with reality is even more obvious when it is a question of the exploitation, suffering, repression, and terror exercised against the "masses." It is as if the masses are prepared to endure the legitimate – legitimate as per the ideological discourse – suffering involved in the "normal" course of things, but will revolt when their suffering becomes intolerable, when it reaches a tipping point that would cause the entire ideological edifice to collapse. In contrast to this mythical image, we should focus instead on the distinction between the factual nature of a social relationship of domination or exploitation and the moment in which this relationship is "experienced" as "unbearable" and unjust (cf. Laclau and Mouffe 2001). The difference between these two levels is radical. A revolt is never inscribed in reality itself, it is never triggered by the "unbearable" nature of "actual suffering" without first being mediated by a symbolic network. Take feminism, for example. It was only in reference to the bourgeois democratic-egalitarian discourse of the "natural rights of the individual" that it became possible for women to experience their condition as "unjust" and articulate their demands.

Lacan's thesis that "History does not exist" should be interpreted as referring to the contingent mode in which reality is symbolized. History is not a homogenous process tied together by a continuity-of-signification that would allow us to totalize its many dead ends and discarded events. It is an "open" process, a contingent succession of "quilting points" that retroactively introduce order under the auspices of "rational" necessity. I want to draw particular attention to the fundamental paradox of the "quilting point." The "quilting point" is a fundamentally *contingent* operation through which the ideological-symbolic field retroactively receives its "reason," its *necessity*, or, to put it in Hegelian terms, through which it posits its own preconditions.

The One and the impossible

In order to define the ideological quilting point precisely, it will be useful to draw on Ernesto Laclau's analysis of fascist ideology (cf. Laclau 1977). The fascist ideological edifice is cobbled together from heterogeneous elements whose "significations" are in no way predetermined (its roots in *Blut-und-Boden*, populist nationalism, corporatism, an elitist ethics of aristocratic-military origin, etc.). Any one of these elements could have been put to use by different ideological projects (populist nationalism could have been used by the left, for example). How does a patchwork like this become a closed and unified edifice? It is necessary for an exceptional-element (a master-signifier) to intervene and serve as the "quilting point," thus totalizing the field and stabilizing its signification. In the case of the Nazis, this role was played by the "Jewish plot," which gave the impasses of everyday life their true signification, just as in Christian ideology the "fear of God" gave meaning to all the travails of earthly life. The "quilting point" is a One, a single element that totalizes the others, that divides them, causing them to undergo a certain kind of "transubstantiation" through which they begin to function as expressions of an underlying Principle (all earthly suffering is an "expression" of divine wrath, etc.).

The One is located at the *intersection* of the internality of ideological meaning and the externality of the automatism, of senseless ritual. From inside the field of ideological signification, the One serves as its constitutive externality. This is the fundamental paradox of the "quilting point." The element of the chain that totalizes and stabilizes its signification, that halts its metonymic slippage, is not the point of "abundant" signification, a Guarantor exempted from the differential interplay of the elements that would serve as a stable and fixed reference point. Rather, it is the element that, from inside the structure of the utterances, plays the role of the process itself of speech. It is the element that, from inside the field of the signified, plays the role of the signifying automatism. It is "pure difference," the element whose role is purely structural, whose nature is purely "performative," which is to say, whose signification coincides with the act of its own utterance – it is the "signifier without the signified." Therefore, the key move in the analysis of an ideological edifice is when one looks behind the blinding and fascinating sheen of the element that totalizes the field and finds its self-referential, tautological, performative content. In the end, a "Jew" is only a person to whom we have affixed the label "Jew": all the phantasy richness of his supposedly characteristic traits (greedy, conspiratorial, etc.) obscures the fact that he serves a purely structural function, not that "in Truth, Jews are different." The "fear of God" is the product of a reversal that takes place purely at the level of signification; all the imagery of divine fury is supported only by a simple structural relocation.

The uniquely "ideological" dimension comes out of a certain kind of "error in perspective." This element that, from inside the field of signification, plays the role of the reference-less signifier, is perceived in the ideological experience as the point of signifying saturation that closes the field of signification. The moment that, in the structure of an utterance, is true only in virtue of the process of its uttering, is perceived through the lens of ideological experience as the transcendent Guarantor of Meaning. The signifier that serves as the lack, that is in fact nothing more than the positivization of lack, is perceived as the point of ultimate fullness – in short, pure difference appears as full Identity exempted from the interplay of differentiation and guarantor of its own homogeneity. We can call this error in perspective "ideological anamorphosis." Lacan referred several times to Holbein's *Ambassadors*, because viewed from a certain angle, a shape in the foreground of the painting turns out to be a skull (cf. Lacan 1998a: 85–9). A "critique of ideology" should perform a similar operation. If we look at the Guarantor of Meaning, the "phallic," erect, extending element, from a different point of view, it reveals itself to be the mark of lack, the empty space of signification.

It is now possible to pin down the relationship between the quilting point as a "pure" signifier and the Real as the traumatic, non-symbolizable kernel. Each socio-ideological field structures itself around an impossible-Real "hard kernel," around an "antagonism," an ungovernable *Spaltung* that extends across the entire structure of society, one variant of which is the "class struggle." The "class struggle" is therefore in no way the "last Signified," the ultimate reference that would guarantee the correctness of our interpretation of the social field (in the sense that "the final signification of all social phenomena comes from their role in the class struggle"), but, on the contrary, it is the Impossible that dooms every ideological totalization of Society and means that each one will necessarily produce a symptom. It is the Impossible that makes it so that *we cannot* reduce the processes of society to a unified field of signification. Class difference would therefore be a little bit like sexual difference for Lacan, an "impossible, non-totalizable rapport." It is worth noting that in both cases – "class reductionism" and "pan-sexualism" – the process of ideologization takes the same form, in which the non-symbolizable "hard kernel" is made into the last Signified, the reference point that guarantees the signification of all of the phenomena in question.

The quilting point's "cleverness" is the fact that it performs what might best be described as a "sleight of hand" with the Real kernel. We pretend that we master the impasse of the Real through the element that, in truth, does nothing more than incarnate, positivize, this impasse as such. When we say "Jewish conspiracy" instead of "class struggle," it seems as if the thing has been mastered; the scission running through the social edifice now seems symbolized, mastered, localized in an existing element. In Nazi discourse, the "Jew" plays the role of the fetish in a strictly Freudian sense. It is the element that both embodies and denies "class struggle" (in the same way that, in analytic theory, the fetish both affirms and denies the castration of the mother). The element that totalizes the ideological field does nothing more than positivize the field's Real kernel, its own impossibility.

The figure of the "Jew," of the "Jewish conspiracy," is therefore *the way in which Nazism presentifies its own impossibility.* The "Jew," in its positive form, is nothing more than the presentification of the fundamental impossibility of the totalitarian project. This is why it is not enough to recognize that the totalitarian project, with its aim of re-establishing a totally transparent and homogenous society and so forth, is impossible. The problem is that, in a certain sense, totalitarianism *knows this*, it has already recognized it, and it includes this knowledge in its system in the form of the "Jew." In this way, the fascist project aims at establishing a non-antagonistic society in which the relationships between its diverse groups would be complementary, working together like the different limbs of a single organism (the capitalists and the workers as the "head" and "hands" of the "societal body," etc.), which is to say that fascism is founded on the rejection of the "antagonistic" character of society (the "class struggle"). And the figure of the Jew, the fetish, embodies this denial of societal antagonism (the Jew is the force behind the decomposition of society, he might be the ruthless capitalist or the communist demagogue who introduces "class struggle" into society from the outside). The fascist ideological perspective is therefore structured as a struggle against the element that plays the role of the impossibility of the fascist project. The "Jew" is just the fetishistic embodiment of a fundamental blockage. Therefore, a "critique of ideology" must, from the very beginning, reverse causality as it is perceived by the totalitarian gaze; the Jew, far from being the actual "cause" of social antagonism, is, in its positive form, nothing but the presentification of this "antagonism," the blockage, the "impossibility" that prevents society from becoming a full and closed totality.

Lacan versus "poststructuralism"

It may seem initially as if the Lacanian logic of the "quilting point" could easily be transposed onto a "poststructuralist" problematic of an open, dispersed, plural process (writing, text, difference, the flux of desire, etc.), which is then "totalized" through a "nodal point." The "*pas-tout*," "feminine" side would be a flux of unassociated elements, "floating signifiers," an interplay of displacements and condensations, etc. (the "primary process"). The intervention of an exceptional-element, a One, then totalizes this free-floating flux, transforming it into a fixed structure. "Poststructuralism" emphasizes that the totalization of the open, plural process through the One, its "suturing," is always destined for failure, that it will always be overturned, pushed aside, and a "symptomal reading" sets about detecting the points in which the cracks in this totalization appear. It ends up in a kind of "bad infinity," in an endless tug-of-war between the quilting point and its subversion. Every text is somewhere between the two, neither completely quilted, sutured, nor totally dispersed (which would be equivalent to psychosis), but rather caught in a back-and-forth in which a quilting point is always followed by its subversion.

Laclau and Mouffe (2001) had just such a model of the operation of the ideological field. For them, the field is made up of unattached elements, "floating signifiers," whose very identity is "open," overdetermined by their entanglement with the other elements, whose "literal" signification rests on their metaphorical excess-of-signification. Take *environmentalism*, for example. The ideological positions with which it will come to be associated are not predetermined. It is easy to imagine strains of environmentalism that would be statist (only state intervention can stave off disaster!), socialist (capitalism is at the root of environment problems!), conservative (what we need is a return to the soil!), and so forth. *Feminism* can be socialist or apolitical; even *racism* can be elitist or populist, etc. etc. The ideological "quilting point" is precisely the totalization that pins down the free-floating ideological elements, roping them into a structured web of signification. Socialism, for example, or the "class struggle," give a specific and stable meaning to the other elements, to democracy (the alleged "true democracy" as opposed to bourgeois "formal" democracy), to feminism (seeing the exploitation of women as the result of the class divisions), to environmentalism (the exploitation of nature by the rule of capital), to the peace movement (the greatest danger is imperialist adventurism), and so on. Of course, Laclau and Mouffe emphasize that a "quilting point" is always temporary, unstable, that the radical contingency of the historical process can at any moment dissolve the dominant network.

How, then, can we exit this "bad infinity"? How does the Lacanian approach deal with this field in which every attempt to "suture" is always in the process of being subverted and split open by the contingency of the textual process? What Lacan points out is that the question is not how to subvert totalization, but rather: how it is that there is even the *possibility* of a "quilting point" in a diffuse text? In passing, I should mention that this is a properly Hegelian shift in focus. For Hegel, the true problem is not overcoming division, but the question, "Where did the division come from?" Not achieving dis-alienation, but rather asking, "Where did alienation come from?" If totalization and the "quilting point" fail, it is because they can only bring about their own existence through an element that incarnates this very impossibility itself. The quilting point, far from immediately establishing the totality, embodies its very impossibility, the totality as an impossibility.

It is therefore superfluous to search for symptomal points, fissures that could cause the totality to collapse. It is superfluous to say that the quilting point tries to totalize the diffuse and diverse field but will always fail – *as if the quilting point itself was not the embodiment, the positivization of this fundamental failure, of this very impossibility as such.* Here we are dealing with a negative version of "Truth is evidence of itself;" the quilting point is the evidence of its own impossibility. In other words, a totality functions such that one element, the exceptional One, carries the totality's impossibility. This is the paradox of the phallus that is itself, in its positive form, the signifier of castration, which is to say, the signifier of its own lack. Here, Lacan differentiates himself from Jung, to whom is attributed the famous quote – and this may be a misattribution, but *se non e vero, e ben trovato* – "What is the penis if not the phallic symbol?" This is the difference between the phallus and the pre-phallic object: the breast and excrement are *lost* objects, while the phallus as a signifier is not simply lost but it is an object that, *through its very presence*, embodies this loss. The phallic signifier is, of course, the "transcendental signifier," but only if we keep in mind the fundamental ambiguity of the concept of the transcendental. The unique feature of this concept is that it makes the radical limitation of the "human condition" into a positive, constitutive power, in other words, it turns the finitude, the closure of the "human condition" into its own positive foundation.[1]

1 This also allows us to examine the question of the subject in a manner that is radically different from "poststructuralism." The key move of "poststructuralism" is the reversal of the motif of the "subject of production" into the "production of the subject." The "subject of production" (that autonomous, active, productive center that objectifies itself and produces its own world) is itself produced, a unique effect of the trans-subjective textual process. The "subjectifying-effect" consists in the different "positions of the subject," the diverse modes of "lived experience," of blindness, through which individuals experience their position in the textual process, the diverse modes through which the individuals see themselves as "actors" in the historical process. As such, the subject is reduced to the "subject of the signified" with a fixed identity. "Poststructuralism" emphasizes the precarious and fragile nature of this identity: the limits of an individual's identity can at any moment be broken down or subverted, the subject can never arrive at a truly stable identity.

A Lacanian theory would accomplish the same reversal as it did with totalization. The signifying structure subjectifies itself through the inclusion of a paradoxical element that plays the role of its impossibility, of its empty space. In other words, through the signifier that represents the subject for the other signifiers. This subject is precisely the empty, impossible "signified" of the quasi-transcendental signifier "One." The subject emerges against the background of its own impossibility, before becoming the identity-in-itself of the productive center, the actor in its own history, it is *stricto sensu* non-historical empty space, it is, so to speak, non-position, pure non-identity. In other words, the limit of the subject of the signified, of its identity, is not its dissolution through the diffuse trans-subjective process, but rather the *subject itself as subject of the signifier.* When we remove the "subject of the signified," all the contents that had given it its identity, the whole "patchwork" of its identification, in this moment in which "nothing takes place but the place," the pure and empty form that remains is precisely the "subject of the signifier."

"There is no metalanguage"

The same aporia is repeated with regard to metalanguage. From the "poststructuralist" perspective, saying "there is no metalanguage" is equivalent to saying that the text and its commentary, which is supposedly its truth, coincide. Literary theory becomes the same thing as its "subject," it becomes part of the literary body, such that we end up with an endless text that presents the perpetually unfinished attempt at its own interpretation. The "poststructuralist" approach fundamentally consists in reading a theoretical text as if it were literature, putting its pretension to truth "in parentheses," and more specifically laying bare the textual mechanisms that produce its "truth-effect." We have a universalized aestheticization that sees "truth" as a stylistic "effect" of the discursive structure (this is the Nietzschean tendency in "poststructuralism," and what is interesting about Lacan is his almost total lack of any reference to Nietzsche). In truth, it was Lévi-Strauss who already – despite his critiques of the poststructuralist "mode" – opened the gates for "deconstructivist" poeticism by reading the theories of the interpretations of myths as new versions of the myths themselves.

In this view, metonymy has a logical primacy over metaphor. The metaphorical cut is only a doomed attempt to stabilize, to channel, to master the metonymic dispersion of the textual flux. From this perspective, Lacan's insistence on the primacy of the metaphor over metonymy, his argument that metonymic slippage must always support itself with a metaphorical cut, only shows that his theory remains influenced by a "metaphysics of presence." Isn't the Lacanian theory of the quilting point, of the phallic signifier as the signifier of lack, an attempt to master the "dissemination" of the textual process, to locate the lack in a signifier, even if it is the signifier of the lack itself? Derrida (1987) criticized Lacan several times for the paradoxical gesture of reducing or canceling lack by means of its very affirmation. Because it is determined as "symbolic castration," because the phallus is its signifier, lack is positioned in a unique external point that guarantees the consistency of all of the other elements.

Even though this might only be at the level of a "naive" reading, it seems difficult to avoid the feeling that there is something "that doesn't hold together" in the poststructuralist position, or perhaps, something that holds together a little *too well*. A view that constantly repeats "there is no text that is completely metaphysical, nor is there any text that is completely non-metaphysical." This view claims, on the one hand, that it is impossible to free oneself from the

metaphysical tradition through the simple act of taking one's distance, that one could not pass outside of metaphysics, because the
very language that we must use is saturated with metaphysics. But it
simultaneously holds that any text, as metaphysical as it may be, will
always produce gaps in which the ruptures in the metaphysical circle
emerge, points where the textual process subverts what the author
"wanted to say." Isn't such a position a little too self-assured, or, to
put it more directly: *doesn't it in fact imply the position of a metalanguage*, one in which the "deconstructionist" can always reassure
himself that "there is no metalanguage," that no utterance means
what it was supposed to mean, that the process of speaking always
subverts what was spoken?

When you observe the passionate way in which the "poststructuralist" insists on the fact that any text, including his own, remains
fundamentally ambiguous and is overwhelmed by the textual process
that it passes through, you cannot help but notice the hint of obsti-
nate *denial*, the barely concealed recognition that one is speaking
from a secure, unimpeachable position. This is why poststructuralism's "poeticism" is fundamentally forced. All the effort put into
writing "poetically," of showing how one's own text is caught up in
a process that overwhelms it, of avoiding the purely theoretical form
by making use of approaches that are normally reserved for literature:
all this only serves to mask a firm theoretical stance, which could be
expressed without residuum in a pure and simple "metalanguage."
This is why so many "deconstructionist" texts – especially those from
the US – feel like a "bad infinity" in the Hegelian sense, a pseudo-
poetic infinite variation on a theoretical motif, a variation that produces nothing new. The problem with "deconstructionism" is not
that it renounces strict theoretical formulation and gives itself up to
poetic aestheticization; rather, its problem is that it is *too* "theoretical" (in the sense that it takes a position that does not engage us,
that does not touch on our subjective position).

How, then, can we avoid this dead end? Here is where we come
to the radical difference between Lacan and "poststructuralism." In
Seminar XI, he begins one of his sentences: "That is precisely what
I mean, and say – for what I mean, I say . . ." (1998a: 218). From a
"poststructuralist" point of view, phrases like these indicate that he
has slipped back into the position of Master. "Saying what I mean
to say" presumes a perfect coincide between what I intended to say
and what I actually said, and isn't that the very definition of the
Master? Doesn't this show that Lacan wanted to keep the position
of the Master for himself, that he acted as if his own text was
exempted from the gap between saying and wanting to say, as if he

could control the effects of his text? However, from the Lacanian perspective, it is precisely this kind of "impossible" utterance – utterances whose logic is the same as the paradox "I'm lying" – which, because they are "impossibility itself," keep the fundamental gap of the signifying process open and prevent us from reverting back into the metalinguistic position. Here, Lacan is being Brechtian. In Brecht's "didactic pieces" from the early 1950s, characters utter "impossible" commentaries on their own actions. An actor comes on stage and says: "I am a capitalist whose goal is to exploit my workers. Now I'm going to approach one of my workers and try to convince him of the rightness of the bourgeois ideology that legitimizes exploitation," then he walks up to a worker and starts talking to him. Such an approach, in which the actor comments on his own acts from the position of a pure metalanguage, helps us understand in a tangible way the fundamental impossibility of such a position. Isn't it, in its very absurdity, infinitely more subversive than the forced poeticism that forbids every "simple," "direct" statement, that always tells us to add yet another commentary, take yet more distance, retreat even further, put even more things in parenthesis, between quotation marks, all of these signs that "we should not take what we are reading directly, literally, as identical to itself . . ."?

The same thing goes for Hegel. The standard critique accuses him of using Absolute Knowledge to "close" the process. Since the momentum of the dialectical process is the discord between wanting to say and actually saying – the fact that we always say something else in regard to what we wanted to say – isn't the last moment of this process, Absolute Knowledge, defined by the perfect conjunction of wanting to say and saying, realized at long last? In this "Twilight of Life," the subject would finally be able to say what he meant to say, and would only mean to say what he actually said. We must therefore break open the "closed circle" of dialectical movement and argue that there is an irreducible de-centering of saying in relation to wanting to say. The radical emergence of a process of differentiation cannot be suppressed in the self-mediation of Absolute self-identity. The subject is traversed by the Other, whose constitutive characteristic is alienation. We have seen how this idea of "opening" the process, this insistence on the irreducible gap, entails a metalinguistic position.

But, if there is no metalanguage, how can we say that the gap between saying and wanting to say is irremediable, that the subject is always left behind and traversed by the de-centered Other? The only way of affirming the "openness" of this process, the irreducible gap that makes the metalinguistic position impossible, is to embody this gap in an "impossible" element. If a metalanguage is impossible, the only way to avoid backsliding into metalanguage by affirming that it doesn't exist or that it dilutes itself in every utterance is to produce the enunciation of a pure metalanguage that, through its own absurdity, demonstrates and materializes its own impossibility, which is to say, a paradoxical element that, in its very identity, embodies the gap, absolute difference. For Derrida, localizing lack in its mark channels it, tames it, limits its dissemination into the textual process, etc., whereas for Lacan, only the presence of this "at least one thing" can keep the radical distance of the gap open.

14

Naming and Contingency: Hegel and Analytic Philosophy

Kripke the Hegelian

For his critics, the image of Hegel as a "panlogicist" functions as the Real, which is to say, the manufactured impossible reference point, the unsettling point that must be avoided, sidestepped, circumvented, in order for their approach to be possible. In other words, this portrayal of Hegel serves to legitimate the historical evolutionism of Hegel's critics, who all repeat the same mantra: "There is no a priori logical schema that binds and constricts the secret contents in some Procrustean manner, instead there is the immanent logic of the development of living, existing history." Through the very move of insisting on the distance between the fundamental necessity of development and all the richness of the detours and accidents through which this necessity came to be realized, Marx erased the radically open, anti-evolutionist nature of the Hegelian dialectical process. When Marx made this step, he posited a necessity that cannot be reduced to a retroactive effect of contingency, which he argues is purely accidental, stemming from accidents on the path to the realization of historical necessity. But Hegel's true view of the relationship between necessity and contingency has survived, albeit in a somewhat unexpected place: the strain of analytic philosophy that is perhaps best exemplified by the work of Saul Kripke.

Kripke's approach to the "skeptical paradox" is profoundly Hegelian (cf. Kripke 1982). What exactly is the skeptical paradox? To summarize it briefly: each exception from a given rule is retroactively explicable if we consider that it follows from a different rule that is consistently applied. Everyone knows the rule of addition; now let us suppose that no one up until now had ever added 63 and 51 together and that, for the first time, someone is asked what the sum of 63 and 51 is. He replies: "63 + 51 = 5." When told he has made a mistake he replies: "But how do you know that I've made a mistake? How can you be sure that all along I haven't been following the rule that corresponds perfectly to the standard rules of addition, except that it says that the sum of 63 and 51 is 5?" Let us call the rule of addition *plus*, and let us call the other rule – which corresponds perfectly to *plus*, with the sole exception of the sum of 63 and 51, which it says is 5 – *quus*. How can I be sure that, when I thought I was following *plus*, I wasn't actually following *quus*? What does a rule consist in if, in the case of any exception, I can affirm the existence of a rule that accounts for it?

According to Searle's (1999) counterargument, it should be easy to show that the "skeptical paradox" can only arise if we are observing the act in question (addition, in this case) externally, which is to say, from the framework of an external description of the act. However, such an approach by definition misses the immanence of the rule in relation to the act; as long as we are dealing with an act that is guided by a properly symbolic rule, the act will always involve a reference to this rule, even if we obtain a result that does not fit with the rule. This is why, if someone tells me "63 + 51 = 5," I don't go searching for another, previously unknown, rule, I simply say that he is mistaken. The *plus–quus* dilemma is therefore false because the rule of addition functions as *a constitutive element of the act of addition itself*. To use Searle's terminology, the rule of addition is part of the *background*, the presupposed backdrop of the act of addition. Therefore, in this case, "rule" is essentially synonymous with the big Other; the very fact of speaking testifies to an a priori belief in the Other's "regularity." This belief in the Other is a precondition for any rational reasoning, because it is its foundation, its background – only the psychotic "doesn't believe in it." As Lacan emphasized, the fundamental characteristic of psychosis is this *Un-Glauben*, this distance that the subject maintains from the universe of symbolic rules, acting as if these rules did not determine the very space from which he spoke. Searle's counterargument, however pertinent it may be at its own level, nonetheless remains at the level of hermeneutics. The big Other that we are dealing with here is the same thing as what Gadamer (1975) called a "horizon of understanding," the preconditional acceptance of certain fundamental propositions that will predetermine the framework in which reflection will take place and outline in advance the shape of the experienced meaning:

> [M]eaning is provided by the sense each of us has of being part of his world, that is, of his little family of everything that revolves around it. Each of you – I am speaking even for the leftists – you are more attached to it than you care to know and would do well to sound the depths of your attachment. A certain number of biases are your daily fare and limit the import of your insurrections to the shortest term, to the term, quite precisely, that gives you no discomfort – they certainly don't change your world view, for that remains perfectly spherical. The signified finds its center wherever you take it. (Lacan 1998b: 42)

Phenomena like slips of the tongue and failed acts already offer sufficient proof that the hermeneutic Other, the Other that is the universe of rules that preordains the field of signification, is not the same as the other of the psychoanalytical process. The hermeneutic Other cannot explain the psychoanalytical other. Isn't a slip of the tongue a perfect example of an act that is a failure from the perspective of its immanent rule, but that nonetheless, in this very failure, is a success from the point of view of *another*, unknown rule (the one that gives this slip of the tongue its meaning)? Isn't the aim of analytical interpretation precisely to reveal the hidden rule that I had been following unconsciously, uncovering regularity where common sense could only make out nonsensical chaos? In other words, it tries to discern a *quus* where common sense saw only a failed attempt at following a *plus*. This is the perspective of the analyst as the subject who supposedly knows, the guarantor of the transformation of a *lawless* series into a *lawlike* series, who guarantees that in the end a Rule will erupt that will retroactively confer signification on all failures and slips (cf. J.-A. Miller 1978).

However, Lacan's last word does not mean that the analyst is the placeholder for the big Other, whose purpose would be to reflect the true meaning of the analysand's own words back to her. Rather, the meaning of Lacan's last word comes from the fact that the Other is lacking, that there is no "Rule," that its emergence always comes out of a retroactive construction that introduces order into an absolutely discontinuous sequence, which is also called the Real (cf. J.-A. Miller 1980). This is why Kripke's conclusion is especially pertinent. The very fact of admitting the eventuality of a retroactive reinterpretation (according to which any exception could turn out to be a regular case) undermines the possibility of any rule at all and breaks down the ordered universe into a contingent constellation. Kripke's examination of how a contingent series is transformed into a rule-governed series is therefore relevant to the core itself of the dialectical process.

Descriptivism versus anti-descriptivism

The problem of the "skeptical paradox" is, in the end, the same as the problem Kripke addresses in his first book, *Naming and Necessity*, namely, how can we ground and legitimate the necessity of a universal rule or of naming? The "skeptical paradox" confronts us with an uncomfortable experience: a universal rule (the rule of addition, for example) can never "cover" the field to which it would seem to apply by immanent necessity. In his critique of descriptivism, Kripke similarly shows how the immanent content of a name (the bundle of descriptions that form its signification) can never "cover" its field of reference by immanent necessity. Another way of putting this is that we can never give a definitive answer to the following question: Why does this name refer to that object? In both cases, because a rule cannot cover the entire field of its application and because a name cannot cover the entirety of its reference, we are left with an agonizing surplus, a breach out of which the dimension of the Real erupts. When applying a rule, we can never be sure that we are truly dealing with an instance of this rule or with something else entirely; when using a name, even if an object possesses all the properties contained by the signification of this name, we can never be sure that we are truly dealing with the referent that belongs to this name or with something else entirely. We could call this problem *The Invasion of the Body Snatchers*, after the 1956 sci-fi movie in which alien invaders take on human form, imitating us perfectly and taking on all the features of the human beings they impersonate, making their strangeness even more terrifying. The same impasse can be found in anti-Semitism. The Jews are "like us," and it is very difficult to recognize and isolate the X, the unary trait that distinguishes them. The greatest strength of Kripke's critique of descriptivism is that it pins down the location of the Real, the small remainder beyond the bundle of descriptors that "changes everything," the surplus, the elusive difference, that we search for in vain within the reality of the object, among its positive properties.

The focus of this "quarrel over descriptions" rests in the following question: How and why do names refer to objects? Why does the word "table" refer to a "table"? Descriptivism answers that each word initially carries a signification, it signifies a series, a bundle, of descriptive properties ("table," for example, signifies an object with a certain shape that is used for certain purposes), and it refers to objects in the world insofar as these objects possess the properties contained in this name's signification. "Table" refers to a table because the real table is included within the framework of the bundle of descriptors that form the signification of the word "table." Comprehension ("connotation") therefore precedes extension ("denotation"). Extension, the ensemble of objects to which a word refers, is determined by comprehension, by the fully general properties described by its signification.

Anti-descriptivism, on the other hand, says that a word bonds to an object through a "primal baptism," and that this bond remains even if the bundle of descriptors that initially comprised the signification of the word changes completely. Here is a simplified version of one of Kripke's examples (1980: 83): For most people, "Gödel" only evokes the description of "the man who discovered the incompleteness theorem"; however, imagine if recent research revealed that it wasn't Gödel who discovered the theorem, but rather one of his friends – let's call him Schmidt – and that Gödel stole the theorem and eliminated Schmidt in order to cover his tracks. In this example, who are we referring to when we talk about "Gödel"? Gödel or Schmidt? According to descriptivism, when we said the name "Gödel," we would really be referring to Schmidt because only Schmidt would satisfy the conditions of the description evoked by the name "Gödel" (the man who discovered the incompleteness theorem), while according to anti-descriptivism, we were always referring to Gödel, even if the descriptors we were evoking did not fit.

Here we have arrived at the heart of the matter. For descriptivists, a word refers to an object out of the *internal, immanent* necessity of its signification, whereas for the anti-descriptivist, the link that bonds the word to the object to which it refers depends on *external* causality that is fundamentally irreducible to the bundle of descriptors of the word's signification. In other words, the descriptivist focuses on the word's immanent "intensional content," and the anti-descriptivist emphasizes the external causal chain of tradition, the way in which the word's use has been transmitted from one subject to another, from one generation to the next. It may seem as if there is an easy way to resolve the difference between the two accounts. Aren't they just referring to two different types of words, general concepts and words in the strict sense? Descriptivism accounts for how references to general concepts work, while anti-descriptivism explains how proper names function. For example, if I refer to someone as "fatso," it's clear that he possesses the property of being corpulent, whereas the name "Peter" does not allow us to deduce any properties about its

bearer – the name "Peter" refers to him simply because he was baptized "Peter."

But what appears to be a solution to the problem through the
introduction of a simple distinction in classification is a red herring,
serving only to conceal the true importance of the debate. Both
descriptivism and anti-descriptivism claim to offer a *general* theory
of how reference works. For descriptivism, proper names are themselves only the abbreviation of the description, whereas for anti-
descriptivism, the external causal chain determines reference in cases
of general concepts as well, at least for those related to natural kinds.
For example, a certain type of object has been baptized "gold," to
which we associated a series of descriptive properties (a heavy, yellow,
shiny metal, etc.). Over the centuries this bundle of descriptors has
increased and been modified in conjunction with the development of
human knowledge (today we would identify gold by its atomic
number). But let us take as a hypothesis that a researcher reveals that
everyone had been mistaken about the effective properties of the
substance called "gold" (the impression that it is yellow in color is
the result of a collective optical illusion, etc.) – in this case, "gold"
would continue to refer to the same substance as before, in other
words, we would say "gold does not possess the properties that we
had attributed to it," rather than "the substance we all thought was
gold turned out not to be gold." Or, in the opposite situation:

> [T]here might be a substance which has all the identifying marks we
> commonly attributed to gold and used to identify it in the first
> place, but which is not the same kind of thing, which is not the same
> substance. We would say of such a thing that though it had all the
> appearances we initially used to identify gold, it is not gold. (Kripke
> 1980: 119)

Why? Because this substance would not be bound to the name "gold"
through a causal chain that would go back all the way to the "primal
baptism." For the same reason:

> [E]ven if archeologists or geologists were to discover tomorrow some
> fossils conclusively showing the existence of animals in the past satisfy-
> ing everything we know about unicorns from the myth of the unicorn,
> that would not show that there were unicorns. (Kripke 1980: 24)

Just because this quasi-unicorn corresponds perfectly to the bundle
of descriptors associated with the word "unicorn" does not mean
that it is the referent for the mythical idea of the unicorn. One cannot
miss the "libidinal" implications of Kripke's argument. Isn't this the

same problem that we find with the "realization of desire"? When you finally find the thing, it has all the properties of the object you fantasized about, but nonetheless "it isn't it," it isn't the referent that was the aim of your desire. And let us not overlook the examples themselves used by Kripke: "gold," the "unicorn," maybe it's not a coincidence that the examples he chose have such libidinal resonance, that they are so easy to turn into metaphors for the object of desire.

What does Lacan have to offer to this "quarrel over descriptions"? Far from "passing beyond" the opposition between descriptivism and anti-descriptivism through some kind of quasi-dialectical "synthesis," Lacan shows how both positions *overlook the same crucial fact*: the radical contingency of naming. The proof of this is that they both felt compelled to construct a fable to defend their position. Searle has the fable of the primitive tribe, and on the other side we have Donnellan's fable of the "omniscient observer of history."

In order to provide a counterexample to anti-descriptivism, Searle tells the story of a small primitive tribe in which everyone knows everyone else, newborns are baptized in front of the whole tribe, and individuals learn the signification of names through direct demonstration ("this is a . . ."). Furthermore, there is an absolute taboo against using the names of the dead. In such a tribe, language functions in a completely "descriptivist" manner, the reference of each name is fixed solely by its bundle of descriptors (cf. Searle 1999: 240).

Now, of course Searle knew perfectly well that such a tribe never existed, but such a tribe only needs to be logically possible in order to prove that this function of language has logical primacy and that all the anti-descriptivists' examples are logically secondary, "parasitic," which is to say that they presuppose a pre-existing "descriptive" function. Let us take the following extreme case of parasitism. All we know about a certain person is that his name is Smith. Searle points out, first, the fact that his name is Smith is a minimally descriptive trait (we know at the very least that he answers to the name "Smith"), and, second, such an extreme case presupposes that there must be at least one other individual for whom the name "Smith" brings to mind a series of properties (a fat man with a beard who teaches a course on the history of pornography, etc.). In other words, the example that the anti-descriptivist sees as a normal case (in which the reference is transferred through an external causal chain, independent of the bundle of descriptors) is only an external presentation (external, which is to say that it abstracts the intentional content tied to the name) of "parasitism," which is logically secondary.

In order to refute Searle, we must show that his fable is *logically* impossible, not just empirically impossible. Derrida's "poststructuralist" approach, for example (cf. Derrida's response to Searle, in Derrida 1977), was to attempt to show the way in which "parasitism" is always already present, even in the supposedly original function of language. For Derrida, Searle has created a fable of pure presence, of perfect transparency to the referent. But language is "originally" the trace of an absence; lacking is the quasi-transcendental "possibility condition" for the establishment of language's differentiating network. A Lacanian would focus elsewhere, on the fact that there is something missing from the way in which Searle tells his story. As soon as we have a language in a strict sense, a language that realizes social ties – and this is true even in the closed universe of an isolated tribe – intersubjective recognition becomes a constitutive part of any and every name, which makes the idea of a "private language" a contradiction *in adjecto*. In the final analysis, a name refers to an object *because others use that name for the object.* These "others," of course, are not reducible to empirical others, to possible interlocutors; they represent the dimension of the big Other, the symbolic order. Here we find the dogmatic mistake specific to the signifier, the mistake that takes the form of the tautology: "table" refers to a table because the table is called "table." To put it differently, the form of language always precedes the way in which it comes to be used. In Searle's example of extreme "parasitism" in its pure and self-referential form, interlocutors use a name but know nothing about the object to which this name refers. The only intentional content that fixes the reference for their usage of this name is "what others mean when they use this name." But Searle's error is that he doesn't see the way in which this self-referential point is the *sine qua non* of the way language "normally" operates.

Searle's mythical tribe would be a little group of psychotics in which, because of the taboo on using the names of dead people, kinship could not function. If the thing that Searle's account overlooks is the dimension of the *big Other*, anti-descriptivism – at least in its dominant form – overlooks the *little other*, the object's status as *Real*. This is why the anti-descriptivist is always searching for the X that would not be reducible to the bundle of descriptors, that would not be found among the given properties of the object, in *reality*, with the result that they construct their own mythical account of an "omniscient observer of history" (Donnellan 2012: 71). Keith Donnellan, the author of this account, starts with a rather amusing fictional example. For most of us, Thales is "the Greek philosopher who thought that all was water." However, suppose first that when Herodotus and Aristotle spoke of Thales, they were actually referring to a well-digger who, on a blisteringly hot day, exclaimed: "Ah, if everything was water, I wouldn't have to dig all these damn wells!" and second that in ancient Greece there was a philosopher hermit who didn't speak to anyone, but who really believed that everything was water. In this situation, to whom would the name "Thales" refer? Certainly not the philosopher hermit, even though he corresponds to the description "the Greek philosopher who thought that everything was water." Rather, "Thales" would refer to the unknown well-digger. The problem is that today, the true referent of the name "Thales" is inaccessible to us. Only an "omniscient observer of history" who could trace back the entire causal chain to its starting point, the moment when the name "Thales" was attached to the unknown well-digger, would be able to pin down the reference.

Donnellan's mistake, which is what compelled him to construct this fable in the first place, is to search for the X that corresponds to the rigid designator – the kernel outside the descriptive properties of the object that would remain the same in all possible worlds – in reality. He saw this X as some existing thing, missing the retroactive nature of naming itself. This surplus, which would be the same in every possible world, corresponds to "the thing in the object that is more than the object," and that is therefore beyond the object's pre-sentation in reality, its positive properties. It is the *object a*. We search in vain for this object in reality just as, to use the Marxist example, we search in vain among the positive properties of gold for the X that makes it the embodiment of wealth, just as we search among the positive properties of a commodity, among the qualities that deter-mine its use value, the X, the commodity's exchange value. Looking at the "impossible" relationship between the rigid designator and the core of the object that would remain the same in every possible world, one cannot help but recognize the relationship between S1, the signi-fier without signified, and the *object little a*.

The fictional "omniscient observer of history" therefore serves exactly the same role as Searle's primitive tribe. In both cases, the goal is to overcome the radical contingency of naming through the invention of an instance that could guarantee its necessity. In one example reference is guaranteed by the immanent "intensional content" of the name itself, in the other by the causal chain that takes us back to the "primal baptism" that bound the name to the object.

Speech acts, real acts

In general, it seems as if analytic philosophy is at its best when it is able to open the chasm that reveals the Real in all its irreducible contingency. Edmund Gettier (1963) brought this to light in regard to questions of knowledge. There are three conditions that must be satisfied for us to be able to say that subject S "knows" proposition P: (1) S must believe P – that there is a table in an adjoining room, say; (2) P must be true – there really is a table in the adjoining room; and (3) S must have good reason to believe P – he has seen the table, someone told him there was a table in the adjoining room, etc. Therefore, if he randomly guesses that there is a table in the adjoining room or if he arrives at his belief through "magic" (psychic visions, etc.), we would not say that "S knows P" in the standard sense. What Gettier then did was construct some complex thought experiments in which these three conditions are fulfilled, but we nonetheless do not want to say that "S knows P" in the standard sense of the word.

The same breach can be found with regard to action. There are three similar conditions that must be fulfilled in order for us to say that subject S accomplished intended act A: (1) S intended to accomplish A, (2) A was accomplished, and (3) S's intention to accomplish A was the reason A was accomplished (for example, even if I have the intention of closing a door, but I do it by accident, we cannot say that this was an intentional act). Probably the most common pastime among philosophers of action is thinking up cases in which these three conditions are fulfilled but we cannot say that S accomplished A in the standard sense of the word. An example of this would be a slight variation on the above example: I was so obsessed with the idea of closing the door that, not knowing what I was doing, I accidentally bumped into the door, shutting it. In this example, my intention of doing A is inarguably the reason that caused A to be accomplished, but nonetheless we cannot say that A was accomplished intentionally. Of course, there are ways of getting out of such dead-ends through further distinctions. Searle (1999), for example, introduced the distinction between *prior intention* and *intention-in-action*. But such distinctions only serve to re-conceal the new world that had become visible, the world of *failed acts*, acts that succeed through their very failure, a strange universe that lies between the "successful" intentional act and pure unintentional dumb luck, and is analogous to the gap between the two deaths. The breach between the conditions for the success of the act and its realization can only be filled when the act fails – in this sense, we could say that each act, as it crosses the threshold of the possible and realizes itself in the full meaning of the term, is fundamentally a failure, will always retain something of the "impossible."

Take this indeterminable surplus that lies beyond the necessary conditions, that must be added to fill the breach, to allow knowledge to become effective knowledge and an act to become an effective act. Doesn't it, in its impossibility, touch the Real, insofar as there is always something improbable, "impossible," about the given form of a thing? We perceive a thing as possible, we wait for its arrival, and despite all that, its arrival, its realization, is shocking. This is the perspective from which we should approach the status of the act in analytical practice and theory.

The first step is doing away with the "naive" contrast between acting and speaking; "when saying is doing." It may seem as if Lacanian theory, with its emphasis on the signifier, is fully inscribed in this contradiction, without remainder. Isn't the only true act in the proper sense the act of language, the founding of a new symbolic reality? And doesn't the non-linguistic act in its essence draw from the category of the "passage to the act," that false exit that represents a failed symbolization of the traumatic kernel? It seems then that psychoanalytic theory turns the folk wisdom of "talking instead of doing" on its head and posits that, in the end, we act instead of talking. We act when our words are lacking, when the path to symbolization is blocked. If, then, the last word of analytic theory is "saying is doing," the end of the analytic process would be the completed integration of the subject into the symbolic order. The aim of analysis would be to produce the master-signifier, the "mandate," that would give the subject its position in the symbolic network and would make symbolic identification possible. Failed acts would be symptomal formations that could be dissolved through successful symbolization. The analyst, whom we identify with the other, plays the role of the "Master of signification"; his job is to reflect the true signification of the analysand's message back to him by situating it in the symbolic network. Basically, the essential feature of the analytical act would be the "miraculous" transformation of chaos into a "new harmony," the establishment of symbolic necessity through the production of a new "quilting point" that would retroactively confer signification onto the symptomal formulations. Initially, it seems as if Lacan's framework of the four discourses leads to the above perspective (cf. Lacan 1998b: 16). Isn't it true that we find a "quilting point," a location of production, an S1, in the analytical discourse? But there is a catch. The analyst, the "agent" in the analytical discourse, is not identified with the big Other, the "Master of signification"; rather, he seems to be the object *a*, which means that his actions are not located on the side of the signifier, but on the side of the object, in the surplus, in the indefinable remainder of the Real (cf. Cottet 1985).

Of course, rehabilitating the non-symbolic dimension of the act does not mean backsliding into the "naive" opposition between acting and speaking. The analyst is far from being a person who "acts instead of talking" – particularly since "the failure is the object" (Lacan 1998b: 58), which is to say that the object's location is created by the failure of symbolization. The analyst's action should not pretend to "go beyond words to the thing itself"; rather, it consists in showing the – so to speak – positive side of symbolization's failure, the empty space enclosed by this failure. In other words, the analyst's act does not take place at the level of "acting" outside of "talking." Instead, he presents a negative act, an act that coincides with the non-act and in this way fixes the location of the foreign body *inside "speaking" itself*. As such, the analyst's act is the opposite of the performative gesture, of the "successful" speech act.

The performative comes from the Master. In the agent's position we find S1, the self-referential signifier that, through the very act of its own utterance, establishes a new social link, the "founding speech" that gives it its symbolic mandate, the famous "you are my master" that makes you my master (and we mustn't forget its complement, "you are the one who will follow me"). S1 represents the subject for the other signifiers, it is the point at which the chain is subjectified, which is the root of its particular illusory effect. It is as if at the single moment of "I want," there is conjuncture between wanting to say and actually saying, between the subject of the utterance and the uttering subject. There is therefore nothing "psychological" about the impression of "sincerity," of "authenticity" that the Master's performative gesture exudes. It is exactly the opposite, it is a necessary structural illusion particular of the S1; the illusion that at this specific point, the subject is "fully in his speech." The Master's gesture gives rise to this illusion almost automatically. As soon as we "understand" this gesture, we have to "take it seriously," because its self-referential function, its "authentic," "sincere," "serious" nature *is part of its very signification*, in the same way that in the ontological proof of God, His existence is part of the definition of God (which is to say, in the end, the signification of the word "God"). The sleight of hand operated by S1 consists precisely in this short-circuit between intention (wanting to say) and the self-referential affirmation of the "sincerity" of this intention. This is why statements in which the subject's division erupts generally take the form of "pragmatic paradoxes" that show a rift in this "sincerity." For example, "there is a table in the adjoining room, but I don't believe it" (as if making the statement: "there is a table in the adjoining room," does not imply a belief in it). One cannot miss the way in which the structure of this sentence corresponds perfectly to the fetishistic disavowal "(of course I know that) my mother doesn't have a phallus, but I don't believe it."

Far from winding up praising the act that inaugurates the Master, Lacanian theory in fact denounces it as imposture. In the matheme of the Master's discourse, the space of production is occupied by the object *a*; what could this mean besides that the performative gesture produces a residuum, an irreducible remainder? The subject does not allow himself to be subsumed under his symbolic mandate without leaving a remainder. This surplus, which eludes the foundational gesture of the Master, divides the subject and triggers the eruption of the hysterical question: "What am I, if I'm what you've just been saying I am?" (Lacan 1997b: 279). In other words, the performative gesture that confers the symbolic mandate upon the subject, that pins it to an S1, simultaneously divides it between S1 and a remainder from which, because it is the space of its truth, it asks the Master the hysterical question. This question defines the status of the subject as a speaking subject, which is to say, a divided subject. The only way to avoid it is to occupy the psychotic position, to cause the symbolic to collapse into the Real (the king who believes himself to be king, which is to say, who thinks that the symbolic mandate "king" is part of his very nature).

From this point of view, the analyst's discourse is the inverse of the Master's performative discourse. The agent's place is occupied by the object *a,* by the waste, by that which, in the speaking subject, escapes from the performative's grasp. In the space of production we find S1 – or, as Jacques-Alain Miller (1980) emphasized, "producing" really means something like externalizing, taking distance, perhaps even liberating. The analytical discourse liberates us from the illusory short-circuit of the Master's gesture, it isolates the S1 and shows it in all its true empty, formal, tautological, self-referential, nature. In short: its stupidity.

The impossible performative

What is it then that the theory of speech acts overlooks? Already in Austin's *How to do Things with Words,* the transition from the opposition performative/constative to the triad locution/illocution/ perlocution and the classification of diverse illocutionary acts reveals a fundamental theoretical impasse. Far from simply building off of the initial intuition that "saying is doing," reformulating the performative into the illocutionary act entails a loss. Even the most "naive" reading would find that the essential feature of the performative disappears in this transition. It is also clear that Austin felt compelled to reclassify things in this way because he saw that his first description of the performative and of the original performative/ constative pairing was lacking. John Searle's taxonomy of illocutionary acts (1985) can help us to locate where exactly this lack lies. Searle produces the point at which Austin-I and Austin-II overlap: "declarations," one type of illocution, are "in a strict sense" the "pure" performative.

Searle's taxonomy is based around the "direction of fit" between words and the world involved in the different types of speech acts. In the case of *assertives*, the direction of fit is from words to the world (if I say "there is a table in the next room," the condition of satisfaction for this proposition is that there really is such a table). With *directives*, the direction of fit is from the world to words (if I say: "close the door!" the condition for satisfaction is that the act realizes these "words" "in the world" – the listener must close the door, and must do it because I told him to and not for other reasons), etc. *Declarations* are the trickiest, because their direction of fit goes two ways, both from the world to words and, at the same time, from words to the world. Take the utterance "the show's over," for example. What does the speaker accomplish by uttering this phrase? Well, he effectively creates a new state of affairs in the world (the fact that the show is over); the direction of fit is therefore from the world to words. How does he do this? By presenting this state of affairs as already being true: he observes that the show is over – *he accomplishes the act by describing it as accomplished*. With declarations, the speaker tries to "*cause something to be the case by representing it as being the case* . . . if he succeeds he will have changed the world by representing it having been so changed" (Searle 1999: 172).

Of course, every utterance accomplishes an act in the sense of its own illocutionary force, but there is nonetheless a key difference between declarations and, say, directives. When I say: "close the door!" I successfully accomplish the act of giving an order, but it remains up to you to actually close the door, whereas if I say "the show's over," I have not only announced that the show is over, but I have effectively ended the show. Only declarations have the "magical power" of realizing their own propositional content. The direction of fit from world to words is not limited to the fact that a new state of affairs follows the words (in the future). The key point is that the causality is immediate, it is the utterance itself that produces the new state of things. As we have seen, the price of this "magic with words" is its repression. We pretend that we are describing a pre-existing state of affairs, we end the show by *observing* that it is over. In order for the performative to be "pure" (a speech act that realizes its own propositional content), it must therefore be divided, it must take the form of its opposite, it must turn itself into a constative.

We can link this split to Searle's theory of "indirect speech acts," which are sentences like "Could you pass me the salt?" in which the primary illocutionary act (the directive, the request for the other person to pass me the salt) is accomplished through a secondary illocutionary act (a question about the other's abilities). Searle calls cases like these "parasites"; they are secondary by nature, they presuppose a preceding logically necessary illocutionary act (in our example, the order "Pass me the salt!"). But aren't declarations in fact examples in which the "parasitism" *comes first*? Their primary illocutionary dimension (the "magic power" of being able to realize their own propositional contents) can only be manifested in the form of an assertive, of a description of "this is how it is." This also allows us to take a new approach to Lacan's thesis that ontology relies upon the discourse of the Master.

> [The discourse of being is] quite simply being at someone's heel, being at someone's beck and call – what would have been if you had understood what I ordered you to do. Every dimension of being is produced in the wake of the master's discourse – the discourse of he who, proffering the signifier, expects therefrom one of its link effects that must not be neglected, which is related to the fact that the signifier commands. The signifier is, first and foremost, imperative. (Lacan 1998b: 31–2)

Why would ontology, which is the discourse about the world as an existing totality, depend upon the Master? The answer is right here in the structure of declaration, the "pure" performative that takes the form of a constative. Ontology is supported by an "indirect speech act" – the assertive, the constative "this is how it is," that conceals its performative dimension. It is blind – and perhaps it even blinds itself – to the way in which its own utterance realizes its propositional content. It is impossible to explain the "magical power" of declarations without reference to the Lacanian "big Other." Searle himself recognized this when he emphasized that, in order for a declaration to be accomplished, there must be "such institutions as the church, the law, private property, the state and a special position of the speaker and hearer within these institutions" (1985: 18).

In *The Emperor's New Clothes*, everyone knows that the emperor is naked, and everyone knows that everyone else knows. Why then, does simply saying in public that "the emperor is naked" have the performative power to explode the established network of intersubject relationships? In other words, if everyone knew it, *who was the person who didn't know?* There is only one possible answer: the big

Other (in the sense of the field of recognized social knowledge). These types of utterances are valuable because they are "ontological proof of the existence of the big Other." Declarations follow the same logic; the show is over when the utterance of the constative statement "the show is over" *brings this to the attention of the big Other.*

And isn't Freudian "original repression," which Lacan specified was the fall of the "binary signifier" (Lacan 1998a: 236), precisely this split inside the "pure" performative (of the declarative), the fact that it can only articulate itself in the form of a constative? The thing that is "originally repressed," the thing that by structural necessity must be missing from the establishment of the signifying network, is the signifier of the "pure" performative that *does not* take the form of a constative. It is out of this impossibility, this scission, that the subject emerges as subject of the signifier. The subject's location is the void opened by the fall of the "impossible" binary signifier, the signifier that, if it were possible, would be the signifier that "belonged to" the subject, the signifier that, instead of simply representing the subject, would guarantee its presence in the signifying chain.

Lacan's S1, the master-signifier that represents the subject for the other signifiers, is, therefore, as a "pure" performative, the point at which the performative and the constative intersect. We can now see what was missing from Austin-I (of the "performative") as well as from Austin-II (of the "illocutionary force"): a paradoxical topological model in which extreme internality (the "pure" performative) would coincide with externality (the constative). This is why the philosophy of speech acts only deals with subjecthood at the level of the imaginary-me, of an interlocutor who supposedly "expresses himself" through his statements, while overlooking the subject of the signifier, the empty space opened at the intersection of the performative and the constative.

I and *a*

S1 is not the key word, the knot of significations, because it is the "richest" word, the word that would condense all the signifying richness of the "quilted" field, but rather because it's the word that "things" themselves refer to in order to recognize themselves in the unity of their own field. Take the famous Marlboro ad campaign. There's a tanned, "rugged" cowboy, open sky over the vast prairie, etc. all of which connotes a well-defined image of America (the country of endless possibility for tough, honest folks, etc.). The "quilting point" effect only occurs at a specific turning point, when "actual" Americans begin to identify themselves with the image created by Marlboro advertisements, when, in their ideological self-representation, in the lived experience of Americans, "real" America is itself represented as "Marlboro-country." A similar turning point exists for everything that could be called "the symbols of the American spirit." Let us take just one of many: Coca-Cola. The essential fact is not that Coca-Cola "connotes" a particular vision of America (the freshness of the cold and bittersweet taste, etc.), but rather that such a vision of America gets its consistency from the signifier "Coca-Cola." We could say *"America is Coca-Cola!"* for example – if we wanted to come up with insipid advertising slogans – but the key fact about this statement would be that *we could not* flip it by saying "Coca-Cola is America." The only possible answer to the question "and what is it that is Coca-Cola?" is the impersonal "that"; "that's Coca-Cola!," the X, the object-cause of desire.

It is precisely because of the surplus X that the quilting point's operation is not circular: it is wrong to say that we don't gain anything from the "quilting" process because Coca-Cola would first connote the American spirit, and that this spirit (which is to say the series of traits that supposedly express it: freshness, youth, etc.) would then condense around "Coca-Cola" as its signifying representation. The thing that we gain is the surplus X, the object-cause of desire, the "unnamable thing" beyond Coca-Cola's positive properties, the thing "in Coca-Cola that is more than Coca-Cola," and which, following Lacan's formulation (1998a: 268), can suddenly turn into shit, into an undrinkable syrupy mess – just try drinking it flat and warm.

The logic of this surplus is particularly visible in the case of anti-Semitism. The Jew initially appears as the signifier that connotes a whole series of "existing" properties attributed to Jews (greedy, dirty, manipulative, cosmopolitan, etc.), but anti-Semitism in its true form only arrives with the reversal of this relationship, when we say "he is greedy/dirty/manipulative – *because he is a Jew.*" At first, this reversal seems tautological; nothing is gained, we could easily reply "of course he is like this because he's a Jew, because 'Jew' in fact signifies 'greedy, dirty . . . .' " But this circularity is an illusion. The signification of "Jew" in the statement "because he is a Jew" cannot be reduced to the series of properties attributed to the Jew. Instead, it refers to the unnamable X that supposedly causes and produces these traits, the thing "in the Jew that is more than the Jew," the unique and unary trait that Nazism worked obsessively to identify, to define and measure, to pin down a positive property that would allow them to "objectively," "scientifically" identify Jews.

We will always search in vain for this unnamable X amid the positive properties of the object because it is produced at the level of "words" and not of "things." The *object little a* is the paradoxical "thing" that receives its entire substance from the hole in the Other, in the signifying network. Whereas, on the other hand, the "pure" signifier, S1, the "quilting point," is produced at the level of "things," which is to say, it comes as the signifying point that serves as a referent so that the field of "things" can recognize itself in its unity.

The key point is the *non-coverage of the symbolic network and the circuit of reality symbolized by this network*; there is a surplus on both sides. The symbolization of reality, the inscription of the circuit of reality in the signifying network, opens the void of the un-symbolizable – the emptiness of *das Ding*, the terrifying Thing – in the form of the Real. On the other side, symbolization necessarily entails a surplus in the signifying network itself, the "at least one" self-referential, "pure" signifier, I (S1), to which nothing in "reality" corresponds. We should not think of the relationship between the I (the "pure" signifier without signified) and the *a* (the un-symbolizable object of desire) as a complementary or parallel relationship analogous to the relationship of an "ordinary" signifier (S2) to the object it designates. In other words, we cannot say "I designates *a*, the thing that falls, the thing that is excluded from the circuit of reality, in the same way that an 'ordinary' signifier designates an object in reality, in the same way that the circuit of reality corresponds to the network of 'ordinary' signifiers." In order to pin down the paradoxical relationship between the I and the *a*, we must look at the famous flattened representation of the Möbius strip (see figure 2).

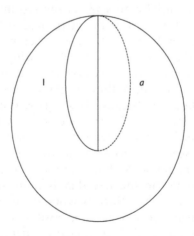

Figure 2

The big circle is simultaneously both the circle of reality and the circle of language; on one side, it's the circuit of reality, on the other it's the linguistic network. In a similar way, in the inner oval we have I on one side and *a* on the other. I is not on the side of language, it is on the side of reality, whereas *a* is on the side of the symbolic network. I (S1) is a signifier on the same surface as reality. If we wish to grasp "reality in its entirety," we must necessarily add a paradoxical *signifier* to it; we will sooner or later stumble across a thing that is, so to speak, "its own sign," that does nothing but positivize its own lack (and this is precisely the definition of the phallic signifier). The only way to close the circle of "reality" is to include an "element" that occupies the space of its constitutive, "primordial" repression. How best to explain the thing that is its own sign? Take the Hegelian distinction between the "bad infinity" and the "true infinity." The "bad infinity" is what we have in the famous paradox of the "painting within a painting" (or the map within the map). If a painting contains a painting of itself, the painting must now also contain itself, and so on; if we wish to draw up a perfectly accurate map of a country, we must include this map in the map itself, leading to a "bad" infinite recursion. But the "true infinite" in Lewis Carroll's paradoxical story about maps is something different altogether. In this story, the English decide to produce a detailed map of their country, but they are unsatisfied with the result: it's not detailed enough. The map keeps getting bigger and more chaotic until one of them comes up with the idea of using *the country itself as its own map*. Even today, England continues to serve as a very satisfactory map of itself. This is the "true infinite." The fall into the "bad infinite" doesn't end when we have reached the unattainable *final* moment (the final image within an image), but when the *first* moment suddenly appears as its own other, when the country becomes a map of itself, when the thing becomes its own sign. This point at which the initial moment reverses itself into its own other through the return-to-self is the point at which the subject emerges. The "subject" is the name of this "nothing," this empty distance that separates the thing from itself as its own sign, the country from itself as its own map.

Contrary to this, *a* is the paradoxical object that lies on the same surface as the signifying network, it is "on the side of words" and not "on the side of things." If we wish to "close the circle of language," we have to put a non-signifying *object* inside of the signifier itself, an object that we encounter on the side of the signifier. If we take the example of film noir, we can see that, in the end, this object is *the gaze itself*. Hollywood film noir from the 1940s and '50s, with its irresistible nostalgic charm, is a perfect example of an object of fascination. What is so fascinating to us about this macabre universe inhabited by all these stock characters, the cynical "fallen souls," the amoral wealthy, the femmes fatales? It is obvious today that we cannot take these films "seriously." One cannot help but laugh during their most tragic scenes. They have been irreversibly lost as objects of desire. The problem is precisely this: how is it that the classic film noir, a lost object of desire, the mark of a blockage, of a fundamental impossibility (the "impossibility of taking them seriously"), still exercises such nostalgic charm, and not despite the features mentioned above, but because of them? From what "impossible object" does this charm arise? The only possible answer is the gaze. Our gaze bases itself on another gaze, one which probably never existed, of the moviegoers of that era who were still able to take film noir "seriously," to find jouissance in it, to be fascinated by it out of their fundamental *naïveté*. When I watch a film noir today, I "see myself seeing myself" – to use Lacan's Valeryan expression (Lacan, *Seminar XI*, 80). I am fascinated by the imaginary gaze that could supposedly be immediately fascinated by film noir, that could enjoy it fully without any ironic distance. This is why, in the phantasy, the object, the little *a* from the matheme $\$ \lozenge a$, is not the scene, but the "impossible" gaze that is fascinated by this scene.

Isn't the "traversal of the phantasy" the experience of the primacy of the gaze over the seen? There is a moment in Hegel's "private life" that seems to provide a confirmation of this. We can pin down pretty much exactly the moment at which Hegel "traversed the phantasy." In one of his letters, he speaks of a period of total depression that he lived through between the ages of 25 and 30: a "hypochondria" that went "*bis zur Erlähmung aller Kräfte*," that was so severe as "to paralyze all his power" (cf. Kojève 1969: 168). He was not ready to pay the price for Absolute Knowledge, which is to say, to make the radical sacrifice, the sacrifice of oneself, the experience of which he describes in *Glauben und Wissen*: "[A]ll the midges of subjectivity are burned to death in this consuming fire, and *the very consciousness of this surrender and nullification is nullified*" (Hegel 1988: 141).

Of course, it is not a coincidence that this crisis came right before the moment in which Hegel "became Hegel," in the years when he was still searching for synthesis in the form of a Totality that could envelop the contradictory moments (Life, Love). Hegel only "became Hegel" when he traversed the phantasy, when he had what we could call the experience of the Other's lack, the recognition that the object only fills an emptiness that is opened by this lack. It was only once he'd seen this that he could describe the space of the subject as an empty space, as a screen on which appear the fragments of a decapitated body, partial phantasmic objects, as the Emptiness that is materialized through the other's gaze, the Emptiness that is the "night of the world," the abyss, the *ex nihilo* that is the only place where new content can be created:

> The human being is this Night, this empty nothing which contains everything in its simplicity – a wealth of infinitely many representations, images, none of which occur to it directly, and none of which are not present. This [is] the Night, the interior of [human] nature, existing here – pure Self – [and] in phantasmagoric representations it is night everywhere: here a bloody head suddenly shoots up and there another white shape, only to disappear as suddenly. We see this Night when we look a human being in the eye, looking into a Night which turns terrifying. [For from his eyes] the night of the world hangs out toward us. (Hegel 1983: 87)

References

Adorno, T. 1970. *Aufsatze zur Gesellschaftstheorie und Methodologie.* Suhrkamp, Frankfurt am Main.

Adorno, T. 1973. *Negative Dialectics*, trans. E.B. Ashton. Continuum Publishing Company, New York.

Adorno, T. 1992. "Fantasia sopra Carmen," in *Quasi una fantasia*, trans. R. Livingston. Verso, London.

Adorno, T. 1993. *Hegel: Three Studies*, trans. N.S. Weber. MIT Press, Cambridge, MA.

Adorno, T. 1997. *Aesthetic Theory*, trans. R.H. Kentor. University of Minnesota Press, Minneapolis.

Althusser, L. 2001 [1971]. "Ideology and Ideological State Apparatuses," in *Lenin and Philosophy and Other Essays*, trans. B. Brewster. Monthly Review Press, New York/London.

Aristotle. 2006. *Physics*, trans. R.P. Hardie and R.K. Gaye. Digireads.com Publishing, Stilwell, Kansas.

Assoun, P.-L. 1975. *Marx et la répétition historique.* Quadrige/Presses Universitaires de France, Paris. [All quotes trans. T. Scott-Railton]

Benjamin, A.E. and Osborne, P. 1994. *Walter Benjamin's Philosophy: Destruction and Experience*. Routledge, London/New York.

Benjamin, W. 1974. *L'Homme, le langage et la culture*, trans. M. de Gandillac. Denoël, Paris.

Benjamin, W. 1992. *Selected Writings* (series), ed. M.W. Jennings. Harvard University Press, Cambridge, MA.

Benjamin, W. 2003. *Selected Writings*, vol. 4, ed. H. Eiland and M.W. Jennings. Harvard University Press, Cambridge, MA.

Benjamin, W. 2009. *On the Concept of History*. Classic Books American, New York.

Chesterton, G.K. 2012 [1901]. *The Defendant*. Dover Publications, New York.

Cottet, S. 1985. "Anatomie de l'acte," *L'Âne*, 23, p. 26.

Dahmer, H. 1973. *Libido und Gesellschaft*. Suhrkamp, Frankfurt am Main.

Danto, A.C. 1972. *Mysticism and Morality: Oriental Thought and Moral Philosophy*. Harper & Row, New York.

Davidson, D. 1980. "How Is Weakness of the Will Possible?" in *Essays on Actions and Events*, Clarendon Press, Oxford, pp. 21–42.

Derrida, J. 1977. "Limited Inc.," *Glyph*, 2.

Derrida, J. 1986. *Glas*, trans. J.P. Leavy and R. Rand. University of Nebraska Press, Lincoln/London.

Derrida, J. 1987. *The Post Card: From Socrates to Freud and Beyond*, trans. A. Bass. University of Chicago Press, Chicago/London.

Descartes, R. 2008 [1901]. *Discourse on the Method and the Meditations*, trans. J. Veitch. Cosimo, New York.

Dolar, M. 1986. "Hinter dem Rücken des Bewusstseins," *Wo es war*, no. 1.

Dolar, M. 1987. "Die Einführung in das Serail," *Wo es war*, nos. 3–4.

Dognin, P.D. 1977. *Les "Sentiers escarpés" de Karl Marx*. Editions du Cerf, Paris. [All quotes trans. T. Scott-Railton.]

Donnellan, K. 2012. *Essays on Reference, Language, and Mind*, ed. J. Almog and P. Leonardi. Oxford University Press, New York.

Fichte, J.G. 1889. *The Vocation of the Scholar*, trans. W. Smith. J Chapman, London.

Foucault, M. 1978. *History of Sexuality*, trans. R. Hurley. Pantheon Books, New York.

Freud, S. 1990. *Inhibitions, Symptoms and Anxiety*, trans. J. Strachey. W.W. Norton & Company, New York.

Freud, S. 2010 [1955]. *The Interpretation of Dreams: The Complete and Definitive Text*, trans. J Strachey. Basic Books, New York.

Gadamer, H.G. 1975. *Truth and Method*. Continuum International Publishing Group, New York/London.

Gettier, E.L. 1963. "Is Justified True Belief Knowledge?," *Analysis*, no. 23.

Grosrichard, A. 1998. *The Sultan's Court: European Fantasies of the East*, trans. L. Heron. Verso, London/New York.

Habermas, J. 1971. *Knowledge and Human Interests*, trans. J.J. Shapiro. Beacon Press, New York.

Hegel, G.W.F. 1911. *Sämtliche Werke*. Hg. Georg Lasson, Leipzig.

Hegel, G.W.F. 1966. "Who Thinks Abstractly?," in *Texts and Commentary*. Anchor Books, Garden City, NY, pp. 113–18.

Hegel, G.W.F. 1977. *The Phenomenology of Spirit*, trans. A.V. Miller. Oxford University Press, Oxford.

Hegel, G.W.F. 1983. *Hegel and the Human Spirit: A Translation of the Jena Lectures on the Philosophy of Spirit (1805–6), with commentary*, trans. L. Rauch. Wayne State University Press, Detroit.

Hegel, G.W.F. 1988. *Faith and Knowledge*, ed. H.S. Harris, trans. W. Cerf. State University of New York Press, Albany.

Hegel, G.W.F. 1991a. *Elements of the Philosophy of Right*, ed. A. Wood, trans. H.B. Nisbet. Cambridge University Press, Cambridge.

Hegel, G.W.F. 1991b. *The Encyclopaedia Logic: Part 1 of the Encyclopaedia of Philosophical Sciences With the Zusatze*, trans. T.F. Geraets, W.A. Suchting and H.S. Harris. Hackett, Indianapolis.

Hegel, G.W.F. 2001. *The Philosophy of History* [electronic resource], trans. J. Sibree. Batoche Books, Kitchener, Ontario.

Hegel, G.W.F. 2010. *The Science of Logic*, trans. G. di Giovanni. Cambridge University Press, Cambridge.

Heidegger, M. 1993. "Letter on Humanism," in *Basic Writings*, ed. D.F. Krell, trans. F.A. Capuzzi. Harper Collins, New York, pp. 213–66.

Heidegger, M. 2002. "Hegel's Concept of Experience," in *Off the Beaten Track*, ed. J. Young, trans. K. Haynes. Cambridge University Press, Cambridge, pp. 86–156.

Henrich, D. 1971. "Hegel Théorie über den Zufall," in *Hegel im Kontext*, Suhrkamp, Frankfurt am Main, pp. 157–86. [All quotes trans. T. Scott-Railton]

Homer. 1999. *The Iliad*, trans. S. Butler. Dover Publications, Mineola.

Homer. 2012. *The Odyssey*, trans. S. Butler. Memoria Press, Louisville.

Hörisch, J. 1979. *Ich möchte ein solcher werden wie . . . Materialien zur Sprachlosigkeit des Kaspar Hauser*. Suhrkamp, Frankfurt am Main.

Kant, I. 1991. *Political Writings*, ed. H.S. Reiss, trans. H.B. Nisbet. Cambridge University Press, Cambridge.

Kant, I. 1992. *Theoretical Philosophy 1755–1770*, trans. and ed. D. Walford and R. Meerbote. Cambridge University Press, Cambridge.

Kafka, F. 1977. *Letters to Friends, Family, and Editors*, trans. R. and C. Winston. Schocken Books, New York.

Kafka, F. 2009a. *The Castle*, trans. A. Bell. Oxford University Press, New York.

Kafka, F. 2009b, *The Trial*, trans. M. Mitchell. Oxford University Press, New York.

Kernberg, O. 1975. *Borderline Conditions and Pathological Narcissism*. J. Aronson, New York.

Kodaï, M. 1984. *Libido Illimited*. Point hors line, Paris.

Kojève, A. 1969. *Introduction to the Reading of Hegel: Lectures on the Phenomenology of Spirit*, ed. A. Bloom, trans. J.H. Nichols, Jr. Basic Books, New York.

Kripke, S. 1980. *Naming and Necessity*. Harvard University Press, Cambridge.

Kripke, S. 1982. *Wittgenstein on Rules and Private Language*. Blackwell, Oxford.

Kristeva, J. 1984. *Revolution in Poetic Language*, trans. M. Waller. Columbia University Press, New York.

Labarrière, P.-J. 1968. *Structures et mouvement dialectique dans la phéno-ménologie de l'esprit de Hegel*. Aubier, Paris.

de La Boétie, E. 2007. *The Politics of Obedience: The Discourse of Voluntary Servitude*, trans. H. Kurz. Black Rose Books, Montréal/New York/London.

Lacan, J. 1987. "Responses to Students of Philosophy concerning the Object of Psychoanalysis," trans. J Mehlman. October, vol. 40, "Television," pp. 106–13.

Lacan, J. 1991a. *The Seminar of Jacques Lacan.* Book I: *Freud's Papers on Technique 1953–1954,* ed. J.-A. Miller, trans. J. Forrester. W.W. Norton & Company, New York/London.

Lacan, J. 1991b. *The Seminar of Jacques Lacan.* Book II: *The Ego in Freud's Theory and in the Technique of Psychoanalysis 1954–1955,* ed. J.-A. Miller, trans. S. Tomaselli. W.W. Norton & Company, New York/London.

Lacan, J. 1997a [1992]. *The Seminar of Jacques Lacan.* Book VII: *The Ethics of Psychoanalysis 1959–1960,* ed. J.-A. Miller, trans. D Porter. W.W. Norton & Company, New York/London.

Lacan, J. 1997b [1993]. *The Seminar of Jacques Lacan.* Book III: *Psychoses 1955–1956,* trans. R. Grigg. W.W. Norton & Company, New York/London.

Lacan, J. 1998a [1981]. *The Seminar of Jacques Lacan.* Book XI: *The Four Fundamental Concepts of Psychoanalysis,* ed. J.-A. Miller, trans. A. Sheridan. W.W. Norton & Company, New York/London.

Lacan, J. 1998b. *The Seminar of Jacques Lacan.* Book XX: *On Feminine Sexuality, the Limits of Love and Knowledge, 1972–1973,* ed. J.-A. Miller, trans. B. Fink. W.W. Norton & Company, New York/London.

Lacan, J. 2006. *Écrits. The First Complete Edition in English,* trans. B. Fink, H. Fink, and R. Grigg. W.W. Norton & Company, New York.

Lacan, J. n.d. *The Seminar of Jacques Lacan.* Book XXII: RSI, 1974–1975, trans. J.W. Stone, with E. Ragland, G. Hyder, F. Kovacevic, and Z. Watson. Unpublished typescript.

Lebrun, G. 1972. *La Patience du concept: essai sur le discours hégélien.* Gallimard, Paris.

Laclau, E. 1977. *Politics and Ideology in the Marxist Theory.* New Left Books, London.

Laclau, E. and Mouffe, C. 2001. *Hegemony and Socialist Strategy.* Verso, London.

Lenin, V.I. 1971. *Lenin Collected Works.* Progress Publishers, Moscow.

Lefort, C. 1981. *L'Invention démocratique.* Paris. [All quotes trans. T. Scott-Railton]

Lefort, C. 1985. *The Political Forms of Modern Society: Bureaucracy, Democracy, Totalitarianism,* ed. J.B. Thompson. MIT Press, Cambridge, MA.

Luxemburg, R. 2011 [1970]. *Reform or Revolution,* trans. Integer. Pathfinder Press, Atlanta.

Marquet, J.-F. 1973. *Liberté et existence.* Gallimard, Paris. [All quotes trans. T. Scott-Railton]

Marx, K. 1968. *Grundrisse I.* Chapitre de l'argent, Paris. [All quotes trans. T. Scott-Railton]

Marx, K. 1992. *Capital.* Volume 1: *A Critique of Political Economy,* trans. B. Fowkes. Penguin Classics, London.

Marx, K. 1993. *Grundrisse: Foundations for the Critique of Political Economy*, trans. M. Nicolaus. Penguin, London.

Marx, K. 2008. *The Class Struggles in France: From the February Revolution to the Paris Commune*. Resistance Books, Chippendale, Australia.

McCullough, C. 1981. *An Indecent Obsession*. Avon Books, New York.

Miller, G. 1975. *Les Pousse-au-jouir du maréchal Pétain*. Livre de Poche, Paris.

Miller, J.-A. 1967. "Action de la structure," *Cahiers pour l'analyse*, no. 9. [Repr. in *Un début dans la vie*, Paris 2002, pp. 57–85].

Miller, J.-A. 1980. "Reveil," *Ornicar?*, nos. 20–21.

Miller, J.-A. 1978. "Algorithmes de la psychanalyse," *Ornicar?*, no. 16.

Miller, J.-A. 1975. "Matrice," *Ornicar?*, no. 4. [Repr. in *Un début dans la vie*, Paris 2002, pp. 135–44].

Miller, J.-A. 1980. *Cinco conferencias caraquenas sobre Lacan*. Caracas, Editorial Ateneo de Caracas.

Miller, J.-A. 1988. "Another Lacan," trans. R. Chipman. Lacan Study Notes, *Hystoria* 6/9. Paris/New York. New York Lacan Study Group. Accessed at www.lacan.com, September 4, 2013.

Milner, J.-C. 1983. *Les Noms indistincts*. Editions du Seuil, Paris. [All quotes trans. T. Scott-Railton]

Milner, J.-C. 1985. *Détections fictives*. Seuil, Paris. [All quotes trans. T. Scott-Railton]

Mocnik, R. 1986. "Ueber die Bedeutung der Chimaren fur die conditio humana," in *Wo es war*, no. 1.

Naveau, P. 1983. "Marx et le symptôme," *Analytica*, no. 33. *Perspectives psychanalytiques sur la politique*.

Nolte, E. 1966. *Three Faces of Fascism*, trans. L Vennewitz. Holt, Rinehart, and Winston, New York/Chicago/San Francisco.

Pascal, B. 2008. *Pensées and Other Writings*, trans. A. Levi. Oxford University Press, New York.

Plato. 1992. *Republic*, trans. G.M.A. Grube, rev. C.D.C. Reeve. Hackett Publishing Co., Indianapolis.

Racine, J. 1825. *Athaliah*, A. Gombert's edition, trans. J. Donkersley.

Regnault, F. 1985. *Dieu est inconscient*. Navarin, Paris.

Riha, R. 1986. "Das Dinghafte der Geléware," *Wo es war*, no. 1.

Schelling, F.W.J. 1856–61. *Sämmtliche Werke*. Augsburg [s.n.], Stuttgart. [All quotes trans. T. Scott-Railton]

Schelling, F.W.J. 1942. *The Ages of the World*, trans. F. de Wolfe Bolman, Jr. Columbia University Press, New York.

Schelling, F.W.J. 1992. *Philosophical Inquiries into the Nature of Human Freedom*, trans. J. Gutmann. Open Court, Chicago.

Searle, J.R. 1985. *Expressions and Meaning: Studies in the Theory of Speech Acts*. Cambridge University Press, Cambridge.

Searle, J.R. 1999 [1983]. *Intentionality: An Essay in the Philosophy of Mind*. Cambridge University Press, Cambridge.

Sohn-Rethel, A. 1970. *Geistige und körperliche Arbeit*. Frankfurt. [All quotes trans. T. Scott-Railton]

Sohn-Rethel, A. 1978. *Intellectual and Manual Labor*, trans. M. Sohn-Rethel. Macmillan Press, London.

Stalin, J. 2013 [1939]. *History of the Communist Party of the Soviet Union (Bolsheviks) Short Course*. Prism Key Press, New York.

Zizek, S. 1983. "Le Stalinisme: un savoir décapitonné," in *Perspectives psychanalytiques sur la politique, Analytica*, no. 33.

Zizek, S. 1985. "Sur le pouvoir politique et ses mécanismes idéologiques," *Ornicar?*, no. 34, pp. 41–60.

Index